MOON HANDBOOKS

TAMPA &
ST. PETERSBURG

AURA REILEY & BOB JENKINS

Here's what people are saying about Moon:

MOON HANDBOOKS

". . . well-written and exceptionally
informative guides."

—THE NEW YORK

MOON METRO

". . . a sleek two-in-one blend of advice a
street maps."

—U.S. NEWS & WORLD R

MOON OUTDOORS

"Well-written, thoroughly researched, an
full of useful information and advice, the
guides really do get you into the outdoor

—GOR

MOON LIVING ABROAD

". . . provides well-rounded insight into the country and
its culture, and then gives you the real scoop on how to
make the best move."

—TRANSITIONS ABROAD

We want to hear from you, too.
Tell us what you have to say: feedback@moon.com

 HANDBOOKS | METRO | OUTDOORS | LIVING ABROAD

HANDBOOKS

TAMPA & ST. PETERSBURG

LAURA REILEY & BOB JENKINS

Contents

Maps

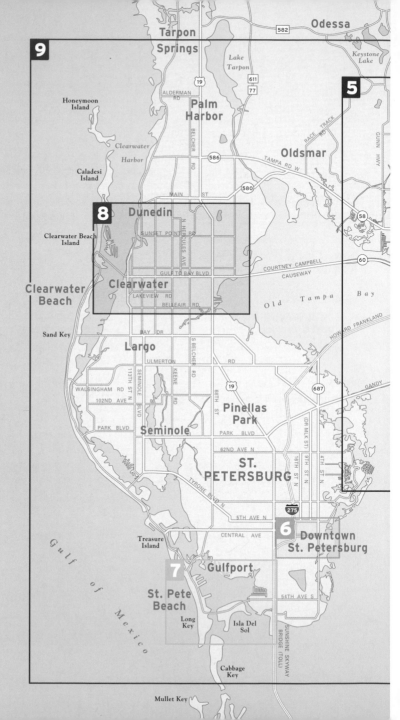

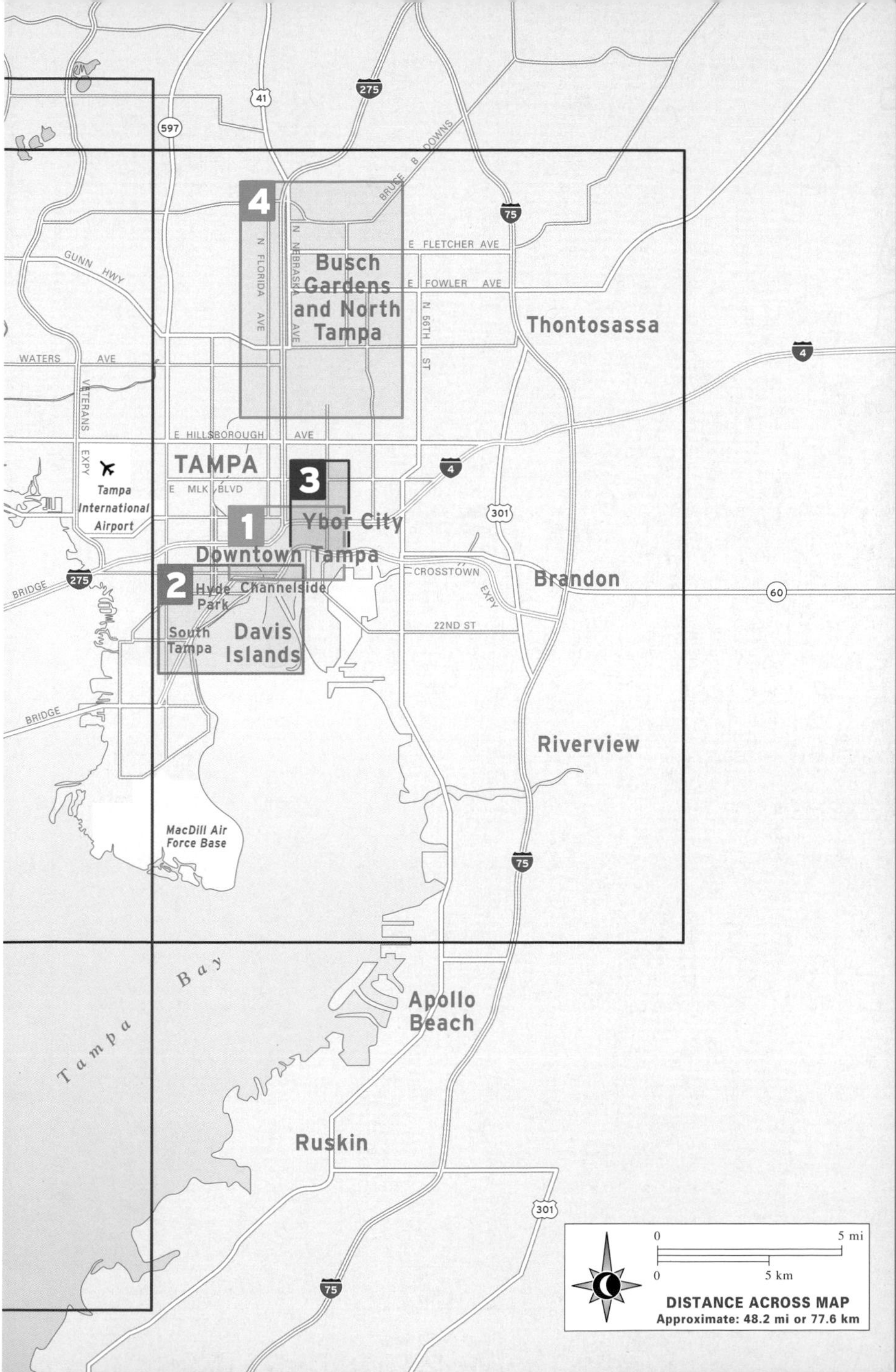

4 Busch Gardens and North Tampa

Thontosassa

TAMPA

3 Ybor City

1 Downtown Tampa

2 Hyde Channelside
Park

Brandon

South Tampa

Davis Islands

Riverview

Tampa International Airport

MacDill Air Force Base

Apollo Beach

Tampa Bay

Ruskin

GUNN HWY

WATERS AVE

VETERANS EXPY

N FLORIDA AVE

N NEBRASKA AVE

N 56TH ST

BRUCE B DOWNS

E FLETCHER AVE

E FOWLER AVE

E HILLSBOROUGH AVE

E MLK BLVD

CROSSTOWN EXPY

22ND ST

BRIDGE

BRIDGE

0   5 mi
0   5 km

DISTANCE ACROSS MAP
Approximate: 48.2 mi or 77.6 km

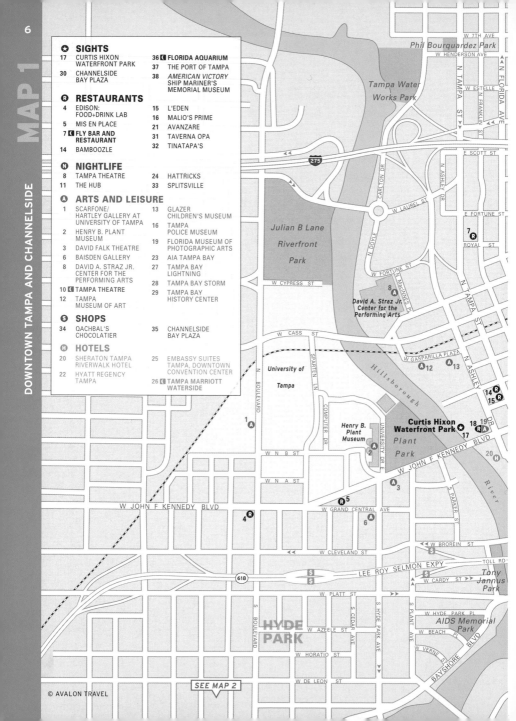

SIGHTS

17	CURTIS HIXON WATERFRONT PARK
30	CHANNELSIDE BAY PLAZA
36	FLORIDA AQUARIUM
37	THE PORT OF TAMPA
38	AMERICAN VICTORY SHIP MARINER'S MEMORIAL MUSEUM

RESTAURANTS

4	EDISON: FOOD+DRINK LAB
5	MIS EN PLACE
7	FLY BAR AND RESTAURANT
14	BAMBOOZLE
15	L'EDEN
16	MALIO'S PRIME
21	AVANZARE
31	TAVERNA OPA
32	TINATAPA'S

NIGHTLIFE

8	TAMPA THEATRE
11	THE HUB
24	HATTRICKS
33	SPLITSVILLE

ARTS AND LEISURE

1	SCARFONE/ HARTLEY GALLERY AT UNIVERSITY OF TAMPA
2	HENRY B. PLANT MUSEUM
3	DAVID FALK THEATRE
6	BAISDEN GALLERY
8	DAVID A. STRAZ JR. CENTER FOR THE PERFORMING ARTS
10	TAMPA THEATRE
12	TAMPA MUSEUM OF ART
13	GLAZER CHILDREN'S MUSEUM
16	TAMPA POLICE MUSEUM
19	FLORIDA MUSEUM OF PHOTOGRAPHIC ARTS
23	AIA TAMPA BAY
27	TAMPA BAY LIGHTNING
28	TAMPA BAY STORM
29	TAMPA BAY HISTORY CENTER

SHOPS

34	OACHBAL'S CHOCOLATIER
35	CHANNELSIDE BAY PLAZA

HOTELS

20	SHERATON TAMPA RIVERWALK HOTEL
22	HYATT REGENCY TAMPA
25	EMBASSY SUITES TAMPA, DOWNTOWN CONVENTION CENTER
26	TAMPA MARRIOTT WATERSIDE

SEE MAP 2

YBOR CITY

TECO

E 8TH AVE
E 7TH AVE
E 6TH AVE
E 5TH AVE
E 4TH AVE
E 3RD AVE
E 2ND AVE
ADAMO DR

NUCCIO PKWY
15TH ST
AVENIDA REP. DE CUBA

Tampa Park
Plaza
Playground

E ESTELLE ST
E SCOTT ST
E KAY ST
E SCOTT ST
INDIA ST
E JOED CT
BURDEN CT
E HARRISON ST

N TALIAFERRO AVE
N MITCHELL AVE
N GOVERNOR ST
CONSTANT ST
N NEBRASKA AVE

E LAUREL ST
N ORANGE AVE

618

SEE MAP 3

Ybor
Channel

E HARRISON ST
E TYLER ST
E CASS ST
E POLK ST
E JACK ST
E JACKSON ST
E TWIGGS
E MADISON
E JOHN F KENNEDY BLVD
N FRANKLIN ST
N FLORIDA AVE
N MARION ST
N MORGAN ST
N PIERCE ST
JEFFERSON ST

9
10
11
16

E JOHN F KENNEDY BLVD
E WASHINGTON ST
E WHITING ST

N MERIDIAN AVE

TECO Streetcar
CHANNELSIDE DR

S CROSSTOWN EXPY

21
22
23
24

DOWNTOWN

S TAMPA ST
N JEFFERSON ST
S BRUSH ST
S NEBRASKA AVE
S CAESAR ST

E WASHINGTON ST
E WHITING ST
E BELL ST
E BROREIN ST
E EUNICE ST
S BROREIN ST

E CUMBERLAND AVE

American Victory
Ship Mariner's
Memorial Museum

Florida Aquarium   36

37   38

USF Park on
the Riverwalk

CHANNELSIDE DR
S MORGAN ST
S FLORIDA AVE
S FRANKLIN ST
OLD WATER ST

Tampa Bay
Times Forum
27, 28

25

26

TECO

CHANNELSIDE

31,32 33
30   34,35
Channelside
Bay Plaza

The Port
of Tampa

29

Garrison   Channel

CHANNELSIDE WALK WAY
HARBOUR PL DR
S BENEFICIAL
S HARBOUR ISLAND BLVD
KNIGHTS RUN AVE

0   200 yds

0   200 m

DISTANCE ACROSS MAP
Approximate: 2.1 mi or 3.4 km

W JOHN F KENNEDY BLVD
W CLEVELAND ST
W PLATT ST
W AZEELE ST
W HORATIO ST
W DE LEON ST
Memorial Hospital
W SWANN AVE
W FOUNTAIN BLVD
W MCKAY AVE
W LYKES AVE
W OAKLYND AVE
W MULLEN AVE
W PARKLAND AVE
W PARKLAND BLVD
EDGEWOOD RD
W SIMMS BLVD

S STERLING AVE
S HIMES AVE
S BEVERLY AVE
W GREY CT
W GABLES CT
S WOODLYNNE AVE
S MACDILL AVE
S LINCOLN AVE
S MATANZAS AVE
HENDERSON BLVD
S GLEN AVE
S ARMENIA AVE
S HABANA AVE
ARRAWANA AVE
S AUDUBON AVE
S TAMPANIA AVE
S MOODY AVE
S HOWARD AVE
S WESTLAND AVE
S ALBANY AVE
S MELVILLE AVE
S FREMONT AVE
S PACKWOOD AVE

Hyde Park Playground

W MORRISON AVE
W JETTON AVE
W WATROUS AVE
W SUNSET DR
W PROSPECT RD
W NEPTUNE ST
W AQUILLA ST
W ESTRELLA ST
W SITIOS ST
W ANGELES ST
W SAN RAFAEL ST
W SAN ISIDRO ST
W SAN NICHOLAS ST
W SAN MIGUEL ST
W SAN CARLOS ST
W SAN JOSE ST
W PALMIRA ST
W BARCELONA ST
W GRANADA ST
W EMPEDRADO ST
W BAY TO BAY BLVD
W SANTIAGO ST
W SAN JUAN ST

Palma Ceia
Golf and Country Club

S STERLING AVE
S FRANKLIN AVE
S STERLING AVE
S HIMES AVE
S ESPERANZA AVE
S FERDINAND AVE
S MACDILL AVE
W JEAN ST
W TEXAS AVE
W PALM DR

LEE ROY SELMON EXPY
TOLL RD
S CROSSTOWN EXPY
DESOTO AVE
BAYSHORE

S HOWARD AVE
S DAKOTA AVE
S DELAWARE AVE
S ALBANY AVE
S HILLS AVE
S GUNBY AVE

W DEKLE ST
W JETTON AVE
W WATROUS AVE

Anderson Park
W BRISTOL ST
S ROME AVE

Bayshore Park
Fred Ball Park
618

MANSON ST
STOVALL ST

Bayshore Park

500 yds
0
0   500 m
DISTANCE ACROSS MAP
Approximate: 3.5 mi or 5.6 km

W EL PRADO BLVD
W WAVERLY AVE
W EUCLID AVE

© AVALON TRAVEL

SIGHTS

22 HYDE PARK VILLAGE
27 BAYSHORE BOULEVARD
39 DAVIS ISLAND YACHT CLUB

RESTAURANTS

2   SQUARE ONE
4   QUEEN OF SHEBA
5   CEVICHE TAPAS BAR & RESTAURANT
7   TC CHOY'S ASIAN BISTRO
8   CHEAP
12 SEVEN 17 SOUTH
13 WATER
14 SIDEBERN'S
16 RESTAURANT BT
17 DATZ

19 BOCA KITCHEN BAR MARKET
21 IRISH 31
28 BERN'S STEAK HOUSE
29 BELLA'S ITALIAN CAFÉ
30 COPPERFISH
32 PANE RUSTICA
33 CAFÉ DUFRAIN
34 JACKSON'S BISTRO BAR & SUSHI
36 ESTELA'S
37 THAI ISLAND
38 220 EAST

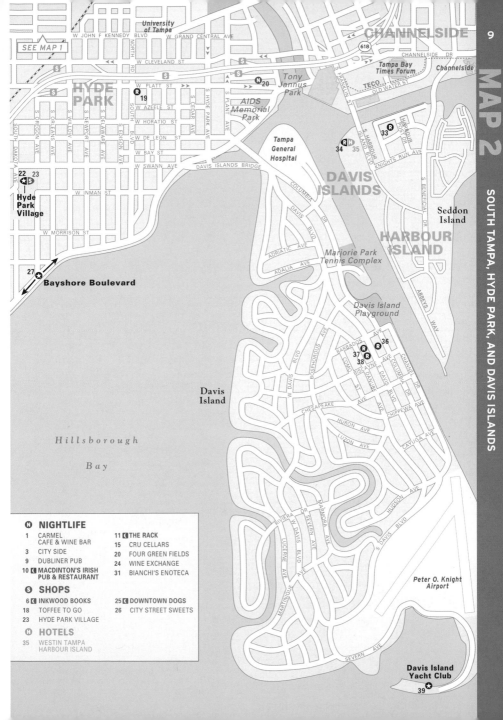

SIGHTS
7 ⬤ 7TH AVENUE (LA SEPTIMA)
13 CENTRO YBOR

RESTAURANTS
12 CARNE CHOPHOUSE
14 SAMURAI BLUE SUSHI AND SAKE BAR
15 TAMPA BAY BREWING COMPANY
22 BERNINI OF YBOR
24 ACROPOLIS GREEK TAVERN
25 COLUMBIA RESTAURANT

NIGHTLIFE
1 NEW WORLD   9 CLUB SKYE
   BREWERY   10 THE RITZ YBOR
2 ORPHEUM   11 ⬤ THE HONEY POT
5 CZAR VODKA BAR   16 CENTRO CANTINA
6 ⬤ G. BAR   18 CLUB PRANA
8 YBOR CITY SOCIAL 21 COYOTE UGLY
   CLUB

ARTS AND LEISURE
17 MUVICO THEATERS
23 YBOR CITY MUSEUM STATE PARK

SHOPS
19 LA FRANCE
20 TAMPA SWEETHEARTS CIGAR CO.

HOTELS
3 DON VICENTE DE YBOR HISTORIC INN
4 HAMPTON INN & SUITES TAMPA/YBOR CITY

DISTANCE ACROSS MAP:
Approximate: .7 miles or 1,145 meters

SIGHTS
9 UNIVERSITY OF SOUTH FLORIDA
17 ADVENTURE ISLAND
19 BUSCH GARDENS
21 LOWRY PARK ZOO

RESTAURANTS
2 ACROPOLIS BAR & GRILL
4 SKIPPER'S SMOKEHOUSE
7 HO HO CHOY
11 PHO QUYEN

NIGHTLIFE
1 PEABODY'S
3 TOAST
5 SKIPPER'S SMOKEHOUSE
16 PEGASUS LOUNGE

ARTS AND LEISURE
8 LETTUCE LAKE REGIONAL PARK
13 UNIVERSITY OF SOUTH FLORIDA CONTEMPORARY ART MUSEUM
14 USF SUN DOME
15 MOSI
20 TAMPA GREYHOUND TRACK

SHOPS
6 SOUND EXCHANGE
10 UNIVERSITY MALL

HOTELS
12 EMBASSY SUITES TAMPA USF
18 LA QUINTA INN TAMPA NEAR BUSCH GARDENS

TAMPA PALMS BLVD W

Lake Forest

BRUCE B. DOWNS BLVD

AMBERLY DR

LIVINGSTON AVE

678

SKIPPER RD

BEARSS AVE E

N 22ND ST

N 46TH ST

N 42ND ST

Lettuce Lake Park

The Claw at USF

275

NORTH BLVD

579

Cedar Lake

Noreast Lake

Pine Lake

Lake Eckels

FLETCHER AVE E

E 131ST AVE

N FLORIDA AVE

N NEBRASKA AVE

N 15TH ST

BRUCE B DOWNS BLVD

Campus Lake

University of South Florida

HOLLY DR

MAPLE DR

ALUMNI DR

University Mall

582

SPECTRUM BLVD

E FOWLER AVE

582

15

E 109TH AVE

N 22ND ST

N 30TH ST

N McKINLEY ST

N 46TH ST

E SERENA DR

E BOUGAINVILLEA AVE

E LINEBAUGH AVE

16

Adventure Island

E LINEBAUGH AVE

E ANNIE AVE

18

Busch Gardens

E BUSCH BLVD

19

E BULLARD PKWY

N 40TH ST

580

NORTH BLVD

275

N 20TH ST

E WATERS AVE

E YUKON ST

Rowlett Park

EAST RIVERHILLS DR

River

20

Eddie Lopez Field

ROWLETT PARK DR

Rogers Park Golf Course

0   0.5 mi

0   0.5 km

Lowry Park

21 Lowry Park Zoo

W SLIGH AVE

E SLIGH AVE

585

DISTANCE ACROSS MAP:
Approximate: 3.7 miles or 6 km

© AVALON TRAVEL

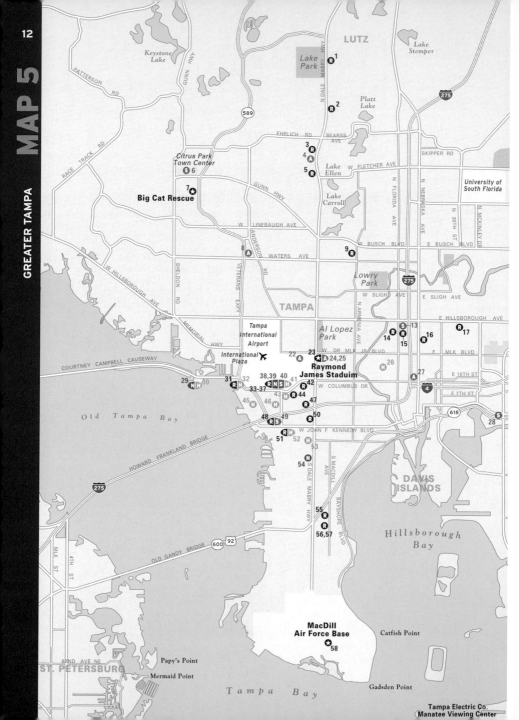

MAP 5

GREATER TAMPA

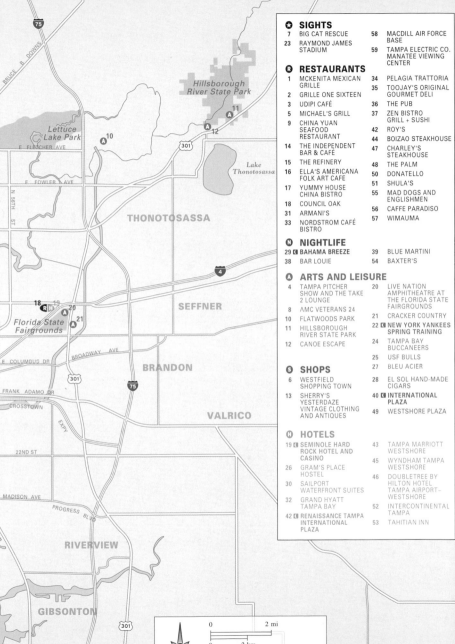

SIGHTS
7 BIG CAT RESCUE
23 RAYMOND JAMES STADIUM
58 MACDILL AIR FORCE BASE
59 TAMPA ELECTRIC CO. MANATEE VIEWING CENTER

RESTAURANTS
1 MCKENITA MEXICAN GRILLE
2 GRILLE ONE SIXTEEN
3 UDIPI CAFÉ
5 MICHAEL'S GRILL
9 CHINA YUAN SEAFOOD RESTAURANT
14 THE INDEPENDENT BAR & CAFÉ
15 THE REFINERY
16 ELLA'S AMERICANA FOLK ART CAFE
17 YUMMY HOUSE CHINA BISTRO
18 COUNCIL OAK
31 ARMANI'S
33 NORDSTROM CAFÉ BISTRO
34 PELAGIA TRATTORIA
35 TOOJAY'S ORIGINAL GOURMET DELI
36 THE PUB
37 ZEN BISTRO GRILL + SUSHI
42 ROY'S
44 BOIZAO STEAKHOUSE
47 CHARLEY'S STEAKHOUSE
48 THE PALM
50 DONATELLO
51 SHULA'S
55 MAD DOGS AND ENGLISHMEN
56 CAFFE PARADISO
57 WIMAUMA

NIGHTLIFE
29 BAHAMA BREEZE
38 BAR LOUIE
39 BLUE MARTINI
54 BAXTER'S

ARTS AND LEISURE
4 TAMPA PITCHER SHOW AND THE TAKE 2 LOUNGE
8 AMC VETERANS 24
10 FLATWOODS PARK
11 HILLSBOROUGH RIVER STATE PARK
12 CANOE ESCAPE
20 LIVE NATION AMPHITHEATRE AT THE FLORIDA STATE FAIRGROUNDS
21 CRACKER COUNTRY
22 NEW YORK YANKEES SPRING TRAINING
24 TAMPA BAY BUCCANEERS
25 USF BULLS
27 BLEU ACIER
28 EL SOL HAND-MADE CIGARS
40 INTERNATIONAL PLAZA
49 WESTSHORE PLAZA

SHOPS
6 WESTFIELD SHOPPING TOWN
13 SHERRY'S YESTERDAZE VINTAGE CLOTHING AND ANTIQUES

HOTELS
19 SEMINOLE HARD ROCK HOTEL AND CASINO
26 GRAM'S PLACE HOSTEL
30 SAILPORT WATERFRONT SUITES
32 GRAND HYATT TAMPA BAY
42 RENAISSANCE TAMPA INTERNATIONAL PLAZA
43 TAMPA MARRIOTT WESTSHORE
45 WYNDHAM TAMPA WESTSHORE
46 DOUBLETREE BY HILTON HOTEL TAMPA AIRPORT– WESTSHORE
52 INTERCONTINENTAL TAMPA
53 TAHITIAN INN

DISTANCE ACROSS MAP:
Approximate: 31.5 miles or 50.6 km

0   2 mi
0   2 km

To
1 Patty & Friends
Antique Mall

9TH AVE N

12TH ST

16TH ST

7TH AVE N

275

689

5TH AVE N

375

4TH AVE N

N 11TH ST
N 10TH ST
CALLA TERRACE N

N 16TH ST
N 15TH ST
N 14TH ST
N 13TH ST

8TH ST

DR MARTIN LUTHER KING S

MIRROR LAKE DR

BURLINGTON AVE
BURLINGTON AVE N

2ND AVE N

2ND AVE N

ARLINGTON AVE

1ST AVE N

N 17TH ST

1ST AVE N

11TH ST

26

CENTRAL AVE

29   30   31

32
N

S 22ND ST
S 21ST ST
S 20TH ST
S 19TH ST

27   28

33

1ST AVE S

DOWNTOWN
ST. PETERSBURG

Tropicana Field

3RD AVE S

S 6TH ST
S 5TH ST

54

4TH AVE S

5TH AVE S

5TH AVE S

175

275

6TH AVE S

ROSER PARK DR S

SIGHTS

| 24 | THE PIER | 43 | DOWNTOWN AREA |

RESTAURANTS

8	MARCHAND'S BAR & GRILL	21	CASSIS AMERICAN BRASSERIE
11	MOON UNDER WATER	37	LA V
12	PARKSHORE GRILL	39	MEZE 119
15	ROLLBOTTO SUSHI	44	WOOD FIRED PIZZA
17	TRYST GASTRO LOUNGE	45	THE AVENUE
18	MFA CAFÉ	46	CAFÉ ALMA
20	BELLA BRAVA	48	GRATZZI ITALIAN GRILLE
		50	Z GRILLE

NIGHTLIFE

4	THE PALLADIUM	40	JANNUS LIVE
16	WINE MADONNA	41	THE GARDEN
32	STATE THEATRE	47	PUSH ULTRA LOUNGE

ARTS AND LEISURE

2	COLISEUM	35	FLORIDA CRAFTSMEN INC.
3	ST. PETERSBURG SHUFFLEBOARD CLUB	36	FLORIDA HOLOCAUST MUSEUM
5	THE PALLADIUM	38	AMERICAN STAGE THEATRE
7	CHIHULY COLLECTION	49	THE MOREAN ARTS CENTER
10	FINN GALLERY	51	TAMPA BAY ROWDIES
14	FLORIDA INTERNATIONAL MUSEUM	52	PROGRESS ENERGY CENTER FOR THE ARTS--THE MAHAFFEY
19	MUSEUM OF FINE ARTS		
23	ST. PETERSBURG MUSEUM OF HISTORY	53	SALVADOR DALÍ MUSEUM
34	THE STUDIO@620	54	TAMPA BAY RAYS

SHOPS

1	PATTY & FRIENDS ANTIQUE MALL	28	MILAGROS
22	BEACH DRIVE NORTHEAST	29	DESIGNERS' CONSIGNER
25	THE PIER	30	PAPER STREET MARKET
26	HASLAM'S BOOK STORE	31	BUFFALO GAL VINTAGE CLOTHING ACCESSORIES AND GIFTS
27	GAS PLANT ANTIQUE ARCADE	33	DADDY KOOL RECORDS

HOTELS

| 6 | LA VERANDA BED AND BREAKFAST | 13 | HOTEL INDIGO |
| 9 | RENAISSANCE VINOY RESORT & GOLF CLUB | 42 | PONCE DE LEON BOUTIQUE HOTEL |

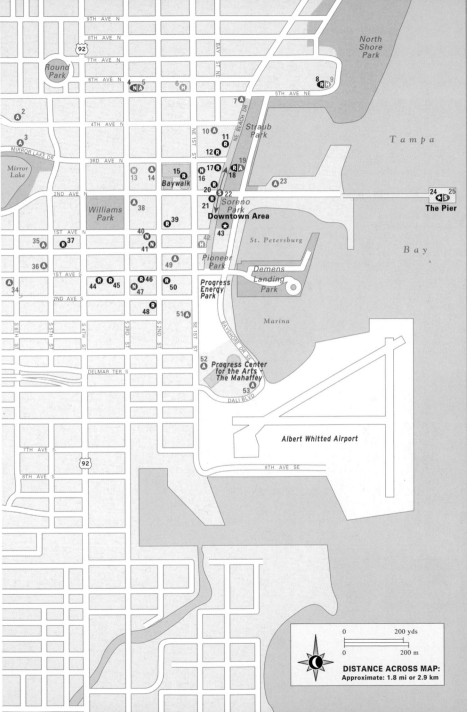

9TH AVE N
8TH AVE N
92
7TH AVE N
6TH AVE N
5TH AVE NE
BAY ST NE
North Shore Park
Round Park
4 5
6 H
N A
8 9
R H
7
4TH AVE N
NE BEACH DR
Tampa
A 2
NE 1ST ST
10 11
Straub Park
A 3
MIRROR LAKE DR
3RD AVE N
12 R
Mirror Lake
N A
13 14
15 R
Baywalk
N 17
16
19
R A
18
A 23
2ND AVE N
20
S 22
24 25
R S
The Pier
A 38
21
Soreno Park
Williams Park
R 39
Downtown Area
42
43
St. Petersburg
Bay
1ST AVE N
40
35 A
R 37
N
41
A H
49
Pioneer Park
36 A
1ST AVE S
A
34
44 R 45
N 46
47
R 50
Progress Energy Park
Demens Landing Park
2ND AVE S
R 48
51 A
Marina
S 6TH ST
S 5TH ST
S 4TH ST
S 3RD ST
S 2ND ST
SE 1ST ST
52 A
Progress Center for the Arts – The Mahaffey
53 A
DELMAR TER S
DALI BLVD
BAYSHORE DR SE
Albert Whitted Airport
7TH AVE S
92
8TH AVE S
8TH AVE SE

0   200 yds
0   200 m

DISTANCE ACROSS MAP:
Approximate: 1.8 mi or 2.9 km

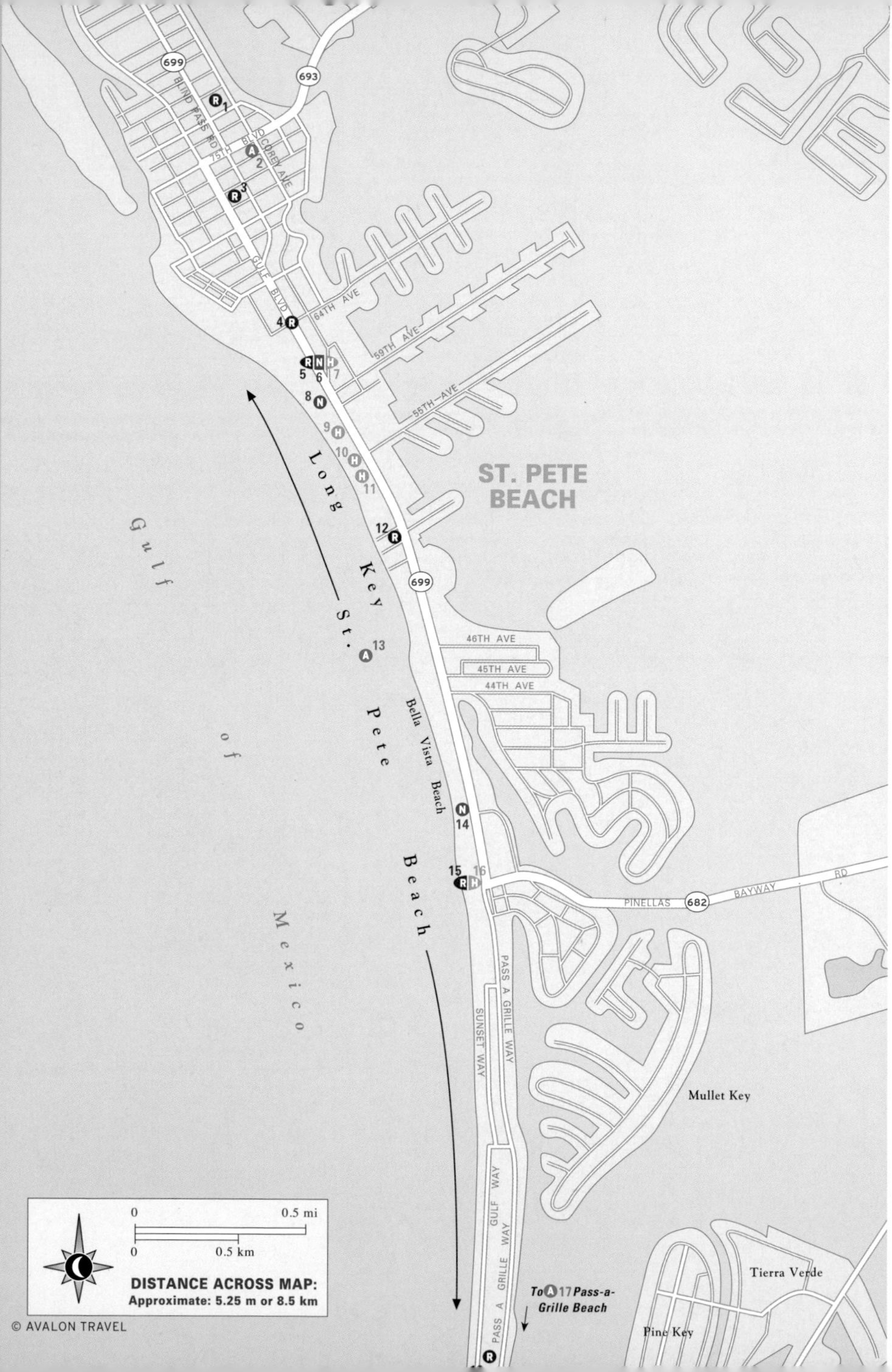

699
693

R 1
2
R 3

699

699

64TH AVE
59TH AVE
55TH AVE

4 R
R N H
5 6 7
8 N
9
10 H
H 11

12 R

ST. PETE
BEACH

46TH AVE
45TH AVE
44TH AVE

A 13

Long Key St. Pete Beach

Bella Vista Beach

N
14

15 R H 16

PINELLAS 682 BAYWAY RD

Gulf

of

Mexico

PASS A GRILLE WAY
SUNSET WAY
GULF WAY

Mullet Key

Tierra Verde

To A 17 Pass-a-
Grille Beach

Pine Key

R

0   0.5 mi
0   0.5 km

DISTANCE ACROSS MAP:
Approximate: 5.25 m or 8.5 km

© AVALON TRAVEL

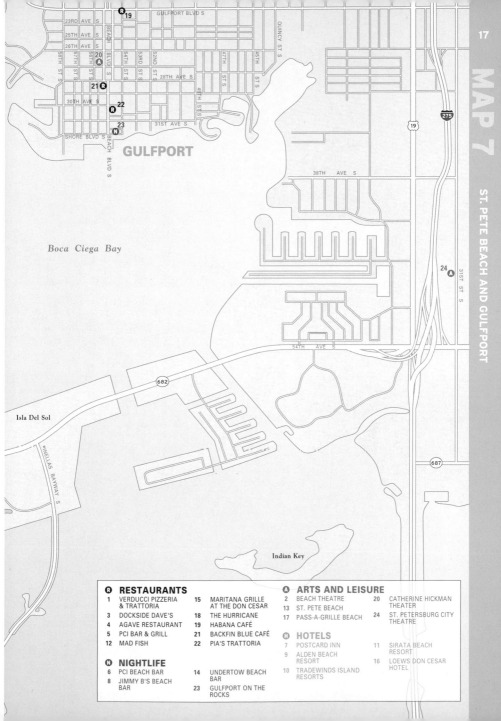

MAP 8

CLEARWATER, CLEARWATER BEACH, AND DUNEDIN

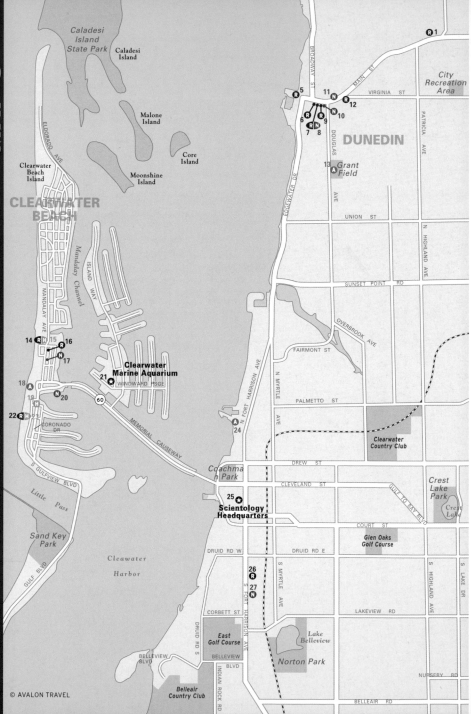

Caladesi
Island
State Park

Caladesi
Island

Malone
Island

Core
Island

Moonshine
Island

Clearwater
Beach
Island

CLEARWATER
BEACH

City
Recreation
Area

DUNEDIN

Grant
Field

Clearwater
Marine Aquarium

WINDWARD PSGE

CORONADO
DR

MEMORIAL CAUSEWAY

Coachman
Park

Scientology
Headquarters

Clearwater
Country Club

Crest
Lake
Park

Crest
Lake

Glen Oaks
Golf Course

Little
Pass

Sand Key
Park

Cleawater
Harbor

East
Golf Course

Lake
Belleview

Norton Park

Belleview
Country Club

© AVALON TRAVEL

MAIN ST
580
Countryside Executive Golf Course
Jerry Lake
GREENBRIAR BLVD
COUNTRYSIDE BLVD
VIRGINIA AVE
19
Lake Chautauque
Spring Lake
N BELCHER RD
Top of the World Golf Course
N KEENE RD
Sylvan Abbey Memorial Park
SUNSET POINT RD
OLD COACHMAN RD
N BELCHER RD
29
Clearwater Airpark
Lake Nature Park
N HERCULES AVE
Clearwater Executive Golf Club
Lickton Field
N SATURN AVE
NE COACHMAN RD
28
Bright House Field
N MCMULLEN RD
BOOTH RD
Park
DREW ST
St. Petersburg College
30
GULF TO BAY BLVD
CLEARWATER
31
BOOTH RD
Old Tampa Bay

DISTANCE ACROSS MAP:
Approximate: 8 m or 12.9 km

0   0.5 mi
0   0.5 km

N MCMULLEN RD

SIGHTS

| 21 | CLEARWATER MARINE AQUARIUM | 25 | SCIENTOLOGY HEADQUARTERS |

RESTAURANTS

1	SPOTOS STEAKJOINT 2	12	MEZZE ON MAIN
2	BASCETTI'S ITALIAN GRILLE	14	CARETTA ON THE GULF
3	IVORY MANDARIN BISTRO	16	KIKU JAPANESE FINE DINING
4	BESA GRILL	22	SHOR AMERICAN SEAFOOD GRILL
5	BON APPETIT	26	CRISTINO'S COAL OVEN PIZZA
6	THE BLACK PEARL	30	LENNY'S RESTAURANT
7	KELLY'S	31	HOOTERS
9	CASA TINA		

NIGHTLIFE

8	CHIC-A-BOOM ROOM	20	SHEPHARD'S BEACH RESORT
10	SKIP'S	27	O'KEEFE'S TAVERN AND RESTAURANT
11	PAN Y VINO WINE BAR		
17	BOBBY'S BISTRO		

ARTS AND LEISURE

13	TORONTO BLUE JAYS SPRING TRAINING	28	PHILADELPHIA PHILLIES SPRING TRAINING
18	CLEARWATER BEACH	29	RUTH ECKERD HALL
24	FRANCIS WILSON PLAYHOUSE		

HOTELS

| 15 | SANDPEARL RESORT | 23 | HYATT REGENCY CLEARWATER BEACH RESORT & SPA |
| 19 | PIER HOUSE 60 MARINA HOTEL | | |

● SIGHTS
- 29 ◨ SUNKEN GARDENS
- 35 ◨ SUNSHINE SKYWAY BRIDGE AND FISHING PIERS

● RESTAURANTS
- 7 BASQUE
- 10 E & E STAKEOUT GRILL
- 12 CARMELITA'S
- 16 ◨ CAFE PONTE
- 22 CAFE VIENNA
- 28 CASITA TAQUERIA
- 31 ALESIA RESTAURANT
- 33 SKYWAY JACK'S RESTAURANT

● NIGHTLIFE
- 9 CLEARWATER WINE BAR & BISTRO
- 37 GEORGIE'S ALIBI OF ST. PETE
- 39 DETOUR
- 40 BEAKS ST. PETE

● ARTS AND LEISURE
- 1 BROOKER CREEK PRESERVE
- 3 ◨ HONEYMOON ISLAND STATE PARK
- 4 ANCLOTE KEY PRESERVE STATE PARK
- 5 ◨ CALADESI ISLAND STATE PARK
- 6 DUNEDIN FINE ARTS CENTER & CHILDREN'S ART MUSEUM
- 13 BEACH ART CENTER
- 14 HERITAGE VILLAGE
- 15 ARMED FORCES HISTORY MUSEUM
- 18 DERBY LANE
- 19 WEEDON ISLAND PRESERVE CULTURAL AND NATURAL HISTORY CENTER
- 20 TAMPA BAY AUTO MUSEUM
- 21 SAWGRASS LAKE PARK
- 30 GREAT EXPLORATIONS CHILDREN'S MUSEUM
- 32 ◨ PINELLAS TRAIL
- 34 BOYD HILL NATURE PRESERVE
- 36 SUNSHINE SKYWAY FISHING PIERS
- 38 CRAFTSMAN HOUSE
- 41 FORT DE SOTO STATE PARK
- 42 EGMONT KEY STATE PARK
- 43 SNEAD ISLAND AND EMERSON POINT PARK

● SHOPS
- 11 ◨ WILLIAM DEAN
- 23 ZBOOKZ NEW & USED BOOKS
- 24 JOHN'S PASS VILLAGE AND BOARDWALK
- 25 TYRONE SQUARE MALL
- 26 BANANAS MUSIC AND MOVIES
- 27 RESOLVE CLOTHING EXCHANGE
- 44 ELLENTON PREMIUM OUTLETS

● HOTELS
- 2 INNISBROOK
- 8 SAFETY HARBOR RESORT AND SPA
- 17 ST. PETERSBURG MARRIOTT CLEARWATER

© AVALON TRAVEL

MacDill Air
Force Base

Tampa Bay

OLD GANDY BRIDGE
Friendship
Trail Bridge

92
600

Weedon
19 Island
Weedon Island Preserve

Papy's Point
Mermaid Point

18

22

687

Coquina
Key

Point Pinellas

Sunshine Skyway Bridge
and Fishing Piers

To ⑫42 Egmont Key State Park,
⑬43 Snead Island and Emerson
Point Park, and ⑭44 Ellenton Premium Outlets

4TH ST N
28
29 30
Sunken
Gardens

16TH ST N

275

SEE
DETAIL

34

62ND AVE S
54TH AVE S

35 36

SUNSHINE SKYWAY
BRIDGE (TOLL)

275

GANDY BLVD N

DR MARTIN LUTHER KING ST
17

Sawgrass
21 Lake Park
20

Pinellas
Park

ST. PETERSBURG

19

19

22ND

5TH   CENTRAL   AVE

19

26
32

33

GULFPORT

Lake
Maggiore

34TH ST N

Boca
Ciega Bay

Isla del Sol

118TH AVE N

118TH AVE N

102ND AVE N

19

PARK BLVD

62ND   54TH

693

689TH

ST

H109

ST

H109

693

38TH AVE N

64TH ST S

64TH ST S

66TH ST S

66TH ST S

31

25

23

TYRONE BLVD N

690

694

SEMINOLE

S BELCHER

DAIRY RD

Lake
Seminole

Seminole

595

SEMINOLE

19

24

113TH ST N

Pinellas
Trail

126TH ST N
102ND AVE N
WALSINGHAM RD

14

233

INDIAN
SHORES

Indian Rocks
Beach

Suncoast Seabird
Sanctuary

REDINGTON SHORES

NORTH REDINGTON
SHORES

Redington Beach

Madeira
Beach

Treasure
Island

St. Pete Beach

PASS-A-GRILLE BEACH

To ⑪41 Fort De Soto State Park

Gulf   of   Mexico

Gulf   of   Mexico

DISTANCE ACROSS MAP
Approximate: 24 mi or 38.6 km

2 mi
0
2 km
0

Seminole
Park

24TH ST N
25TH ST N
40
26TH ST N
3RD AVE N
BURLINGTON AVE N
CENTRAL AVE
39
2ND AVE N
1ST AVE N
1ST AVE S
38
1ST ST N
37
31ST ST N

Discover Tampa & St. Petersburg

Except for Alaska, Florida has the longest coastline of any state: 1,350 miles. The majority of that length is on the Gulf side, the west coast of Florida—a maze of barrier islands, intracoastal waterways, shallow shorelines, and deep bays. And so much of life here centers on all that sustaining water. In fact, the greater Tampa Bay Area, the second-largest metro area in the state, is a region made up of many distinct communities built around the bay, the Gulf of Mexico, and waterways like the Hillsborough River, all laced together with bridges and causeways.

Still, Tampa in Hillsborough County and St. Petersburg in Pinellas County have distinct relationships with all that water. Tampa fronts Tampa Bay, not the Gulf of Mexico. With a huge working port, it doesn't have any beaches to speak of. From the distinct Latin roots of Tampa's historic Ybor City to the high-rises downtown, from the thrills of Busch Gardens to the many spectator sporting opportunities, Tampa is nonetheless a slick vacation destination.

Across the bay, St. Petersburg and Pinellas County share Tampa's geography and climate, but both offer a more low-slung and historic spin on sun and sand. On the bay side, St. Petersburg is a draw for museum buffs, while those nearly in the buff come to sunbathe on the west side of the peninsula in St. Pete Beach, Clearwater Beach, and all the Gulf-side communities in between. Pinellas claims 35 miles of Gulf Coast beaches, drawing more than five million overnight visitors a year to toast in the sun, dodge summer rain squalls, and visit such special museums as the Salvador Dalí Museum, the Chiluly Collection, and the Florida Holocaust Museum.

But it is still the beachy beauty of west-central Florida that offers the kind of rough-edged, front-row view into the natural world that is hard to come by these days. Add to that posh and culturally rich neighborhoods, enduring historical sites, as well as family-friendly attractions to rival Disney, and it's clear that Tampa and St. Petersburg are the Sunshine State's most delectable destinations.

Planning Your Trip

► WHERE TO GO

Downtown Tampa and Channelside

Like a number of American cities, Tampa's downtown is waking up. It's been the city's financial and cultural center for decades, but only in the new millennium have people begun moving into downtown condo high-rises. The city's downtown infrastructure of restaurants, shops, and other amenities has had to keep pace.

Located dockside at the Port of Tampa, where all the cruise ships come in, the shopping/dining/entertainment complex called Channelside has a fun upscale bowling alley, little boutiques, and about a dozen restaurants. The Tampa Bay Times Forum, venue for the 2012 Republican National Convention and home to Tampa's professional hockey team, the Tampa Bay Lightning, is also located

here. This waterfront district is the location for many hotels and is about 15 minutes from Tampa International Airport.

South Tampa and Hyde Park

The city's first residential suburb, Hyde Park was, and still is, the residential area of choice for prominent citizens. Many of the 19th-century bungalows and Princess Anne–style cottages are still occupied today, and the Hyde Park Village collection of boutiques and restaurants is one of the city's better draws.

Davis Islands

Two little islands off downtown Tampa, where the Hillsborough River empties into Hillsborough Bay, became booming real estate developments at the turn of the 19th

downtown Tampa and the harbor

bridge to the beach, Pinellas County

Clear water stretches for miles along the beautiful Gulf of Mexico.

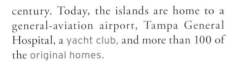

century. Today, the islands are home to a general-aviation airport, Tampa General Hospital, a yacht club, and more than 100 of the original homes.

Ybor City

Party central in Tampa, the century-old cigar-rolling center of town exhibits little of its Cuban heritage these days. The main drag is 7th Avenue, also known as La Septima, closed off to cars on weekend evenings for the throngs of revelers. During the week, the area is more sedate, a better time to try out one or more of the restaurants that range all over the gastronomic map: Among the prime cuisines are Spanish and Cuban.

Busch Gardens and North Tampa

Busch Gardens is located 20 minutes north of downtown in an area that for a long time was not much more than cow pastures and the slowly spreading campus of the University of South Florida. The university has blossomed in recent years, now offering more than 230 degree programs; enrollment hovers around 50,000. The area to the north of USF has become among the most desirable residential communities in the Bay Area.

Greater Tampa

Thanks to the abundance of wealthy international air travelers, the area to the southwest of downtown is chock full of business-friendly hotels and fine shopping. With anchor stores Neiman Marcus and Nordstrom, International Plaza gets the nod for fanciest shopping. This posh assembly of stores is served by an open-air village of restaurants called Bay Street. About four minutes away, Westshore Plaza features more than 100 similarly fancy specialty shops and four major department stores, including a lovely Saks Fifth Avenue.

Pier 60 at Clearwater Beach

Downtown St. Petersburg

St. Petersburg is Florida's fourth-largest city, the anchor of Pinellas County. The city's downtown—on the bayside, not the Gulf side—has seen lots of new growth, from pricey condos to the recently renamed and renovated Shops at St. Pete, a retail, restaurant, and multi-screen complex. There are romantic bed-and-breakfasts, fine restaurants, and cultural attractions.

St. Pete Beach

St. Pete Beach is an autonomous barrier-island town southwest of St. Petersburg. It's a classic Florida beach town, with late-night waterside clubs, deep-water fishing charters, and low-slung motels with views of the beach.

Gulfport

Gulfport is known as the Gateway to the Gulf, as it is the point of departure for the Gulf of Mexico. It faces Boca Ciega Bay, which

leads to the Gulf. It has a sleepy, old-timey yet slightly bohemian charm that lures many snowbirds into staying year-round.

Clearwater and Clearwater Beach

Clearwater Beach offers a wide, inviting shore, serious beach volleyball, and loads of nightlife and casual seafood restaurants. It has perhaps the densest concentration of beachside accommodations, often tall resort hotels and condos right on the beach. Clearwater's downtown, on the other hand, is dominated by the spiritual headquarters of Scientology.

Dunedin

One of the oldest towns on the west coast of Florida, Dunedin has a wooded and subtropical setting with four miles of picturesque waterfront. The closest the Gulf Coast comes to hippie culture, Dunedin boasts a relaxed boat-centric lifestyle, with comfy bars and

windsurfers in front of St. Petersburg's Sunshine Skyway Bridge

flip-flop–wearing denizens. Just off the coast of Dunedin are two of Florida's most wonderful beaches: Honeymoon Island and Caladesi Island State Parks.

▶ WHEN TO GO

This part of Florida is a year-round destination. A huge family draw, partly because of its big airport and proximity to Orlando, the area is at its busiest during school vacations. Thanksgiving–Easter are peak visitor times, but numbers also spike during summer vacation. But be prepared: Summer weather here is like hot breath on your neck all the time, and there are gloomy, stormy skies many afternoons.

This area is also a huge draw for Grapefruit League spring training devotees. The month of March sees many baseball fans cheering on their beloved teams: the Phillies and Blue Jays in Pinellas; the Yankees near downtown Tampa.

Snowbirds also bump up the local population in the winter months (especially on the Pinellas County side). Their timing isn't arbitrary—February, March, and April along much of Florida's Gulf Coast are magical. Temperatures are in the high 70s, with a little breeze, low humidity, little rain, and the Gulf water is just warm enough for swimming.

That said, if you visit just after the snowbirds fly home and before summer sets in, you'll find plenty of accommodations, unoccupied tables in restaurants, and room to roam unhindered on the beaches. You may also find that it's a little cheaper after Easter. The same can be said of the fall, before the huge winter influx of visitors. September and October are lovely in the Tampa Bay Area, but it's also hurricane season, something not to be taken lightly.

Bromeliads are a common sight in Tampa and St. Petersburg.

► BEFORE YOU GO

Tampa International Airport is the largest on the Gulf Coast, clean, organized, and a regular award-winner because it is easy to navigate. Rental cars can be reserved in advance from the airport. Cabs, buses, and shuttles will also ferry you from the airport to your hotel, but the Tampa/St. Petersburg area is very difficult to navigate if you don't have your own wheels.

As for what to pack: Very few places require a jacket and tie, but for nicer restaurants you may feel more comfortable in something festive. The preponderance of outdoor activities also necessitates a change of shoes: something for dinner, sneakers for hiking or athletics, and swim shoes or flip-flops.

Even if you're visiting in the summer, bring a sweater. Everything is over-air-conditioned. In the winter, a long-sleeved pullover with light slacks is usually fine.

If you aim to take full advantage of the area's outdoor allures, bring sunscreen, binoculars, polarized sunglasses (for seeing depth when you fish), and a bird book. Once you're here, you can rent bikes, scooters, skates, strollers, beach chairs, boogie or surf boards, fishing equipment, snorkeling gear, motorboats, Jet Skis, kayaks, canoes, and sailboats.

Explore Tampa & St. Petersburg

▶ THE BEST OF TAMPA AND ST. PETERSBURG

Day 1

▶ Start your vacation by visiting a fairly urban city beach, Clearwater Beach, a long, wide stretch offering showers, restrooms, concessions, cabanas, umbrella rentals, volleyball, and metered parking. Pier 60, where the beach meets the causeway, has a regular sunset celebration with entertainers and live music. But this is the warm-up, just to get your feet wet, so to speak.

▶ If you have a little more time on your hands, head to Caladesi Island in Dunedin, which frequently makes it onto the lists of top beaches in the world. It is only accessible by ferry from Honeymoon Island State Park off Alternate Highway 19 in Dunedin. Caladesi is 3.5 miles long, with a marina and swim beach right near where the ferry lets you off, but the rest of the island remains undeveloped. The bay side of the island is worth exploring, with a mangrove shoreline and seagrass flats (rent canoes and paddle the 3.5-mile canoe trail that meanders through the bay side).

▶ All that paddling will certainly make you ravenous. Dunedin's Main Street is not far away, with a wealth of dining options. Whet your appetite with a little spicy Mexican fare, especially veggie, at Day-of-the-Dead-themed Casa Tina.

Caledesi Island and Honeymoon Island State Parks

WHERE THE HEART IS: TAMPA BAY'S MOST ROMANTIC SPOTS

There's been a lot of talk about some crafty chemical in chocolate simulating the feeling of being in love. Who knows if that's true, but chocolate is indubitably a good way to begin an amorous foray. Even more so if it's Choco-late-Chocolate-Chocolate. That's actually the name of the demure chocolate-shellacked cylinder packing chocolate cheesecake, chocolate mousse, and chocolate pie into one deadly package served with aplomb at **Harry Waugh Dessert Room** at Bern's Steak House. And if the romance leaves you cold, the sheer quantity of sugar, high-octane coffee, and gorgeous after-dinner drinks are bound to give you a little thrill.

On the other hand, nothing gets the heart pumping like a brush with danger. **Big Cat Rescue,** the world's largest accredited sanctuary for big cats, lets you and your sweetie stay overnight with the jaguars and snow leopards. Just hope you're not breakfast in bed. On the third hand (now that's extremely handy), **Skydive City** in Zephyrhills (in Pasco County,

to the north of Tampa) is one of the world's most famous "drop zones." Why here? According to owner T.K. Hayes, "It's in the middle of nowhere, with not a single picturesque thing about it. It's really about the people—Zephyrhills is the largest skydiving place in the world." Tandem jumping (where a rookie jumps physically harnessed to an instructor) has opened skydiving up to people who might never have otherwise taken the plunge.

Then again, you could take to the sea. Ahoy, mates and would-be mates. Climb aboard **Yacht StarShip,** Tampa's premier dining yacht, while the sunset casts its sherbet hues across the Bay.

So far, this is mostly stunt-romance. For Old School champagne-and-caviar, culminating in good bed linens and discreet room service, head to the **Renaissance Vinoy Resort & Golf Club,** St. Petersburg's exquisitely restored Mediterranean Revival resort that exudes the kind of rarefied glamour that helps put life's quotidian woes behind you.

▶ Cap it all off with a nightcap and a little hip-swiveling at the whimsical Chic-a-Boom Room.

Day 2

▶ Probably worth a whole day in its own right, Busch Gardens has must-sees that include the Montu, the ShieKra, the Kumba, and the tooth-rattling Gwazi, in descending order of priority. For a truly different experience, first check the live cheetahs racing along nearby and then board the Cheetah Hunt coaster. Busch is a park for all ages, with a mix of big, scary coasters and sweet animal attractions. And, for lunch, the on-site concessions are better than they need to be (the truly hungry can opt for the all-day dining deal; $32.99 adult, $14.99 child age 3–9).

▶ Right across the street from Busch Gardens is Tampa's Museum of Science & Industry (MOSI), probably the best science museum on the Gulf Coast. It's majorly ambitious to combine this in a day with Busch Gardens, but it can be done.

▶ Alternatively, skip Busch Gardens and pair a visit to MOSI with a half day spent wandering the Florida Aquarium.

▶ Stop for lunch across the street at the port-side dining/entertainment complex of Channelside.

▶ In the late afternoon, take one of the aquarium's Wild Dolphin Cruise Eco-Tours out into the bay to get an eagle-eye view of dolphins, manatees, and migratory birds.

downtown St. Petersburg

▶ And before you hit the hay, experience a Florida original Cracker-style institution: Try the gator nuggets at Skipper's Smokehouse while watching a live blues performance.

Day 3

▶ Spend your third day immersed in the area's arts offerings. Drive over the Howard Frankland bridge to downtown St. Petersburg.

▶ Wander the galleries of the expanded Museum of Fine Arts, followed by a little lunch in its MFA Café.

▶ Then cross Beach Drive to take in glassworks maestro Dale Chihuly's art in its only purpose-built gallery outside his Washington state studio. It takes about an hour to see it all, with fascinating docent-led tours.

▶ Still in an artsy mood? Barely a half-mile south is the fascinating Salvador Dalí Museum, opened in its new home in January 2011 to display the world's largest private collection of the Surrealist genius's works.

▶ Head from any of these museums to Central Avenue, to do a little window shopping or credit-card calisthenics.

▶ As the afternoon wanes, catch a show at the American Stage Theatre or the city-owned Mahaffey Theater.

▶ Music fans should attend a concert outdoors at rock-centric Jannus Live.

▶ There are several worthy restaurants on Beach Drive and within a block or two of Central Avenue that offer tables on the sidewalk.

FOUL-WEATHER FUN

Salvador Dalí Museum

Tampa Bay in the storm season can be a bummer, with every afternoon given over to an impressive deluge or, at the very least, some ominous gloom. But you don't need much to help you while away a wet afternoon. Here are just a handful of ways to keep away those rainy-day blues.

First stop: University of Tampa. Regal yet totally out of place with its minarets, keyhole arches, and ornate Moorish revival architecture, the opulent restored rooms (with original furnishings) of the university's **Henry B. Plant Museum** provide a window to America's Gilded Age, Tampa's history, and the life and work of Henry Plant.

Now head north to University of South Florida. An enormous institution that casts its imposing shadow over the cultural scene of Tampa, it nonetheless is seldom visited by locals who aren't lugging backpacks and books. A visit to the **University of South Florida Contemporary Art Museum** is a good excuse to explore the university campus before parking at the small gallery containing a permanent collection of sculpture multiples by artists such as Roy Lichtenstein, Robert Rauschenberg, and James Rosenquist.

Or skip the studious route and spend some time in rented shoes. **Splitsville** is Tampa's finest bowling alley-cum-restaurant. It has good food, a whimsical environment, and the coolest bowling shoes ever.

But what's more appropriate in moist conditions than swimming with the fishes? At the **Florida Aquarium** anyone six and older can do just that in the coral reef exhibit, and the **Clearwater Marine Aquarium** is a working research facility and home to rescued and recuperating marine mammals, including the world-famous prosthetic-tailed dolphin named Winter.

Speaking of drippy conditions, to see some of the world's most famous molten clocks, head to St. Petersburg's **Salvador Dalí Museum,** the most comprehensive collection of permanent works by the famous Spanish master who himself is the most recognized artist in history (the waxed mustache and arched eyebrows certainly help with that).

SIGHTS

From Busch Gardens to Ybor City, to the lovely beaches on the Gulf Coast, the Tampa and St. Petersburg area has much to offer. In terms of sightseeing, the region has more of a recreational spin, but don't let that be misleading. A walk along Bayshore Boulevard allows one to soak up the riches of Tampa, from the stately homes in Hyde Park to a stunning view of the downtown skyline. Busch Gardens is a family dream come true—but if culture is what you seek, Ybor City's Cuban influence still holds strong not far from downtown. Ybor City is the place to experience the shrinking legacy of the Cuban cigar industry. Are animals more your thing? The Lowry Park Zoo is the perfect place to spend an afternoon watching white tigers and learning about manatee rehabilitation. If you've got kids in tow, don't miss the Museum of Science and Industry—guaranteed to entertain even the most finicky of children with a plethora of hands-on exhibits.

At first glance, St. Petersburg and surroundings may seem to be all about their 20-plus miles of Gulf of Mexico beaches, but Pinellas County is a treasure trove of riches, including St. Petersburg's park-lined waterfront in the tourist-friendly downtown area. Add to that a myriad of museums—including renowned, stand-alone collections of works by Salvador Dali and Dale Chihuly and a moving Holocaust museum—and you won't lack for things to do and see.

COURTESY OF VISITSTPETECLEARWATER.COM

HIGHLIGHTS

LOOK FOR ◖ TO FIND RECOMMENDED SIGHTS.

COURTESY OF VISIT FLORIDA

Florida Aquarium

◖ **Best Place to Go Eye-to-Eye with a Goliath Grouper:** The **Florida Aquarium** is a marvelous Tampa attraction: a 152,000-square-foot center that focuses on Florida's relationship to the Gulf, estuaries, rivers, and other waterways, with a strong environmental message (page 35).

◖ **Best Place to Puff a Local Smoke: 7th Avenue (La Septima)** in Ybor City was once known as the "Cigar Capital of the World," with nearly 12,000 cigarmakers producing 700 million cigars a year. Now Tampa's Latin Quarter is a National Historic Landmark District, offering historic shops by day and the city's most vital nightlife after the sun goes down (page 37).

◖ **Best Loop-the-Loops:** Thrill seekers won't need to be reminded to visit **Busch Gardens.** The park is an unusual mix of thrill rides, entertainment, and animal attractions (it was the first in the U.S. to create an open-range animal habitat) (page 38).

◖ **Best Way to Wander Through a Verdant Yesteryear:** It puttered along as a kitschy Old Florida attraction for years, until the City of St. Petersburg restored **Sunken Gardens,** four-acre tropical gardens, to their former glory (page 46).

◖ **Best Bridge:** The bright yellow **Sunshine Skyway Bridge and Fishing Piers** is the world's longest cable-stayed bridge, the world's longest fishing pier, and a Pinellas County icon (page 46).

Downtown Tampa and Channelside   Map 1

AMERICAN VICTORY SHIP MARINER'S MEMORIAL MUSEUM

705 Channelside Dr., 813/228-8766,
www.americanvictory.org

HOURS: Tues.-Sat. 10 A.M.-5 P.M., Sun. and Mon. noon-5 P.M.

COST: $10 adult, $8 senior and veteran, $5 child, free child 3 and younger

Liberty ships were sitting ducks: They traveled a maximum speed of 11 knots, easy targets for WWII submarines. Thus the Victory ship was born. These newcomers zipped along at 17 knots thanks to cross-compound steam turbine engines that delivered 6,000 or 8,500 horsepower. They were 455 feet long and 62 feet wide. They had reinforced hull plates and included one five-inch stern gun, one three-inch bow antiaircraft gun, and eight 20-milimeter machine guns at various locations onboard.

To explore one of these feats of engineering, visit the SS *American Victory,* one of just four fully operational WWII ships in the United States. This merchant ship served during World War II and the Korean and Vietnam Wars as a military cargo carrier. It is tied up in the Channelside district of downtown Tampa, offering self-guided tours of the ship and guided tours that illuminate the restoration process. It also displays traveling marine exhibits.

CHANNELSIDE BAY PLAZA

615 Channelside Dr., 813/223-4250,
www.channelsidebayplaza.com

HOURS: Operating hours vary according to the store, restaurant, or attraction, generally daily 11 A.M.-11 P.M.

COST: Free

Located dockside at the Port of Tampa where all the cruise ships come in, the shopping/dining/entertainment complex Channelside Bay Plaza has a 10-screen movieplex, including one screen that is 72 feet tall, plus a full-service bar, a fun upmarket bowling alley whose menu runs from sushi to steaks, little boutiques, and nearly a dozen themed restaurants and cafés.

CURTIS HIXON WATERFRONT PARK

600 N. Ashley Dr.

HOURS: Sunrise-sunset

COST: Free

The eight-acre Curtis Hixon Waterfront Park is a great feature of the Tampa Riverwalk. Designed by the New York–based landscape architect Thomas Balsley, the park has become the gathering place for such disparate groups as Occupy Tampa and a massive weekend outdoor ashtanga yoga class. With public performance art and an ice rink erected in winter, the park features a great sloping lawn with two fountains, a children's playground (featuring an interactive NEOS 360 Ring, which combines video games with aerobic exercise and is the first of its kind in the southeast United States), public boat docks along the Hillsborough River, a dog park, seat terraces, a pavilion, and café.

⟨ FLORIDA AQUARIUM

701 Channelside Dr., 813/273-4000,
www.flaquarium.org

HOURS: Daily 9:30 A.M.-5 P.M.

COST: $21.95 box office adult, $19.75 online adult; $18.95 box office senior, $17.05 online senior; $16.95 box office child age 3-11, $15.25 online child age 3-11; free for child 2 and younger

Efforts to gussy up the Florida Aquarium in the past few years with a two-acre outdoor water play area have resulted in an aquarium that doesn't want for anything. Opened in 1995, the 152,000-square-foot aquarium focuses on the waters of Florida. It doesn't contain an exhaustive catalog of the world's aquatic creatures, but tells a very compelling story about Florida's relationship to the Gulf, estuaries, rivers, and other waterways. There are some exotic exhibits (the otherworldly sea dragons, like sea horses mated with philodendrons), but the best parts are the open freshwater tanks of otters, spoonbills, gators, Florida soft shell turtles, and snakes. The aquarium manages to convey a very strong environmental message in its natives-versus-exotics exhibits, but it's all fun, never seeming pious or heavy-handed. There's also a wonderful, big shark tank, a colorful coral grotto, a sea urchin touch tank, and a daily penguin promenade, when the tuxedo-clad birds do a brief walkabout. It's a small enough aquarium that three hours is plenty of time, and not so crowded that kids can't do a little wandering on their own. Regularly scheduled shows involve native Florida birds and small mammals, as well as shark feeding. In fact, the aquarium offers "swim with the fishes" wetsuit dives into the shark tank for the stalwart over 15 years old. A recent cell phone audio tour may be the coolest thing yet.

After perusing the marine life within the eye-catching shell-shaped building, you can take your newfound knowledge out on the bay with one of the aquarium-run **Wild Dolphin Cruise Eco-Tours** ($37.95 adult, $33.95 senior, $29.95 child under 12). You'll head out in a 72-foot catamaran watching for dolphins, manatees, and a huge number of birds. Tampa Bay is home to more than 500 bottlenose dolphins. Tickets are available at the aquarium box office the day of the tour only.

THE PORT OF TAMPA

Seaport Street Terminal, 651 Channelside Dr., Pier #2, 813/905-7678, www.tampaport.com
HOURS: Port offices 7:30 A.M.–5 P.M.
COST: Free

The Port of Tampa typically has four cruise ships calling at its busy port, with a passenger count going from 200,000 in 1998 to just about 900,000 in 2011. There are newer and larger vessels steaming into the downtown Channelside port all the time. A number of lines head out of Tampa on 4-, 5-, 7-, 14- and even 21-day itineraries.

Tampa is now a home port for three cruise lines: Carnival Cruise Lines, Holland America, and Royal Caribbean, with winter-season departures by Norwegian Cruise Line.

The Port's cruise terminals include customer-friendly information areas, full passenger amenities, and on-site parking ($14/day, no reservations are needed). Valet services are also available. The port is in close proximity to Tampa's downtown interstates and within 15 minutes of Tampa International Airport.

South Tampa, Hyde Park, and Davis Islands   Map 2

BAYSHORE BOULEVARD

Swann Ave. to Interbay Blvd.
HOURS: Daily 24 hours
COST: Free

Bayshore Boulevard may be the world's longest continuous sidewalk as it is often labeled. It borders Hillsborough Bay for nearly five miles without a break in the gorgeousness. Joggers, walkers, skaters, and bikers dot its length, which goes from downtown through Hyde Park. Home to the fanciest homes in Tampa, the boulevard was named one of AAA's "Top Roads" for its panoramic views. Even if you don't feel like walking it, it's Tampa's most signature drive. (Also, Tampa Preservation has an excellent driving tour of Hyde Park and a walking tour of part of the neighborhood geared for younger readers; for copies call 813/248-5437.)

DAVIS ISLAND YACHT CLUB

1315 Severn Ave., 813/251-1158, www.diyc.org
HOURS: Spring-fall Thurs. 7 P.M., winter Sun. 2 P.M.
COST: Free to watch

Drive over the causeway to Davis Islands, then across the length of the island to the unassuming, squatty Davis Island Yacht Club. It's free to watch racing, even free to crew for the evening if you have experience and a skipper will take you on. In the winter, the races take place at 2 P.M. on Sundays, but in the warm weather you can watch different classes of sailboats heading out into the bay on Thursday nights at 7 P.M. with the backdrop of Tampa's downtown bathed in a rosy sunset glow. It's beautiful, especially when all the colorful, billowing spinnakers head out.

HYDE PARK VILLAGE

W. Swann Ave., S. Dakota Ave., and Snow Ave., 813/251-3500, www.hydeparkvillage.net
HOURS: Vary
COST: Free

Tampa's downtown doesn't really have a retail center. For that, you need to visit Hyde Park. It's not vast, but the outdoor shopping/dining area is the most appealing shopping destination in town, especially when the weather is nice. There's a large covered parking garage, free to shoppers, and a lovely landscaped plaza at the center. Pottery Barn and Williams-Sonoma are among the bigger stores, with other name brands such as Brooks Brothers, Anthropologie, and Tommy Bahama. Top restaurants include the Cal-Ital Wine Exchange and the indoor-outdoor, Sinatra-infused Timpano Italian Chophouse. In the summer, Hyde Park Village hosts a free, monthly, live music performance, and there's a fresh market each Sunday. The area has seen a great deal of flux in the past couple of years, with stores playing musical chairs, buildings torn down, and condos going up.

Ybor City   Map 3

CENTRO YBOR

1600 E. 8th Ave., 813/242-4660, www.centroybor.com
HOURS: Vary by business
COST: No entrance fee, some clubs have cover charges

Given up for ages as a slightly seedy adult playground at night, Ybor City has become more family friendly with the addition of Centro Ybor, which opened at the beginning of the millennium in the former Centro Español social club. It's a shopping, dining, and entertainment complex right at the pulsing heart of the neighborhood. None of the restaurants here will stir you to poetic excess, but the complex is anchored by the Muvico Centro Ybor 20 theaters, with a GameTime location, The Improv for nighttime adult comedy, and Tampa Bay Brewing Co. pub. There are few shops. The complex has its own

parking structure and is on the TECO streetcar line.

7TH AVENUE (LA SEPTIMA)

7th Ave. from 13th to 23rd Sts.
HOURS: Vary by business
COST: Free

During the day, visitors to Ybor City's 7th Avenue district can still see cigars being hand-rolled and munch a Cuban sandwich, while at night Ybor is the city's nightlife district, drawing 40,000 visitors on weekends to dine at sidewalk cafés and drink and dance at nightclubs. Whether you explore during the day or at night, park your car in one of the many parking lots or garages (metered parking is strictly enforced 24 hours) and walk around or take the Ybor City trolley. You can still see a few little cigar shops and Latin social clubs mixed in with tattoo parlors and restaurants along La Septima (7th Ave.).

You get the most three-dimensional look at Ybor just by walking around: Walk by La Union Marti-Maceo tile mural (226 7th Ave.), pick up a copy of *La Gaceta* (the neighborhood's Spanish-language weekly for nearly 80 years), and walk by the restored former cigar workers' casitas on your way to buy a cigar at **Metropolitan Cigars** (2014 East 7th Ave., 813/248-3304), a 1,700-square-foot walk-in humidor, or to get a Cubano sandwich. A Cubano is a long loaf, 36 inches long, with a thin flaky crust and soft, pillowy interior. This gets piled high with roast pork and Genoa salami (a strictly Tampa twist), Swiss cheese (some say Emanthaler), sour pickles, and spicy mustard; the whole thing is warmed and flattened in a special hot-press. The outside is crisp, the inside warm and a little gooey. It's perfection.

La Septima is also the locale of some of the city's biggest parties: Gasparilla Sant'Yago Night Parade in February, Guavaween in October, the Rough Rider's St. Patrick's Night Parade, and the Tampa Cigar Heritage Festival in mid-November.

Busch Gardens and North Tampa   Map 4

ADVENTURE ISLAND
4500 E. Bougainvillea Ave., 813/987-5660, www.adventureisland.com
HOURS: Mar.-Oct., hours and days vary; closed Oct.-early Mar.
COST: $49.99 adult, $45.99 child age 3-9, free for child 2 and younger

Adventure Island will wet your whistle, and pretty much everything else. It's a 30-acre water park, with slides, corkscrews, waterfalls, a monstrous 17,000-square-foot wave pool, and a children's play area. There are 50 lifeguards on duty, but it's still only appropriate for the truly water-safe. There's also a championship white-sand volleyball complex. If you buy a ticket to Busch Gardens, you can combine it with a ticket here for a discount.

◖ BUSCH GARDENS
E. Busch Blvd. and 40th St., 888/800-5447, www.buschgardens.com
HOURS: Winter daily 9 A.M.-6 P.M.; summer daily 9:30 A.M.-10 P.M.
COST: $81.99 box office adult, $71.99 online adult; $73.99 box office child age 3-9, $63.99 online child age 3-9; free for child 2 and younger; $14 parking

Busch Gardens is expensive. Is it worth it? Definitely. It is a wonderful full-day extravaganza for people of any age. Busch Gardens can entertain you for a full two days, but if you do just one day, everyone will be clamoring for more. A 14-day 6 Park Orlando FlexTicket ($329.95 adult, $309.95 child) is a fairly good deal if you have the stamina to hit SeaWorld Orlando, Universal Studios Florida, Aquatica, Islands of Adventure, and Wet 'n' Wild along with Busch Gardens.

Rides for Little Kids: The amusement park has a huge section of the park geared to children ages 2–7 called **Sesame Street Safari of Fun** (to the far left when you're looking at the map), near **Stanleyville**, as well as in sections near the **Congo**. This is one of those parks where there are those vexing height limitations that preclude you from riding if you're *taller* than the marker.

Rides for Big Kids: Major coasters are the biggest draw for those over 48 inches tall (or over 54 inches for Montu, Kumba, and SheiKra roller coasters) and with no serious health problems. The rides at Busch Gardens are either little-kiddie or pee-your-pants huge. The following are the roller coasters, in descending order of excellence. The **Montu,** at the far

COURTESY OF VISIT FLORIDA

the Kumba roller coaster at Busch Gardens

right of the park, is one of the tallest and longest inverted roller coasters in the world. You are strapped in from above, so your feet dangle while you travel at 60 mph through 60-foot vertical loops and stuff. The **SheiKra** has an incredible 90-degrees-straight-down-from-200-feet-up thrill at the beginning, an underground tunnel, speeds of 70 mph, and water features late in the ride, but overall the ride is too short. It went "floorless" a few years back to add another level of thrill, but it still doesn't make top billing in our book. **Kumba** is third best, with a full three seconds of weightlessness, an initial 135-foot drop, and cool 360-degree spirals. It has good speed, a long ride, and one of the world's largest vertical loops. And the **Gwazi** is for purists: An old double wooden coaster, it's got that tooth-rattling charm as it barrels over the boards in 7,000 feet of track. Opened in early 2011, the newest coaster is **Cheetah Hunt,** which zips riders up to 60 mph three different times over a track

stretching more than 0.8 miles. Paired with the ride are live cheetahs, trained to race along for up to 200 yards, next to a glass-walled observation area.

Beyond the coasters, the **Tanganyika Tidal Wave, Stanley Falls,** and **Congo River Rapids** boat rides are guaranteed to saturate you with water—so time them for the hottest part of the day.

Animal Attractions: Busch Gardens contains about 2,700 animals. Colorful lorikeets will land on your shoulder or flirt shamelessly with you in the **Lory Landing** aviary. There's a **Myombe Reserve,** which lets you get up close with gorillas and chimps. But the best animal attraction is the **Serengeti Plain,** which really takes up the whole right half of the park—you see it all by getting on the Serengeti Express Railway (or the Skyride or a Serengeti Safari). Ostriches may race the train; there are big cats, huffing rhinos, and gracefully awkward giraffes. It's thrilling *and* a wonderful

TALL TALE

Anyone who's spent time in the Tampa Bay area has idly wondered about the big white tower off I-275. What does it do? How did it get there? And most people never get to the bottom of the 231-foot-tall mystery at the corner of Florida Avenue and Bird Street. But you will, now.

The **Sulphur Springs Water Tower** was a North Tampa landmark almost instantly upon its completion in 1927. Like a lot of construction around that time, it was aimed at the state's new vacationing hordes. The introduction of Henry Ford's affordable $400 Model-T just after the turn of that century triggered the phenomenon of road tripping, folks hopping in the car in search of sun, sand, and a little fun. Because they often slept in or next to their cars, they were dubbed "tin-can tourists."

And Josiah Richardson aimed to be ready for them. He built a hotel and tourist cottages along the Hillsborough River. He built a mammoth waterslide with a spring-fed swimming hole, a bathhouse, a shopping arcade, and an alligator farm. Just one problem: Richardson needed a reliable water source for the complex, which he called Sulphur Springs Hotel and Arcade.

So he mortgaged the whole kit and caboodle and hired Grover Pool to build a water tower for him. They excavated 45 feet down into the rock, with eight-inch-thick poured concrete walls reinforced with railroad rails. When it was finished, it stored 125,000 gallons of water from nearby artesian springs.

The pressure was great, the water clear, the supply dependable. If only everything were so steadfast: In 1933 the Tampa Electric Co. dam collapsed and the complex was flooded. Coupled with the Great Depression, the disaster brought the Sulphur Springs complex to its knees. Richardson lost everything.

But the water tower did last. Through the 1960s it provided water to some of the neighborhood that bears its name. In the 1970s, dry at last, it became the architectural icon of the Tower Drive-In theater, graffiti slowly adding a lacy filigree across the tower's white surface. A sheen of fresh, graffiti-proof paint in 1979 failed to change the tower's plight; drugs and crime in the area ensured that it remained overlooked until Walgreens put in a bid to buy the 13-acre spot in 2002.

The hue and cry of Tampa residents made it clear that this tall drink of water was locally beloved. A grassroots group called Save Our Tower sprung up overnight, cajoling and nudging city officials. The City of Tampa bought the site the next year, and renamed the surrounding area River Tower Park. Soon after came ambitious plans—a boardwalk, a botanical garden, a jogging trail. That has not come to pass, but the lush bit of green space in Sulphur Springs still is likely be presided over by the stalwart water tower of Josiah Richardson's abandoned dream.

opportunity to sit down a spell and regroup. (The lamest attraction at the park, though, is Rhino Rally. Don't bother.)

The four-acre **Jungala** is set in the Congo area and has guests mingling with exotic creatures, exploring a "village" hidden deep in the jungle, and connecting with the inhabitants of the lush landscape through up-close animal interactions, multi-story family play areas, rides, and live entertainment.

If you visit in the summer, count on heavy rains in the afternoon. Bathrooms are plentiful and clean, there are scads of strollers to rent,

the food is much better than it needs to be (and there's an all-day dining deal that seems reasonable if you're spending all day at the park), and they even have a dog kennel to watch your pet while you enjoy the rides.

LOWRY PARK ZOO

1101 W. Sligh Ave., 813/932-0245,
www.lowryparkzoo.com
HOURS: Daily 9:30 A.M.–5 P.M.
COST: $23.95 adult, $21.95 senior, $18.95 child age 3-11, free child 2 and younger

This zoo has recently made the overt decision

to take it to the Big Time, going mano a mano with San Diego and the other big zoo kahunas. To this end, they imported four African elephants (for a stunning account, read the *Tampa Bay Times*'s nine-part series on the subject) and created a huge habitat for them.

For years this zoo languished at the bottom of the heap with old-school cages and dubious animal husbandry. All that has changed: *Child* as well as *Parents* magazines have appropriately ranked it in the top ten zoos for families. Little kids want to see the animals up close and personal. At the Lowry Park Zoo, habitats are naturalistic and nicely landscaped, while still designed for maximum viewing. There are around 1,500 native and exotic animals (Malayan tigers, African penguins, and pygmy hippo among them) organized into sensible housing developments. Lots of shade provided by big lush tropicals seems to keep all species fat and sassy, even in the fairly substantial summer heat. One of the zoo's highlights is its Manatee and Aquatic Center, one of only three hospitals and rehabilitation facilities in the state of Florida for lugubrious, sick sea cows.

Tampa's Lowry Park Zoo and Sunline Cruises have come together to present the **River Odyssey Ecotour** ($14 adult, $13 senior, $10 child) on the Hillsborough River. A ride on the *Sirenia* gives visitors a chance to spot the many species of animals that live in and near the river.

UNIVERSITY OF SOUTH FLORIDA
4202 E. Fowler Ave., 813/974-2011, www.usf.edu
HOURS: Daily 24 hours
COST: Free

The University of South Florida (USF) is one of the nation's top 50 universities in expenditures for research, having spent $385 million in 2010. USF offers 219 degree programs at the undergraduate, graduate, specialist, and doctoral levels, including the doctor of medicine. It serves more than 46,000 students on campuses in Tampa, St. Petersburg, Sarasota-Manatee, and Lakeland.

All that said, it's not the most gorgeous campus you've ever strolled. It was originally a commuter school, with parking lots spread across a wide, 1,700-acre campus for all those cars. There's no real central quad, the place where you think "this is the center of all academic shenanigans," no ivy-draped buildings or older men in tired tweed smoking pipes. Still, it's a member of the Big East Athletic Conference and thus has a wealth of spectator sporting options. It also hosts lecture series, concerts at the newly refurbished Sun Dome, and exhibits in the Contemporary Art Museum.

Greater Tampa   Map 5

BIG CAT RESCUE
12802 Easy St., Tampa, 813/920-4130,
www.bigcatrescue.org
HOURS: Regular tour Mon.-Wed. and Fri. 3 P.M., Sat.-Sun. 10 A.M. and 1 P.M.; children's tour Sat.-Sun. 9 A.M.; feeding tour Wed. and Fri.-Sat. 4:30 P.M.; Big Cat Keeper tour Sat.-Sun. 2-4 P.M.
COST: Regular tour $29 (age 10 and older); children's tour $19; feeding tour $55; Big Cat Keeper tour $110; Wild Eyes at Night tour $55

Proclaiming itself the world's largest accredited sanctuary for big cats, Big Cat Rescue provides a permanent retirement home to more than 200 animals, including 14 species of cats. For the visitor, the 20-year-old center offers tours, outreach presentations, animal interaction, and the opportunity to spend an evening in the heart of the sanctuary. On the last Friday of each month, register for the Wild Eyes at Night tour, in which guests roam the grounds equipped with flashlights that illuminate the hundreds of shining eyes in the cat enclosures. Or be a zookeeper for a couple of hours on the Big Cat Keeper tour. You'll get an education in animal husbandry, care, and feeding, and if you plan it for the last Friday of the month, you can combine it with the exciting night-time tour.

MACDILL AIR FORCE BASE

Public Affairs Office, 813/828-2215, www.macdill.af.mil
HOURS: Tours first and third Fri.
COST: Free

Tampa is fairly urban to the south, where it runs into MacDill Air Force Base, which takes up the entire southern third of the Tampa peninsula and is home to the United States Central Command (coordinating all U.S. military operations in Africa and the Middle East). Used as a staging area as far back as the Spanish-American War, it wasn't formally given to the War Department until 1939 and dedicated in 1941. The base trained air crews for overseas deployments in World War II and was crucial during the Cuban Missile Crisis and the Cold War.

Base tours are conducted on an extremely limited basis due to security measures in place since 9/11. Tours are provided only for groups of 25–40, so individuals or families must join one of these tours. Tours last approximately four hours and are scheduled on a first-come, first-served basis. The tour schedule fills up quickly, so contact MacDill Public Affairs early. Priority scheduling is given to Junior ROTC students and other youth groups serving high-school-age students. Military reunions, civic and business organizations, or senior citizen groups are also welcome. Walking and stair-climbing are part of the tour, so those with mobility issues must state that on the tour-request form, available online; modified tours may be arranged to accommodate those with disabilities.

RAYMOND JAMES STADIUM

4201 N. Dale Mabry Hwy., Tampa, 813/350-6500,
http://raymondjamesstadium.com

HOURS: Walk-up tours usually offered Tues.-Thurs. at 2 P.M.
COST: $6 adult 16 and older, $4 senior and child age 6-15, free for child 5 and younger

Raymond James Stadium is a wonderful venue in which to see Tampa's NFL entry, the Buccaneers, or the USF Bulls football teams. Popularly called the RayJay, the stadium was completed in 1998. It holds more than 66,000 fans—52,000 in general seating, the rest in blessedly air-conditioned suites—with a cool, 103-foot-long mock pirate ship that blasts its air cannons (confetti and foam footballs) every time the Bucs score. The tours run from the field into a locker room, a suite, and to Buccaneer Cove, the fan zone that includes the ship and souvenir stores. Group tours are held in the mornings Tuesday–Thursday, but must be arranged at least two weeks in advance (813/350-6545) and must be for at least 10 participants.

TAMPA ELECTRIC CO. MANATEE VIEWING CENTER

6990 Dickman Rd., Apollo Beach, 813/228-4289,
www.tampaelectric.com/manatee
HOURS: Nov. 1-Apr. 16 daily 10 A.M.–5 P.M.
COST: Free

Let's be honest: the manatee is the Ringo Starr of the aquatic mammal world—so homely it is adorable. And gentle, too, which might also be the case with Ringo.

The big herbivores are protected by state and even federal law, mainly by trying to control the speed of the manatees' only true enemy, the yahoos driving their speedboats too fast in the manatees' freshwater or brackish habitat. The boats' fast-spinning propellers gouge the backs of the big guys and gals as they surface for air. You can usually find a few injured manatees rehabbing at Lowry Park Zoo.

But for about a quarter of a century, one of the two local electric utilities has offered a free viewing platform where manatees cluster for the warmth of the plant's cooling-water outflow pipes. Visitors can stroll a 900-foot-long walkway to observe the manatees quite close by, wander through a butterfly garden, or even experience a mild version of a hurricane—that's to illustrate the challenges faced by all of Florida's utility plants.

Downtown St. Petersburg Map 6

DOWNTOWN AREA
Along Bayshore Dr., Beach Dr., 1st St., and 2nd St.
HOURS: Daily 24 hours
COST: Free

St. Petersburg has a charming waterfront downtown area, which is tourist friendly and rich in architecture, historic buildings, attractions, and water vistas. Most of the museums, The Pier, and several public parks (most notably **Vinoy Park** and **Straub Park**) are here. The city owns miles of bay front, which allows for pleasant strolling, biking, rollerblading, and, of course, people-watching. Parking and traffic can be a challenge due to the recent surge in upscale restaurants. But offsetting the parking issue (there are public and private garages, as well as metered spaces) are the sidewalk dining opportunities—and even more people-watching. On Central Avenue, between 2nd and 7th Streets, there are assorted galleries, boutiques, cocktail lounges, and restaurants. A fun way to sample the downtown is aboard a **Segway tour** (149 1st Ave. N, 727/498-2322, Mon.–Sat 11 A.M., 2 P.M., and 5 P.M., Sun. noon and 3 P.M., $55 for 90 minutes, $65 for two hours). Tours include a 20-minute training class beforehand.

The Looper is also a super way to get around downtown. Hop aboard the red-over-yellow

COURTESY OF VISITSTPETECLEARWATER.COM

downtown St. Petersburg

motorized trolleys, and enjoy a half-hour tour of St. Petersburg's top attractions, museums, and hotels. There are 15 stops along the way, and the fare is $0.50 each time you step aboard ($0.25 for seniors). The Looper connects with the Central Avenue Trolley (Central is the east-west boulevard across the peninsula) that runs from the edge of Tampa Bay, downtown, to the picturesque Gulf of Mexico community, Pass-a-Grille. To cross the peninsula on this trolley, the fare is $2.50 ($1.50 for seniors).

THE PIER

800 2nd Ave. NE, 727/821-6443, www.stpete-pier.com

HOURS: Vary by business

COST: $3 parking, $2 aquarium

For decades, the Pier was the heart and soul of visitor activity in St. Petersburg, looking like a five-story inverted pyramid, or the good guys' home base in a sci-fi movie. New museums, savvy lounges, and upscale restaurants and boutiques have taken over the role as the prime reason to be downtown. And because of deterioration in its structure, the Pier was torn down in mid-2013, with the new Pier scheduled to open in 2015.

During its time, The Pier has been a place to rent bikes; grab a rental rod and reel and fish off the end; depart from the Pier on a sightseeing boat charter or on the *Dolphin Queen* (727/647-1538, $22 adult, $19 senior and military, $14 child age 3–12) a 44-foot, 70-passenger catamaran that sails several times daily on 90-minute trips; rent a 24-foot-long electric boat at **The Electric Marina** (727/898-2628) for half an hour, one hour, or all day; dine in the family-friendly food court; or browse the complex's shops. No matter whether the new structure is finished or not, the views of the bay and the waterfront are always delightful, with pelicans and dolphins cavorting nearby.

Clearwater and Clearwater Beach   Map 8

CLEARWATER MARINE AQUARIUM

249 Windward Passage, 727/441-1790,

www.seewinter.com

HOURS: Mon.-Sat. 9 A.M.-6 P.M.

COST: $19.95 adult, $17.95 senior, $14.95 child age 3-12

Just over the bay in Tampa, the Florida Aquarium usually gets the bulk of the kudos. But that aquarium isn't home to a movie star—and a heart-warming one, at that. Clearwater Marine Aquarium was always a less touristy, more modest facility, though one of its missions was to save and rehabilitate injured marine life. And that's where the Clearwater aquarium got its big boost: A young female dolphin, her tail mangled by a crab trap, was brought to this facility. Without a functioning tail, the dolphin, named Winter by aquarium staff, would have died. Instead, the staff found a prosthetics doctor who agreed to create a tail for Winter. Her story, hyped only a little, was turned into the movie *Dolphin Tale,* released in 2011. That isn't the end of Winter's story, however: News reports spread of her adaptation to her prosthetic tail, and numerous people, from children with disabilities to wounded military vets, have come to Winter's pool to be encouraged by what they see. Now she has her own webcam. Clearwater Marine Aquarium has also broadened its outreach, focusing extra-price tours on its status as a working research facility and home to other recuperating/rehabbing dolphins, whales, otters, and so on. For the visitor, the thrust is on education, with more than two dozen daily animal-care and training presentations and exhibits on rescue, rehabilitation, and release—and how the public can help to protect

COURTESY OF VISITSTPETECLEARWATER.COM

Winter the dolphin, Clearwater Marine Aquarium

and conserve endangered marine life. It's like the ACLU for fish. The aquarium offers on-site feeding and care programs for interested guests and operates a daily two-hour-long **Sea Life Safari** (25 Causeway Blvd., Slip #58, Clearwater Beach, 727/462-2628) that takes visitors around the Clearwater estuary and Intracoastal Waterway, with commentary by a marine biologist. The basic admission price includes a sort of museum of props and sets used in creating the film; a shuttle transports guests between that museum, on the edge of downtown Clearwater, and the aquarium, on the causeway approaching the barrier island of Clearwater Beach.

SCIENTOLOGY HEADQUARTERS

210 S. Fort Harrison Ave., Clearwater, 727/467-5000, www.scientology.org

HOURS: By appointment

COST: Free

The "worldwide spiritual headquarters" of the Church of Scientology is known as "Flag Land Base," located in downtown Clearwater, most notably in the historic Fort Harrison Hotel. Since the 1970s, Scientology has purchased large tracts of land in the downtown and waterfront Clearwater area. The religion has a slightly fractious relationship with local government and local media, like the award-winning *Tampa Bay Times* that included details of the recent construction of a massive "Super Power Building" topped with a Scientology cross.

Greater Pinellas County   Map 9

◖ SUNKEN GARDENS

1825 4th St. N., St. Petersburg, 727/551-3102,
www.stpete.org/sunken

HOURS: Mon.-Sat. 10 A.M.-4:30 P.M., Sun.
noon-4:30 P.M.

COST: $8 adult, $6 senior, $4 child age 2-11

Sunken Gardens was snatched from the jaws of death in 1999, nursed back to health under the careful ministrations of the city of St. Petersburg. Nothing a little nurturing and $3 million couldn't fix. It's a four-acre plot of land, much of it 100 years old and counting. There are 50,000 tropical plants and flowers, demonstration gardens, a 200-year-old oak tree, cascading waterfalls, flamingos, and more.

It's more than a garden, though—it's St. Petersburg's most beloved Old Florida attraction. In 1903, a plumber named George Turner, Sr. bought the property, which contained a large sinkhole and a shallow lake. By dint of effort and a huge maze of clay tile, he drained the lake and prepared the soil for gardening. He sold tropical fruit that he grew here at a roadside stand, but folks liked walking through the tranquil greenery so much that he started charging admission. By 1935, the garden was officially opened as Turner's Sunken Gardens (because of the former lake and sinkhole, the whole thing sits down low in a basin), attracting approximately 300,000 visitors per year. It was followed by some other attractions of dubious taste: the World's Largest Gift Shop and the King of Kings Wax Museum. It was one of those places that had loud, modestly literate billboards on the southbound highway up through a couple of states.

But its business fell off as more glitz was mandated by ever more sophisticated patrons. The city felt compelled to help, also restoring the

gift shop/wax museum space to its former glory. Sunken Gardens is beautiful, ever so slightly campy, and a definite slice of local history.

◖ SUNSHINE SKYWAY BRIDGE AND FISHING PIERS

I-275 South toward Bradenton

HOURS: Daily 24 hours

COST: $1

The cable-stay Sunshine Skyway Bridge, the largest in the world, is at the southern end of St. Petersburg and connects the city with Manatee County. It is a serious bridge—29,000 feet long and, depending on the Tampa Bay tides, about 191 feet above the water. The design allows stunning, unobstructed views of the water. However, this bright-yellow beauty, repainted in 2007, is not for those with a fear of heights: Bridge workers are sometimes called to bring down white-knuckled drivers frozen by the view downward.

You cannot stop on the skyway to take pictures or admire its golden cables. However, there is nearby parking. The old Sunshine Skyway was demolished in 1991 after a ship hit one of its support piers and 35 people drove off the bridge in a blinding rainstorm, plunging to their deaths. The approach ends of that original span are now the 0.75-mile-long North Pier and a 1.5-mile-long South Pier—together said to be the world's longest fishing pier, although they are miles apart. You can drive your car onto the pier and park it right next to your fishing spot, parallel parking on the left lane, with room for cars to drive and walkways on either side of the span. There are restrooms on both piers, and bait shops sell live and frozen bait, tackle, drinks, and snacks. They also rent rods. The North Pier has a large picnic area next to the bait shop.

RESTAURANTS

The Tampa Bay area is the home base of numerous national and regional chains: Hooters, Durango Steakhouse, Beef O' Brady's, Checkers, Shells' Seafood Restaurant, Carrabba's, Outback Steakhouse, and that's just the tip of the iceberg. Maybe it's residents' deep streak of loyalty, maybe their plodding constancy, but marketing geniuses have determined that Tampa Bay is the perfect test market for new chain restaurant concepts. They are trotted out here, and if they fly, launched in the rest of the country.

Still, the past number of years has seen the arrival of a raft of new unique, discrete, and more-or-less independently owned restaurants. Chefs on both sides of Hillsborough Bay are beginning to question where their product comes from, to espouse the virtues of local, sustainable, organic, and naturally raised foods. Trends and culinary fads from elsewhere in the country require a bit longer to take root here, and there's not that frenetic Cult of the New that one sees in many big metro areas. Meaning, reservations aren't impossible at the temple of the latest macaroni maestro or the newest sushi shaman.

In terms of cuisine, Tampa Bay is something of a generalist. St. Louis boasts the legendary toasted ravioli. In Philly, it's all about the cheesesteak. Let other cities each have their personal gastronomic monomania, here it's a little bit of everything, impacted by the availability of fresh Gulf of Mexico seafood.

COURTESY OF VISITSTPETECLEARWATER.COM

HIGHLIGHTS

LOOK FOR 【 TO FIND
RECOMMENDED RESTAURANTS.

【 **Best Way to Spy on Visiting Dignitaries:** Maryann Ferenc and Marty Blitz's **Mise en Place** is the go-to place for thoughtful fine dining. It's also where local big shots and visiting celebs break bread and make deals (page 48).

【 **Best Place to Indulge Your Urge to Graze:** At downtown Tampa's **Fly Bar and Restaurant** you don't have to choose between the kobe sliders or baby beets with a mantle of Humboldt Fog goat cheese (page 49).

【 **Best Place to See Two Cuisines Coexist:** B.T. Nguyen's **Restaurant BT** draws from classic Vietnamese and classic French, with a few dishes that cross over (page 51).

【 **Best Use of Local Produce: Boca Kitchen Bar Market** is a relative newcomer on the scene, drawing from the increasing number of local farms (and owner Gordon Davis's own good dirt) for an ever-changing menu (page 52).

【 **Best Steak with Side Order of Kitsch: Bern's Steak House** has been a Tampa institution for more than 50 years, making national "best steak" lists the whole time. It's a bordello-like warren of rooms, with flocked wallpaper and ornate gilt mirrors, and an over-the-top romantic dessert room upstairs (page 55).

【 **Best Place to Practice Saying "Bruschetta":** A local watering hole and slick sidewalk-table Italian restaurant, downtown St. Petersburg's **Bella Brava** does a fabulous fritto misto calamari and addictive thin-crust pizzas (page 70).

【 **Most Red Haute Fare:** Chris Ponte's calling card at **Cafe Ponte** is Cal-Ital, sometimes with hints of Mediterranean, but always luxurious and sophisticated (page 83).

Downtown Tampa and Channelside   Map 1

AMERICAN
EDISON: FOOD+DRINK LAB ❸❸
912 W. Kennedy Blvd., 813/254-7111, http://edison-tampa.com
HOURS: Mon.-Thurs. 11:30 A.M.-2:30 P.M. and 5-10 P.M., Fri.-Sat. 11:30 A.M.-2:30 P.M. and 5-11 P.M.

Here's what is so smart about Jeannie Pierola's new Edison: It's funny. Its full name sets up expectations of beakers and lab coats and very serious scientific inquiry. The celebrated former chef at Bern's and SideBern's is having a whale of a time at her new place, riffing on contemporary trends in the culinary world, freestyling on current fetish ingredients and faddish techniques, and all at a price point that makes Edison an everyday prospect for most Tampa Bay diners. Menu categories would stymie Thomas Edison and probably his buddy Henry Ford, too: "spark," "cold start," "soluble or solid," "constants,"

and "C8H10N4O2" (that last one means caffeine). The basic idea is some things are hot, some are cold, some are a little bigger, all of them are totally mix and match, suited to a shared noshing approach. Small plates are the new black around here.

【 MISE EN PLACE ❸❸❸
442 W. Kennedy Blvd., 813/254-5373, www.miseonline.com
HOURS: Tues.-Thurs. 11:30 A.M.-2:30 P.M. and 5:30-10 P.M., Fri. 11:30 A.M.-2:30 P.M. and 5:30-11 P.M., Sat. 5-11 P.M.

Mise en Place has been at the cutting edge of Tampa dining for years; Marty Blitz is a local culinary legend. Look out at the minarets of the University of Tampa as you scroll through the oversized one-page menu. It's hard to characterize the sensibility in the kitchen when the menu, changing weekly, ranges from pizza with

PRICE KEY

$ Most entrées less than $10
$$ Most entrées $10-25
$$$ Most entrées more than $25

chorizo, roast corn, chilies, and manchego to mole spice–rubbed seared tuna with purple potatoes, vanilla bean pineapple salad, and a prickly pear habanero vinaigrette. They also take great care to accommodate folks with special diets and it's one of the only places in town with a sophisticated cheese program: maybe a firm, smoky, aged sheep's milk cheese, a Grafton Cloth Bound cheddar, and one most excellent runny-stinky selection from the Cote d'Or.

ECLECTIC

◖ FLY BAR AND RESTAURANT $$

1202 N. Franklin St., 813/275-5000, www.flybarandrestaurant.com/tampa

HOURS: Mon.-Thurs. 11:30 A.M.-3 P.M. and 5:30 P.M.-midnight, Fri. 11:30 A.M.-3 P.M. and 5:30 P.M.-1 A.M., Sat. 5:30 P.M.-1 A.M.

The Fly's buzz is deafening. The brainchild of Tampa native Leslie Shirah, this bastion of hip has a devoted following among Tampa foodies and revelers. Shirah honed the concept during a 15-year stint in San Francisco, where she still owns three restaurants. The concept is this: a share-it-with-friends approach to international small plates; suave cocktails; a little live music; and a minimalist-hip decor. Chef Fred Quinones has raised the bar further: Tiny golden and red beets are roasted, herbed, and given a molten blanket of tangy Humboldt Fog goat cheese. A delicious contrast of flavors, it's rivaled by a bowl of caramelized brussel sprouts, their earthiness accented with a sharp grain mustard vinaigrette. He has added fish tacos with fruity tomatillo salsa, an heirloom tomato salad, and

YACHT STARSHIP

Ahoy, mates and would-be mates. Climb aboard Yacht StarShip (departs from 603 Channleside Dr., 813/223-7999, www.yachtstarship.com, dinner cruise $60, departs 5 P.M., returns 7:30 P.M.), Tampa's premier dining yacht, while the sunset casts its sherbet hues across the Bay. It's the *Love Boat,* only not as interminable and without all the crew in white knee socks. Imagine yourself plowing into hand-carved beef tenderloin with garlic mashed potatoes napped with wild mushroom demi-glace, or maybe grilled swordfish nestled under a tomato-caper beurre blanc and served with sautéed spinach. Now add in a little gentle rocking, the salty sea air, and a tangerine sunset illuminating the downtown Tampa skyline. In 2.5 hours, you can have the cruise of a lifetime aboard this three-story, 180-foot yacht. Arrive a half-hour before departure to sign in and board. The boat does not wait for latecomers!

tucked onions and cheddar cheese in the center of the lush kobe sliders.

FRENCH

L'EDEN $$

500 N. Tampa St., 813/221-4795, http://dine-at-leden.com

HOURS: Mon.-Tues. 8 A.M.-3 P.M., Wed.-Thurs. 8 A.M.-3 P.M. and 5-9 P.M., Fri.-Sat. 8 A.M.-3 P.M. and 5-11 P.M.

The tiny French bistro L'Eden has charm. It seems most thronged for weekday lunch, when soups, crepes, and salads fuel downtown workers. At night, service can be very mixed and the small-plate approach contains some oddities ("India curry chicken" ends up being tiny croissants containing chicken salad with curry-flavored mayonnaise—not what you'd expect, but tasty). Dessert crepes, a nice meal ender, come with several choices of fillings.

RESTAURANTS

GREEK

TAVERNA OPA $$

615 Channelside Dr., Ste. 123, 813/443-4821, www.tavernaoparestaurant.com/tampa

HOURS: Mon.-Thurs. 11 A.M.-10 P.M., Fri.-Sat. 11 A.M.-1 A.M.

An outpost of the concept that began in 1998 in Hollywood, Florida, Taverna Opa serves good Greek food right on the water in Channelside. It has views, it has belly dancing, plus napkin tossing and people yelling "Opa!" and, yes, it has great Greek salads, eggplant dip, and chicken souvlaki. A number of family-style menus ($25–40 pp) allow you to try a range of hot and cold meze offerings along with meat and seafood platters and planks of delicious lemon-roasted potatoes and spinach leek rice. If you're going to order à la carte, grilled octopus with olive oil, vinegar, and oregano is done well, and if your appetite is mondo, the moussaka, the size of an old-school boom box, is rich with bechamel, velvety soft eggplant, and ground beef.

ITALIAN

AVANZARE $$$

Hyatt Regency Tampa, 211 N. Tampa St., 813/225-1234

HOURS: Daily 6-10 A.M., 11:30 A.M.-2 P.M., and 5-11 P.M.

Situated blocks from Tampa Bay Performing Arts Center, the Hyatt's Avanzare is dreamy for dinner and a show. A waterfall cascades in the five-story atrium, but the restaurant maintains a relaxed intimacy common to fine Italian trattorias. At breakfast and lunch it's straight-ahead American with fillips of Mediterranean, but in the evening Avanzare goes upscale and sinfully Italian. The kitchen meanders across the geography of Italy, sending out inspired regional dishes to folks celebrating special occasions or those sophisticates who just choose to indulge like this for no particular reason.

STEAKHOUSE

MALIO'S PRIME $$$

400 N. Ashley Dr., 813/223-7746, www.maliosprime.com

HOURS: Mon.-Thurs. 11 A.M.-11 P.M., Fri. 11 A.M.-midnight, Sat. 4 P.M.-midnight

He knew everyone, made people feel good, and greeted the ladies with a kiss: Malio Iavarone was the consummate restaurateur and showman, his restaurant Malio's Steakhouse an iconic dining destination. It opened in 1969 and closed in 2005, a long run in restaurant years. And now it's back, kind of. Malio's son, Derek, and a buddy launched Malio's Prime in downtown Tampa's 31-story Rivergate Tower (the one that looks like a beer can). It's an anchor of sorts for the whole Riverwalk initiative, a riverfront renaissance that recently became a reality. It's a gorgeous space, with a familiar menu of steaks and chops, but as evening progresses in the 8,000-square-foot restaurant, the noise level swells, making lingering somewhat unattractive.

TAPAS

TINATAPA'S $$

615 Channelside Dr., Ste. 120, 813/514-8462

HOURS: Mon.-Thurs. 4-11 P.M., Fri. 11 A.M.-2 A.M., Sat. noon-2 A.M., Sun. noon-10 P.M.

One of the few remaining restaurants in the beleaguered Channelside these days, Tinatapa's is named in homage—just a tongue-twister away—to the famous Tipatina's in New Orleans, so if you know your Big Easy, you'll know Tinatapa's is going to be a fun, loud, raucous place to end an evening. Barcelona mosaics and logs for rafters give the spare, round room a decidedly European feel. There isn't total verisimilitude with some of the Spanish small plates: Baked goat cheese with tomato sauce and salmon with a horseradish glaze might flummox the average barfly in Madrid. Still, flavors are bright and assertive, prices are low, and sharing makes it an adventure (but for those who have trouble sharing, house specialties come in full entrée sizes, paired with black beans and Spanish rice).

VIETNAMESE

BAMBOOZLE ⊕

516 N. Tampa St., 813/223-7320,
www.bamboozlecafe.com
HOURS: Mon.-Fri. 11 A.M.-2 P.M.

Bamboozle packs them in downtown at noon.

Quick and healthy Vietnamese fusion has charmed office workers at lunch, with classic pho and traditional noodle salads, followed up by the oh-so-sweet Vietnamese coffee, lush with sweetened condensed milk. It's very vegetarian friendly.

South Tampa and Hyde Park   Map 2

AMERICAN

DATZ ⊕⊕

2616 S. MacDill Ave., 813/831-7000, http://datzdeli.com
HOURS: Mon.-Sat. 7 A.M.-10 P.M., Sun. 8:30 A.M.-3 P.M.

At Datz, Suzanne and Roger Perry and their crew seem in a state of perpetual motion: "Eh, minimize the deli, now it's a gastropub, let's do cheese-making classes, oh, and cask cocktails, er, can we fit a case in here for macarons and super-fancy William Dean chocolates?" The sandwiches are jaw-stretching with stacked meat on great homemade bread, with solidly tasty condiments, a marvelously real half-sour pickle, and deeply russet homemade chips (perfectly salted, greaseless, with a drizzle of addictive blue cheese aioli). But still, that's not even the best part. It's the vast beer and wine list and a willingness to experiment with the latest culinary trends that keeps Datz perennially fresh (and swamped with diners).

SQUARE ONE ⊕⊕

3701 Henderson Blvd., 813/414-0101,
www.square1burgers.com
HOURS: Sun.-Thurs. 11:30 A.M.-10 P.M., Fri.-Sat. 11:30 A.M.-midnight

Bill Shumate opened his first burger joint in 1964 in Norman, Oklahoma. Many restaurants and concepts later (like Bella's on S. Howard), he and his partner Joanie Corneil have returned to these roots, back to square one with, um, Square One. It's burgers and lots of them, with nine basic types (Meyer Angus beef, kobe, sashimi tuna, portobello)

with a whole passel of toppers (teriyaki ginger sauce, roasted black bean and corn salsa) and three types of buns. The menu shows admirable focus, but these are fancy burgers: Think Angus beef topped with caramelized onion, sun-dried tomatoes, and Brie. They have nearly the best burger in Tampa (despite the fact that the fries need another minute in the fryer). This is often a mob scene of young families.

ASIAN

◖ RESTAURANT BT ⊕⊕⊕

2507 S. MacDill Ave., 813/258-1916,
www.restaurantbt.com
HOURS: Mon.-Thurs. 11:30 A.M.-2:30 P.M. and 5:30-9:45 P.M., Fri.-Sat. 11:30 A.M.-2:30 P.M. and 5:30-10:30 P.M., Sun. 11:30 A.M.-2:30 P.M.

B.T. Nguyen has been at the forefront of Tampa's gastronomic scene for nearly 20 years, with a number of restaurant ventures. At Restaurant BT, classic Vietnamese and French dishes appear in a swirl of lemongrass and hot chiles, always innovatively presented in stylish, architectural flights of fancy that echo the sophistication of the indoor/outdoor dining room. Trained as a sommelier, Nguyen's wine list is also laudable, which explains the locale's popularity as an evening gathering place for the city's beautiful people.

TC CHOY'S ASIAN BISTRO ⊕⊕

301 S. Howard Ave., 813/251-1191, www.tcchoysbistro.com
HOURS: Mon.-Thurs. 11:30 A.M.-2:30 P.M. and

RESTAURANTS

5:30–10 P.M., Fri. 5:30–11 P.M., Sat.-Sun. 11 A.M.-3 P.M. and 5:30–11 P.M.

Remember when salsa supplanted ketchup as America's favorite condiment? Wasabi has to be nipping at salsa's heels. Sushi turns up everywhere, from the ballpark to convenience stores to—and here's the strange part—a whole bunch of different kinds of Asian restaurants. It's part of a recent trend to purvey a greatest-hits list of pan-Asian dishes under the same roof, an enticing mélange of pad Thai, tekka maki, and kung pao chicken sure to please everyone. TC Choy's Asian Bistro in Hyde Park is a textbook example of the species. Anchoring a long row of restaurants along South Howard Avenue, TC Choy's traffics in carefully constructed dishes from Thailand, Singapore, China, Japan, and Malaysia, all served in an oversized, stylish dining room. The best offerings are noonday dim sum, with big tables perfect for large parties.

WATER ❸❸

1015½ S. Howard Ave., 813/251-8406, www.ciccioandtonys.com
HOURS: Daily 6-10 P.M.

Dead center on Restaurant Row, Water is a savvy Japanese-inspired seafood joint and a late-night hangout for the neighborhood's beautiful people. Water specializes in rice paper rolled sushi (no nori) paired with punchy sauces and dynamic side dishes. A minimalist design aesthetic and a no-reservations policy cannot douse the enthusiasm for vibrant combos like unagi, banana, and avocado.

ECLECTIC

◖ BOCA KITCHEN BAR MARKET ❸❸

901 W. Platt St., 813/254-7070, www.bocatampa.com
HOURS: Sun.-Thurs. 5-11 P.M., Fri.-Sat. 5 P.M.-midnight

Along with a growing group of Tampa Bay restaurants, the new Boca Kitchen Bar Market isn't satisfied with a little local lettuce and some backyard herbs: It sources locally. The locavore

fervor wouldn't mean much if what Boca did with all this bounty was ho-hum. Executive chef Ted Dorsey and chef de cuisine Chad McColgin are brilliant. And it's hip. Gordon Davis's old Smoke BBQ has been enclosed, with lots of wood and cozy hightops in the bar area and two intimate dining rooms with glamorous lighting and cool rock posters (Wilco, Flight of the Conchords, etc.). Bathrooms are funky-posh, and there's free valet parking. It feels like the kind of neighborhood cult find you'd see in San Francisco or Brooklyn. The menu's most provocative item is an unspecified "staff meal, $16." With Dorsey and McColgin at the helm, it's bound to be local, thoughtful, and, most importantly, delicious.

PANE RUSTICA ❸❸

3225 S. MacDill Ave., 813/902-8828, www.panerusticabakery.com
HOURS: Tues. 8 A.M.-6 P.M., Wed.-Sat. 8 A.M.-10 P.M., Sun. 8 A.M.-3 P.M.

A thin-crust pizza hotshot by day, Pane Rustica hosts some of the most sophisticated Cal-Ital dinners around from Wednesday to Saturday, with full table service and an elegant short wine list. You can still opt for one of those luscious thin-crust pizzas (maybe one with a mantle of gorgonzola hiding sweet lengths of caramelized shallot? or perhaps ricotta salata enlivened with olive tapenade and sun-dried tomatoes?) or even a laid-back burger gussied up with Brie and roasted red peppers. But the breadth of alluring choices might sway you toward something a bit more refined. Don't miss Kevin and Karyn Kruszewski's stupendous cookies, cakes, and other homemade confections for dessert.

SEVEN 17 SOUTH ❸❸❸

717 S. Howard Ave., 813/250-1661, www.717south.com
HOURS: Mon.-Fri. 11:30 A.M.-2:30 P.M. and 5-10 P.M., Sat. 5-10 P.M.

Two fully realized culinary strategies are adopted simultaneously at Seven 17 South, each separate but equal. One side of the menu deals in kicky pan-Asian dishes as the other offers up sturdy Italian classics (lasagna, veal scaloppini). There's something for everyone, but not all on the same schizophrenic plate. Its success isn't just about the food: A sleek, clubby interior (visit just for a peek at the stunning art deco canvasses set against deep lapis lazuli walls) draws a hip, fashion-forward crowd. Service is warm and attentive, with glamorous hostesses bustling around as each evening amps up. The bartenders' mixology skills don't hurt, either, to lure a robust bar business most nights. Not every dish is a slam-dunk, but most diners' desires can be satisfied somewhere in the pages of the long menu.

SIDEBERN'S ❸❸❸

2208 W. Morrison Ave., 813/258-2233, www.siderns.com

HOURS: Mon.-Thurs. 5-10 P.M., Fri.-Sat. 5-11 P.M.

If the steakhouse Bern's doesn't sound like your

cup of tea, try the more contemporary approach at the affiliated SideBern's. Chef Chad Johnson has been nominated for a James Beard award, and general manager/bartender Dean Hurst has garnered all the kudos a mixologist can. The daily-changing selection of breads is absolutely knockout (curry sesame flatbread, kalamata and fig loaf). Veggies are first rate: a first course salad of sliced roasted red beets, goat cheese, and spring mix in a lovely Dijon vinaigrette; a heavenly cipollini onion soup with white truffle foam. Chef Johnson experiments with his own charcuterie and brings in as much local produce as possible. Cocktails are pricey but worth a splurge.

ETHIOPIAN
QUEEN OF SHEBA ❸

3636 Henderson Blvd., 813/872-6000, http://ethiopianrestauranttampa.com

HOURS: Daily 11 A.M.-10 P.M.

Queen of Sheba's location is one of those

SideBern's

Bermuda Triangle sites that has seen the demise of a number of restaurant ventures. Queen of Sheba will stick, though, on the basis of its huge family-style platter of spiced legume or meat stews called wats, its chicken drumsticks, and the hard-boiled eggs. The platters are lined with injera, a staple Ethiopian bread made of tef flour (gluten-free, a boon to wheat allergies or celiac disease sufferers). Spongy and elastic, more injera doubles as a utensil, with tiny pieces used to scoop dabs of stew.

IRISH

IRISH 31 $

1611 W. Swann Ave., 813/250-0031, www.irish31.com

HOURS: Mon.-Wed. 11 A.M.-1 A.M., Thurs.-Sat.

11 A.M.-2 A.M., Sun. 10 A.M.-midnight

Opened in 2011 in the building occupied by the original Wine Exchange, Irish 31 took over what has always been a wonderful space, on a corner with big windows and an inviting patio, adjacent to what is now CineBistro. Owners Jay and Bianca Mize have made it even better, with gorgeous wood floors, rustic light fixtures that look straight from nearby Restoration Hardware, cool tables with attached, fold-out stools, and a wall of vintage Tampa black-and-white photos. The menu is a savvy mix of traditional Irish pub fare and its classic American counterparts: shepherd's pie and lamb stew alongside burgers and fat Reuben sandwiches. At night the draw is live music in the courtyard.

ITALIAN

BELLA'S ITALIAN CAFÉ $$

1413 S. Howard Ave., 813/254-3355,

www.bellasitaliancafe.com

HOURS: Mon.-Fri. 11:30 A.M.-midnight, Sat.-Sun.

4-11 P.M.

Joanie Corneil and Bill Shumate opened Bella's more than 25 years ago. At the time it was the fifth restaurant between Kennedy and Bayshore Boulevards. Six or seven years later that number had swelled to 29. The place has had two

remodels in its lifetime and still manages to be comfortable but upscale enough to host date night elegantly. Servers are warm, portions are ample, and the place shimmers with the patina of Tampa tradition.

The food at Bella's is geographically indistinct, more the idea of Italian food that we hold dear. Regulars swear by the Confetti Spaghetti, a creamy basil tomato sauce dotted with bacon, tomato concasse, onion, basil, and green peas creeping around a zillion strands of soft spaghetti. And with already reasonable markups on wine, Wednesdays make it a serious bargain with all bottles half off.

SEAFOOD

COPPERFISH $$

1502 S. Howard Ave., 813/251-6789,

www.copperfishtampa.com

HOURS: Mon.-Sat. 5-11 P.M., Sun. 10 A.M.-3 P.M. and

4-10 P.M.

Gordon Davis's Copperfish opened in mid-2013, after incarnations are Le Bordeaux, St. Bart's Island House, Ceviche, and Samba Room. This iteration is of the "less is more" school, with simple dishes like local fish grilled over pecan and fruit wood. Copperfish also offers grilled oysters and an expansive raw bar.

SPANISH/TAPAS

CEVICHE TAPAS BAR &
RESTAURANT $$

2500 W. Azeele St., 813/250-0203, www.ceviche.com

HOURS: Tues.-Thurs. 5-11 P.M., Fri.-Sat. 5 P.M.-3 A.M.

Despite a recent move, Ceviche hasn't skipped a beat, serving its namesake citrus-cured fish, sea scallops with manchego, and an array of little dishes with addictive olives and almonds, all in a sleek nightclub atmosphere. Its new location has a great bar for live music and dance, a suave late-night hangout for Hyde Park's hipsters, purple-mouthed from pitchers of delicious sangria. There is also a location in downtown St. Petersburg (10 Beach Dr., 727/209-2302,

I SCREAM!

The Tampa Bay area has undergone something of a fro-yo invasion in the past two years, with Pinkberry clones and top-your-own emporiums dotting strip malls on both sides of the bay. And gelato seems to have carved itself a foothold, from Paciugo in St. Petersburg to the equally delicious Gelateria del Duomo at International Plaza. But let us pay homage to the old-fashioned independent ice cream parlor, preferably with a walk-up window, a splintery picnic table, and swirled soft-serve dipped in warm chocolate to make an instant shell that still seems magical.

Bo's (7101 N. Florida Ave., Tampa, 813/234-3870) has been around for 50-plus years. The guys behind the counter aren't speedy, so you may find yourself striking up a conversation while enduring the dense fog of mosquitoes and no-see-ums. There are diehard fans of the upside-down banana split (served in three sizes, from doable to truly unsettling to think about): sliced banana, ice cream, hot fudge, pineapple topping, whipped cream, nuts, cherries, and so forth, all rammed deep in a Styrofoam cup.

Dairy Joy (3813 S. Manhattan Ave., Tampa, 813/839-5485) has stayed the course over time, with vanilla, chocolate, and twist soft-serve at the core. In recent years they've added 10 flavors of hard ice cream, with sno-cones for the

kids and a quarter-pound beef hotdog. The banana split is a big seller, with several variations, and waffle bowl sundaes are nearly as popular.

Dairy Kurl (1555 Gulf-to-Bay Blvd., Clearwater, 727/446-1549) is a classic soft-serve palace where not much has changed in decades, including the sticky picnic tables and the owner. Soft-serve can be dipped, sprinkled, sauced (the peanut butter sauce rules), or blended with candy as a shake. These are all good options.

Old Farmer's Creamery (2531 4th St. N., St Petersburg, 727/896-2827) looks just like the Fisher-Price red barn with white trim. It's not cheap, but they make their own ice cream in a huge range of flavors (plenty of chocolate permutations), with tons of brightly colored kiddie flavors. The young counter staff contends ably with crowds despite what must be some harrowing scooper's arm (think carpel tunnel but a little colder).

Twistee Treat (6900 Gulf Blvd., St. Pete Beach, 727/367-7690) is a beacon, shaped like a giant vanilla twisty soft-serve. It's so visually arresting it starred briefly in the upcoming James Franco vehicle *Spring Breakers*. They go light on the hard ice cream (8 flavors) and have a soft-serve machine to which they can add 66 different flavors. Twistee is also dip-crazy, with a traditional chocolate dip, caramel, and even cherry.

Sun.–Mon. 5–10 P.M., Tues.–Thurs. 5 P.M.–midnight, Fri.–Sat. 5 P.M.–1 A.M.).

CHEAP $
309 S. Howard Ave., 813/258-5878,
www.cheapinsoho.com
HOURS: Tues.-Sat. 5 P.M.-2 A.M.

Cheap has most of the elements of an exciting small-plate restaurant, but it needs to tinker with its menu. An industrial-chic, low-light, loud-music place with good buzz, the space has a high funk-factor provided by wonderful found-object murals and the use of minivan banquettes in the booths, complete with seatbelts. Cheap boasts colorful mix-and-match

china, gorgeous sangria pitchers, and lovely swirled stemware. Half the menu is *crudos,* cold raw seafood dishes like tartares, ceviches, and sashimis. The other half is *epulae* (a Latin word that loosely means "feast"). On either side, most dishes lack textural contrast of something crunchy, and vegetarian options are limited.

STEAKHOUSE
BERN'S STEAK HOUSE $$$
1208 S. Howard Ave., 813/251-2421,
www.bernssteakhouse.com
HOURS: Daily 5-11 P.M.

Bern's is the biggest gorilla of them all on the

RESTAURANTS

Tampa dining scene. The restaurant known around the world is on what is now a slightly seedy stretch of South Howard Avenue, but fans are undeterred. Founded in 1956, the landmark has a wine list that could break a toe and a menu that reaches new levels of hyperbole. Waiters go through a grueling years-long apprenticeship, resulting in a staff that could, and does, quote verbatim from the offerings. Steaks are so lovingly described that it wouldn't be surprising to hear the eye color, hat size, or hobbies of the cows in question. It's prime beef, aged and nurtured in Bern's own meat lockers, and you dictate the size, cut, and cooking temperature. You gotta go to Bern's, if only to revel in the bordello-like decor of gilded plaster columns, red wallpaper, Tiffany lamps, and murals of French vineyards. After dinner take the tour of the kitchen and wine cellar.

Then head upstairs to **The Harry Waugh Dessert Room at Bern's Steak House.** Nothing prepares you for it, not even the rococo excess of Bern's downstairs. You dine in individual hollowed-out wine casks. There are individual wall-mounted radios to set the mood at your table. You hear a rumor about an accordionist, maybe something about flambéing waiters. The romantic date-night possibilities of this dessert-only upstairs of Bern's (named after a wine-writing crony of Bern himself) get the heart racing. If that's not enough, there's Chocolate-Chocolate-Chocolate. That's the name of the demure chocolate-shellacked cylinder packing chocolate cheese pie, chocolate mousse, and chocolate cheesecake into one deadly package.

Davis Islands   Map 2

AMERICAN
CAFÉ DUFRAIN 🅢🅢
707 Harbour Post Dr., 813/275-9701,
www.cafedufrain.com
HOURS: Mon.-Sat. 11:30 A.M.-10 P.M.
Café Dufrain's executive chef Ferrell Alvarez has big news. Together with partners Ty Rodriguez and Cathy Hume, they've launched *Local Dirt,* a quarterly magazine about sustainability and locally sourced foodstuffs. Alvarez's passion is clear from the menu at the charming 10-year-old Harbour Island original, with more than 80 percent of the menu comprised of local and sustainably sourced foods.

220 EAST 🅢🅢
220 E. Davis Blvd., 813/259-1220, www.220east.com
HOURS: Mon.-Thurs. 11:30 A.M.-3 P.M. and 5-10 P.M., Fri. 11 A.M.-3 P.M. and 4-11 P.M., Sat. 11 A.M.-11 P.M.
Nestled in the cute street-that-time-forgot business district of Davis Island, the longtimer 220 East beckons with a cheery turquoise-and-grape awning. Opinions are divided about the best tables—out front at one of the handful on the patio, or inside at one of the deep green booths. Either way, most tables are full of islanders and pilgrims from elsewhere in the Bay Area eager for a friendly face and a fairly priced, unfussy meal that ranges affably through American, Asian, and even Cajun dishes.

ASIAN/ECLECTIC
JACKSON'S BISTRO BAR & SUSHI 🅢🅢🅢
Wyndham Harbour Island Hotel, 601 S. Harbour Island Blvd., 813/277-0112, www.jacksonsbistro.com
HOURS: Mon.-Thurs. 11:30 A.M.-2:30 P.M. and 5-10 P.M., Fri. and Sat. 11:30 A.M.-2:30 P.M. and 5-11 P.M., Sun. 10:30 A.M.-2:30 P.M. and 5-10 P.M.
Really on Harbour Island, an adjacent tiny island within a stone's throw of Davis Islands, Jackson's opened in 1997 and has waited for everything, and everyone, around it to arrive at its sophistication level. Judging from the hip, bustling crowd, they've arrived. And the

sleek restaurant embraces the throngs with a laudably broad wine list and a something-for-everyone culinary approach that includes pistachio-crusted red snapper, lush prime rib eye steaks, and a smart array of familiar *nigiri* and *makimono* sushi rolls. There's also an attached lounge for nightly entertainment. It's a vast, clubby, mahogany-lined room containing a lengthy three-sided bar and some of the city's most diehard revelers. Despite its island locale, Jackson's is one block from the Tampa Convention Center, Marriott Waterside, and the Hartline Trolley.

MEXICAN
ESTELA'S ❸
209 E. Davis Blvd., 813/251-0558, www.estelas.com
HOURS: Mon.-Fri. 11 A.M.-10 P.M., Sat.-Sun. 11 A.M.-11 P.M.

Across the street from 220 East and equally beloved, Estela's is known for exemplary carne asada (a rib eye with lots of thinly sliced onions and a limey piquancy, served with a cheese enchilada and refried beans) and chocolate tacos.

Margaritas are big and quenching; there's mariachi on the weekends. Unsurprisingly, Estela's has spawned additional locations in New Port Richey, St. Petersburg, and Brandon.

THAI
THAI ISLAND ❸
210 E. Davis Blvd., 813/251-9111
HOURS: Mon. 11:30 A.M.-2:30 P.M., Tues.-Fri. 11:30 A.M.-2:30 P.M. and 5-10 P.M., Sat.-Sun. 5-10 P.M.

Thai Island has the sweet charm of a beloved neighborhood place. It's not fancy; the decor is simple and homespun. The service is as personal as it gets—if it's not Clay McElmurray making suggestions and zipping over a tray, it's his wife, co-owner Penn Karach. Karach's mother, Pat, is often in the kitchen. What elevates Thai Island above plenty of other area Thai restaurants is breadth of menu and quality of ingredients. They have the familiar curries (green, red, panang, massaman), but the salad and appetizer sections of the menu pack some unusual finds.

Ybor City   Map 3

AMERICAN
CARNE CHOPHOUSE ❸❸
1536 E. 7th Ave., 813/341-9555, www.carnechophouse.com
HOURS: Mon.-Thurs. 11 A.M.-10 P.M., Fri.-Sat. 11 A.M.-11 P.M., Sun. 4-10 P.M.

It's official. Jason Fernandez has an empire. Bernini, Green Iguana, and Hot Willy's in Ybor City were joined in 2012 by Carne Chophouse in the historic 1912 El Centro Español Building. Steaks and chops take center stage, supported by nostalgia-inducing classics like garlicky escargots and trout almondine. But it's affordable, with a few nods to Ybor's past (a little chimichurri, some sofrito potatoes). Fernandez understands a couple of things clearly. People are looking for value: Entrées

come with a soup, Caesar or wedge salad, and a choice of side dish. And people in Ybor like their cocktails: The new restaurant has an extremely well-outfitted bar, with a savvy list of signature cocktails (the Ybor Rough Rider features Southern Comfort, amaretto, and sour) and, as at Bernini, there are $2 Finlandia martinis 11:30 A.M.-7 P.M.

TAMPA BAY BREWING COMPANY ❸❸
Centro Ybor, 1600 E. 8th Ave., 813/247-1422, www.tbbco.com
HOURS: Mon.-Tues. 11 A.M.-11 P.M., Wed.-Sat. 11 A.M.-2 A.M., Sun. 1 P.M.-midnight

One of Tampa's beloved brewpubs, Tampa Bay Brewing Company moved from elsewhere in Ybor City to anchor the Centro Ybor. And it's a welcome addition. There's good live music, excellent proprietary brews (watch the Redeye Ale, it's a humdinger), and an ambitious American bistro menu.

GREEK
ACROPOLIS GREEK TAVERN $$
1833 E. 7th Ave., 813/242-4545,
www.acropolistaverna.com
HOURS: Mon.-Thurs. 11 A.M.-midnight, Fri. 11 A.M.-3 A.M., Sat. noon-3 A.M., Sun. noon-midnight

Picture belly dancers Fridays, Saturdays, and Sundays; a frenetic bouzouki band; or the stirring Greek song stylings of Babi Lavidas. Add to that people leaping up to gyrate through a quick *zeibekiko* or *sousta*, punctuated by the occasional sound of plates breaking, and you have yourself a Hellenic hootenanny at Acropolis Greek Tavern. Tables outside are nice, but you might miss out on the action in the columned dining room. Owners Sam and Costa Waez have taken a traditional Greek taverna set-up

and infused it with Ybor fun. The menu is all that the blue-and-white color scheme promises, with gyros, spanakopita, moussaka, and such. Vegetarians will be especially pleased at their range of options: tahini-lush hummus and baba ganoush; a roasted veggie sandwich anchored by nutty eggplant; falafel offered as a wrap or app, drizzled with more tangy tahini sauce.

ITALIAN
BERNINI OF YBOR $$$
1702 E. 7th Ave., 813/248-0099, www.berniniofybor.com
HOURS: Mon.-Thurs. 11:30 A.M.-10 P.M., Fri.-Sat. 11:30 A.M.-midnight, Sun. 4-10 P.M.

People-watching is a robust pastime in Ybor City, with occasional catcalling and trash-talking adding a fillip of drama. For the best sidewalk seat in town, pull up a chair at Bernini. It's set in the historic Bank of Ybor City building and serves sophisticated Cal-Ital cuisine—salmon carpaccio, lemon-scented calamari, and filet mignon sparked with a wild mushroom

restauranteur Richard Gonzmart in the wine cellar at Columbia Restaurant

risotto and topped with heady truffle butter. It attracts a more mature crowd than the bars and clubs all around it, partly because of the thoughtful wine list and partly because the mixologists know their way around the bar. Given Bernini's namesake painter, Bernini's Italian chocolate kiss martini is suitably over-the-top, go-for-Baroque, pairing Ketel One vodka, Godiva white and dark liqueurs, and a hint of Frangelico, all sealed with a kiss. Certainly easier on the breath than the punchy puttanesca pizza (olives, anchovy, capers, etc.), but it all depends on your priorities.

JAPANESE
SAMURAI BLUE SUSHI
AND SAKE BAR $$
Centro Ybor, 1600 E. 8th Ave., 813/242-6688, www.samuraiblue.com
HOURS: Mon.-Fri. 11:30 A.M.-midnight, Sat. 5 P.M.-1 A.M., Sun. 5-11 P.M.

A longtimer in the ever-changing lineup of Centro Ybor restaurants, Samurai is a big, frenetic joint serving sake bombers, "spontaneous combustion rolls," and other kooky spins on Japanese bar staples. You've had better chilled soba noodles and tekka maki, but it doesn't matter much once you've relaxed with something from the suave saketini menu.

SPANISH/CUBAN
COLUMBIA RESTAURANT $$$
2117 E. 7th Ave., 813/248-4961
HOURS: Mon.-Thurs. 11 A.M.-10 P.M., Fri.-Sat. 11 A.M.-11 P.M., Sun. noon-9 P.M.

The Columbia bears the distinction of being the oldest restaurant in Florida (started in 1905) and the nation's largest Spanish/Cuban restaurant (13 rooms extending one city block). Frankly, the food is not spectacular these days, but the experience is worth picking through ho-hum paella or sipping pedestrian sangria. Some of these waiters have been here a lifetime, the many rooms manage to stay packed, and there are stirring flamenco shows Monday–Saturday nights.

Busch Gardens and North Tampa   Map 4

AMERICAN
SKIPPER'S SMOKEHOUSE $$
910 Skipper Rd., 813/971-0066, www.skipperssmokehouse.com
HOURS: Tues.-Fri. 11 A.M.-10 P.M., Sat. noon-11 P.M., Sun. 1-10 P.M.

New Tampa (the residential area northeast of downtown), as the name indicates, is all new. The upside is that things are clean, pristine, and hygienic; the downside is that there's no sense of history, no gritty, timeworn ambience. If you are jonesing for something that seems older than a decade or so, Skipper's Smokehouse has the ambience of a place 10 times its age. It's Tampa's best live music venue (blues, alt rock, Tuvan throat singers, the gamut), with concerts held outdoors under the canopy of a huge, moss-festooned live oak. It has a lively 30s-and-up bar scene (with a mighty fine mojito), and a ramshackle restaurant serves a wonderful blackened grouper sandwich, gator nuggets, and black beans.

CHINESE
HO HO CHOY $
1441 Fletcher Ave. E., 813/962-2159, www.hohochoychinese.com
HOURS: Sun.-Thurs. 11 A.M.-10 P.M., Fri.-Sat. 11 A.M.-11 P.M.

Relocating from a spot on Dale Mabry Highway, Ho Ho Choy is a purveyor of appealing and straightforward Chinese dishes as well as an array of less familiar dim sum. The fried and steamed dumplings are served all day (whereas in China the small dishes are served

RESTAURANTS

primarily for lunch), offered in small, individual portions. Ho Ho Choy's fried sesame ball is prototypical, featuring a crunchy, sesame seed–coated exterior giving way to a smooth red bean paste center. An order of pork buns brings airy, soft white bread cradling a sweet, electric-pink barbecued pork filling. The pan-fried dumplings are the best, with their crisp fried exteriors contrasting the rest of the slithery dumpling, and a savory, gingery ground pork filling.

GREEK
ACROPOLIS BAR & GRILL ⑤⑤
14947 Bruce B. Downs Blvd., 813/971-1787,
www.acropolistaverna.com
HOURS: Mon.-Thurs. 11 A.M.–midnight, Fri.-Sat.
11 A.M.–3 A.M., Sun. noon-midnight

The staff at Acropolis Bar & Grill is young, attractive, and prone to launching into a fit of grapevine dancing at the slightest provocation. They yell "Opa" and break plates, a belly dancer undulates on the weekends, and a DJ spins world music late into the night. The same menu at lunch and dinner means it's a little splurgy at lunch, but consummately affordable at dinner. The owners have stayed focused in the kitchen, ditching things that may not be accessible to timid palates (fishy taramasalata) and keeping the Greek crowd pleasers (flaming cheese, watch the eyebrows). Generally, portions

are big and entrées come with a choice of soup or salad—hard to choose, because the soup is often a delicious lemony avgolemono (like eggdrop soup, Greek-style) and the salad is a generous Greek salad topped with a wedge of perfect feta.

VIETNAMESE
PHO QUYEN ⑤
2740 E. Fowler Ave., 813/632-3444, www.phoquyen.com
HOURS: Sun.-Thurs. 10:30 A.M.–9 P.M., Fri.-Sat.
10:30 A.M.–10 P.M.

Pho (pronounced FUH—say foot without the *t*) is the Vietnamese national breakfast. Pho Quyen provides a glorious introduction to the species. In the little shopping center near USF shared by Staples and JoAnn Fabrics, this Southeast Asian restaurant, at the site of a former Chinese eatery, has filled a void, bringing the clean, vibrant flavors of Vietnam to New Tampa, all at very affordable prices. Food fiends claim that pho, like Japanese miso or Jewish chicken soup, functions as an analeptic, stimulating the central nervous system when you're sick, sad, or hung-over. Who knows if that's true, but there's just about nothing else more wholesome. Pho Quyen's interior is simple and utilitarian, with green vinyl booths, a few huge silk orchids, and jolly green plaid tablecloths that gussy up the spare dining room of peach and green walls.

Greater Tampa   Map 5

AMERICAN
ELLA'S AMERICANA FOLK ART CAFE ⑤⑤
5119 N. Nebraska Ave., Tampa, 813/234-1000,
www.ellasfolkartcafe.com
HOURS: Tues.-Thurs. 5-11 P.M., Fri.-Sat. 5 P.M.–midnight,
Sun. 11 A.M.–8 P.M.

The walls of Ella's are covered with outsider art and on the weekends co-owner Ernie Locke can sometimes be seen with his band Nervous

Turkey. But what has really charmed Seminole Heights at this independent-minded charmer is its cool spins on down-home classics like chicken and waffles.

GRILLE ONE SIXTEEN ⑤⑤⑤
15405 N. Dale Mabry Hwy., Tampa, 813/265-0116,
http://grilleonesixteen.com
HOURS: Sun.-Thurs. 11 A.M.–9 P.M., Fri.-Sat. 11 A.M.–10 P.M.

Grille One Sixteen has made waves with its hip,

FLORIDA FOODS

What is Florida cuisine? The beneficence of the Gulf of Mexico and the absurd number of sunny days provide a number of indigenous delicacies.

ALLIGATOR

Head to the venerable **Skipper's Smokehouse** (910 Skipper Rd., Tampa, 813/971-0666, www.skipperssmokehouse. com), Tampa's beloved indoor-outdoor live blues venue, where a huge, moss-festooned live oak provides shade. They offer gator a few ways: in chili, as part of a gator tail dinner with hush puppies and a couple of sides; as a sandwich; or just as a nugget appetizer. It's a novelty item worth trying once.

SMOKED FISH SPREAD

At **Ted Peters Famous Smoked Fish** (1350 Pasadena Ave., South Pasadena, 727/381-7931, www.tedpetersfish.com) they'll smoke your catch, fillet it, throw it over a smoldering red oak fire in the smokehouse, then package it up for you to take. But even non-anglers should angle for a visit. It's prized for its laidback style and inviting picnic tables. The smoked fish spread with saltines is good, the salmon is excellent, and the mullet is an intensely fishy acquired taste. This is a beer-drinking establishment, it gets fairly busy, and it closes early. Credit cards are not accepted.

STONE CRAB

One of Florida's favorite delicacies is a renewable resource. During the October–May season, fisherfolk haul the crabs up, yank off one claw, and throw them back to grow another.

One of the local heavy hitters for these crustaceans is **Frenchy's Café** (41 Baymont St., Clearwater Beach, 727/446-3607, http://frenchysonline.com). The original Frenchy's Café opened in 1981. Since then, several other businesses have been opened by the same owners (Frenchy's Saltwater Café, 419 Poinsettia Ave., Clearwater Beach, 727/461-6295; Frenchy's Rockaway Grill, 7 Rockaway St., Clearwater Beach, 727/446-4844; and Frenchy's South Beach Café, 351 S. Gulfview Blvd., Clearwater Beach, 727/441-9991), all fueled by their own fleet of commercial fishing boats. Eat stone crab

like the locals, chilled with mustard sauce. It's not gauche to ask for them hot, adorned with only a squeeze of lemon and a pool of clarified butter.

ORANGE JUICE

Citrus is Florida's leading cash crop, producing 90 percent of the country's orange juice (almost all Florida oranges are juiced, not sold whole). To get a sense of the full range of the state's wonderful citrus, head south over the Sunshine Skyway Bridge to the **Citrus Place** (7200 U.S. 19, Terra Ceia, 941/722-6745). There are navel oranges in the fall, honeybells coming soon after the new year, followed by temple oranges, honey tangerines, and Valencia oranges. White and pink grapefruits are available nearly year round.

CUBAN SANDWICH

In Tampa, the Cuban is the king of sandwiches. Go to **La Segunda Central Bakery** (2512 N. 15th St., Ybor City, 813/248-1531, http://lasegundabakery.com) for an audience with the king. The bakery turns out 6,000 Cuban loaves daily: 36 inches long, with a zipper-like seam down the top, with the remnants of a palmetto leaf charred along the seam. The pillowy interior of the loaf is piled high with roast pork and Genoa salami (that's a Tampa twist), Swiss cheese (some say Emanthaler), sour pickles, and spicy mustard. The whole thing is warmed and flattened in a special hot press. It has to be ruthlessly pressed to render the outside crisp and the inside majorly gooey.

KEY LIME PIE

Key lime pies are way more Floridian than all-American apple. Graham cracker crust cradles a piquant filling of egg yolk, condensed milk, and the juice of tiny key limes. It's not complex, but it is divine when it's good. **Mike's Pies** (Fresh Market, 3722 Henderson Blvd., Tampa, 813/875-7400, www.mikespies.com) in Tampa makes 30 kinds of pies, selling between 4,000 and 6,000 each week. Mike Martin's biggest seller is key lime by a good bit, but he has won more than a dozen national championships at the annual Great American Pie Festival for a range of pies, some from family recipes dating back more than 100 years.

RESTAURANTS

Miami-like design. House music pulses; waiters scoot around in mod all-black; an elegant long bar is packed with the glamorous or at least fashion-intrepid. The kitchen has a strong New American palette with a world-beat sense of play. Not every time at bat yields a home run, but the chef usually gets on base.

THE INDEPENDENT BAR & CAFÉ ❸
5016 N. Florida Ave., Tampa, 813/341-4883,
www.independenttampa.com
HOURS: Mon.-Thurs. 9 A.M.-midnight, Fri.-Sun.9 A.M.-3 A.M.

The beer-intensive Independent only recently began serving food. For a while the converted gas station that became the Independent was so deadly serious about craft beer that they sold nothing else. Since then they've added this: a grilled cheese that will blow your mind, with molten gouda on rye bread with pears sautéed in honey and five spice. There are other things on the menu (a liverwurst sandwich, a vegan BLT), but it's hard to get beyond the grilled cheese.

MICHAEL'S GRILL ❸❸
11720 N. Dale Mabry Hwy., Tampa, 813/964-8334,
www.michaelsgrill.com
HOURS: Mon.-Thurs. 11 A.M.-9 P.M., Fri.-Sat. 11 A.M.-10 P.M.

In the sophisticated neighborhood of Carrollwood, Andrea and Michael Reilly's little Michael's Grill has become an institution, as much for the warm greeting and neighborly service as it is for the convivial patio and spare, brasserie-style dining room. You can eat your French onion soup or penne Bolognese at the bar and take in all the drama of the bustling open kitchenb but through the French doors and out onto the leafy patio the well-heeled crowd always seems to be having more fun.

NORDSTROM CAFÉ BISTRO ❸❸
International Plaza, 2223 N. Westshore Blvd., Tampa,
813/875-4400
HOURS: Mon.-Sat. 10 A.M.-9 P.M., Sun. noon-6 P.M.

When Nordstrom has an especially good shoe sale you don't want to get too far from the action. Sophisticated salads and brick-oven pizzas emanate from a lively demonstration kitchen. Ladies who lunch and fatigued shopping casualties enjoy the respite on Nordstrom's upper level.

THE REFINERY ❸❸
5137 N. Florida Ave., Tampa, 813/237-2000,
thetamparefinery.com
HOURS: Tues.-Thurs. 5-10 P.M., Fri.-Sat. 5-11 P.M., Sun. 11 A.M.-3 P.M.

The Refinery's Greg and Michelle Baker have been a catalyst for the Tampa food scene, bringing a level of hipness and forward-thinking sourcing that is unprecedented. Housed in a charming Victorian bungalow in the idiosyncratic neighborhood of Seminole Heights, this James Beard nominee reinvents itself every week with an all-new menu that pushes the envelope in its juxtapositions as well as its focus on local farms and purveyors. This is where Mario Batali chose to eat on a recent visit, hanging out in the upstairs bar that is every bit as cool as something you'd find in Portland or Brooklyn. With serious tats and an affection for organ meats, Baker is a chef's chef, with the closely held conviction that great food shouldn't be the purview of only the one percent.

BRAZILIAN
BOIZAO STEAKHOUSE ❸❸❸
4606 W. Boy Scout Blvd., Tampa, 813/286-7100,
www.boizao.com
HOURS: Sun.-Thurs. 11 A.M.-2:30 P.M. and 5-10 P.M., Fri. 11 A.M.-2:30 P.M. and 5-11 P.M., Sat. 5-11 P.M.

Eating at a classic Brazilian *churrascaria* like Boizao is a little like fielding a series of telemarketing calls during dinner. Every minute or two you have to stop what you're doing— eating, talking, whatever. Only in this case, it's because someone is repeatedly offering you meat on a long skewer: Oh, yes, please. No, none of that, thanks. Each diner gets a tabletop card: Green side means go, red side means stop.

The Refinery, downtown Tampa

Pronounced boy-ZOUN, this newcomer seems to draw the expense-account businessfolk who stay in nearby Tampa International Airport/ Westshore hotels. It's a vast, slick space with a festive, all-you-can-eat party vibe. The waft of rotisseried meats greets you at the door; a huge salad bar buffet anchors the airy room; the lavish glassed-in wine cellar holds enticing heavy-hitters and oversized bottles.

BRITISH
MAD DOGS AND ENGLISHMEN $$

4115 S. MacDill Ave., Tampa, 813/832-3037, www.maddogs.com

HOURS: Mon.-Thurs. 11 A.M.-10 P.M., Fri.-Sat. 11 A.M.-11 P.M., Sun. 10 A.M.-10 P.M.

Mad Dogs and Englishmen has a sense of humor, which may explain its longevity. Celebrating its twentieth year, its 2011 menu sported the old joke: "Two cannibals eating a clown. One says to the other, 'Does this taste funny to you?'" Co-owner Wilton Morley

seems to do things his own way, and that has worked out just fine. This is a family place, a casual indoor-outdoor spot to meet for a pint and a nibble on the odd Tuesday night. The beer list favors Britain, the wine list is more global (prices are very reasonable; by-the-glass pours are very generous), and the servers and bartenders seem to be from all over the place. The menu features British pub staples (fish and chips, chicken curry) with some more eclectic offerings like red Thai curry and innovative homemade ice cream.

CHINESE
CHINA YUAN SEAFOOD RESTAURANT $

8502 N. Armenia Ave., # 1A, Tampa, 813/936-7388, http://chinayuanrestaurant.com

HOURS: Mon.-Thurs. 11 A.M.-10 P.M., Fri. and Sat. 10:30 A.M.-11 P.M., Sun. 10:30 A.M.-10 P.M.

China Yuan was always good, its burnished-skin ducks practically flying out of their glass

FAST FOOD FAVORITES

The Virginia-based **Five Guys Famous Burgers and Fries** (2702 E. Fowler Ave., Tampa, 813/977-4400, www.fiveguys.com; 7054 U.S. 19 N., Pinellas Park, 727/526-7800; 13149 N. Dale Mabry Hwy.; 3841 W. Kennedy Blvd., Tampa) is gaining market share locally due to its free in-the-shell peanuts, spectacular fries, and burgers lavishly accessorized then packaged in no-frills, no-logos, brown-paper bags like the olden days.

Chipotle (2662 Gulf to Bay Blvd., Clearwater, 727/724-1768, www.chipotle.com; 3700 Park Blvd., Pinellas Park, 727/525-2484; 780 4th St. N., St. Petersburg, 727/895-6050; 309 N. Westshore Blvd., Tampa, 813/289-9820; 533 S. Howard Ave., Tampa, 813/254-6450; 2576 E. Fowler Ave., Tampa, 813/971-4360; 12827 N. Dale Mabry Hwy., Tampa, 813/961-1444) is a recent fastie that's doing some things right, emphasizing spice and health in their burrito bowls.

The same could be said of Miami-based **Pollo Tropicale** (3900 Park Blvd., Pinellas Park, 727/362-9600, www.pollotropical.com; 6276 W. Waters Ave., Tampa, 813/319-6360; 3285 W. Hillsborough Ave., Tampa, 813/319-1850), trafficking in Caribbean-style, citrus-marinated grilled chicken served in a clean, bright environment.

By most accounts it's still working out the kinks, but PF Chang's fast concept, **Pei Wei Asian Diner** (12927 N. Dale Mabry Hwy., Tampa, 813/960-2031, www.peiwei.com; 1402 66th St., St. Petersburg, 727/347-1351) stays focused on healthful choices with its wok-cooked Thai, Vietnamese, Japanese, and Chinese noodle and rice dishes.

A fast-food chain launched by an Outback Steakhouse co-founder, **PDQ** (2207 S. Dale Mabry Hwy., Tampa, 813/254-7373, www.eatpdq.com) is about as narrowly focused as they come, like the In-N-Out Burger of chicken. The core is chicken tenders made with white meat chicken that are moist and wholesome-tasting, with a fairly heavy, crunchy batter. These fried tenders come sliced as toppers on the crispy chicken salad or in a crispy chicken sandwich. Milkshakes—chocolate, vanilla, strawberry—are thick (more dessert than beverage) and served in a small enough portion that you won't be queasy by the last pull on the straw. The fresh-squeezed lemonade is old-timey and quenching. And this place is fast: Whether you drive through or walk in, you'll have your bag of goodies in a disorientingly short amount of time.

---

case and onto plates of the eager and the lucky. But the dining room was punitively bright, barebones, a little cold, and a lot cramped. All that changed a few years ago when the doors reopened after an expansion and major remodeling. The new space is airy, fronted by a bank of windows, and populated by generous round tables suitable for big parties. An array of dim sum, not cart service, brings delicate shrimp har gow and cup-shaped meat siu mai, roast pork buns (like meat-filled doughnuts, what's not to like?), and flaky fried chive dumplings. This major carb-load is best mitigated with an order of spicy eggplant with garlic or sautéed pea sprouts.

YUMMY HOUSE CHINA BISTRO ⑤

2620 E. Hillsborough Ave., Tampa, 813/237-3838, http://yummyhousechinabistro.com

HOURS: Daily 11:30 A.M.-2:30 P.M. and 5:30-9:30 P.M.

This second Yummy House venture purveys just about the best Chinese food we've had in years. The kitchen traffics in bright sautéed greens, still-crisp veggies, burnished-skin ducks, and cracked crabs redolent of ginger and scallion, served to a mostly Chinese clientele. The place has a huge and devoted fan base, people who recognize that there is real Hong Kong know-how at work in the kitchen. It's packed on most nights, the lovely dining room loud with the raised voices of big families and gastronomic enthusiasm. Just slightly understaffed, the few waiters seem always at a near-jog, brusque but efficient in their task of bringing and taking away. The original location is on Waters Avenue (2202 W. Waters Ave., 813/915-2828, www.yummyhousetampa.com).

DELI

TOOJAY'S ORIGINAL GOURMET DELI $

International Plaza, 2223 N. Westshore Blvd., Tampa, 813/348-4101, www.toojays.com

HOURS: Sun.-Thurs. 8 A.M.-9 P.M., Fri.-Sat. 8 A.M.-10 P.M.

TooJay's serves fat, old-school New York–style deli sammies, no froufrou chutneys here. Go for corned beef or the Italiano. There are 24 locations, only in Florida, and all are very family-friendly. The chicken noodle soup and blintzes will cure the shopping-trip blues and not set you back much.

GASTROPUB

THE PUB $$

International Plaza, 2223 N. Westshore Blvd., Tampa, 813/443-5642, www.experiencethepub.com

HOURS: Mon.-Wed. 11:30 A.M.-midnight, Thurs. 11:30 A.M.-1 A.M., Fri.-Sat. 11:30 A.M.-2 A.M.

An outpost of a small chain of English gastropubs clustered in Ohio, Kentucky, and Florida, The Pub took over the Bamboo Club space at International Plaza, with great outdoor tables, cozy leather booths, and lots of bar seating. It's a sprawling place, with emphasis on what's on tap and with a menu that is fittingly pub grub (bangers and mash, shepherd's pie). The weekday drink deals can streamline decision-making: on Tuesdays it's $4 pints; on Wednesdays it's half-price bottles of wine; on Thursdays there are $4 martinis and cocktails. Monday night is quiz night, with half-price fish and chips to sustain the quizzlers.

INDIAN

UDIPI CAFÉ $

14422 N. Dale Mabry Hwy., Tampa, 813/962-7300, www.udipiusa.net

HOURS: Tues.-Sun. 11:30 A.M.-9:30 P.M.

Forget lamb vindaloo—south Indian vegetarian will blow your taste buds sky-high with spicy eggplant curry. Udipi is a barebones setting for an exotic cuisine, so don't expect a gastronomic tour guide. Go for the masala dosa, a huge, thin rice-and-lentil pancake rolled into a tube so it looks like a sleeping bag on a platter, served with curry-spiked potato and onion paste, coconut chutney, and sambar. Or head for one of the *uthapam,* a soft white pancake in which things like tomato, peas, cilantro, and onion are embedded. Easiest eaten in triangular wedges dotted with sauce, it's like an Indian spin on pizza. There is no alcohol here.

ITALIAN

ARMANI'S $$$

2900 Bayport Dr., Tampa, 813/207-6800, http://hyatt.com/gallery/tparw_armanis

HOURS: Mon.-Thurs. 6-10 P.M., Fri.-Sat. 6-11 P.M.

When you want to get a sense of Tampa's scale, distance, and scope, you have to dig deep into your wallet and head to Armani's atop the Grand Hyatt Tampa Bay. It's the undisputed top special-occasion and god-I-need-to-clinch-this-deal restaurant in town, partly for the view, partly for the solicitous service, and partly for the scaloppine Armani (thin-pounded veal sautéed with wild mushrooms and cognac in a creamy truffle sauce) or the grilled duck breast stuffed with liver pâté and dried cherries in a subtle vanilla sauce. The wine list shows depth and breadth, with an emphasis on important California/French wines.

CAFFE PARADISO $$

4205 S. MacDill Ave., Tampa, 813/835-6622

HOURS: Mon.-Sat. 5:30-10 P.M.

"Are you ready to hear the evening's specials?" Sure, why not, how ready do we have to be, we thought. After about the tenth dish, we started panicking. What was that first one again, with the fish? Did he say something about

RESTAURANTS

manicotti? Not to worry, the waiter was patient with us, repeating as necessary. Giving advice, cajoling gently to ensure we'd ordered well. Caffe Paradiso is that kind of place: friendly, casual, with comforting Italian cuisine served up by folks who, if they aren't Italian, have the warmth and tendency to gesticulate that makes them seem so. It's the kind of place that's familiar and reminiscent of home—regardless of your heritage. It's nothing too snazzy from the outside, just a little storefront in the St. Croix Plaza on South MacDill Avenue. Inside, it's comfy and dark, with crisp linens and lots of regulars.

DONATELLO $$$

232 N. Dale Mabry Hwy., Tampa, 813/875-6660, www.donatellotampa.com
HOURS: Daily 5:30-10 P.M.

The blush is not off the rose at Donatello, a Tampa original since 1984. In the dining room, tuxedoed waiters perform with the assurance only longtime employment provides, whether that's guiding guests through the menu or whipping up a tableside Caesar (the best in town). The food is rigorously traditional Northern Italian, with just about everything made in house (all right, not the penne or other macaroni). The wine list is stunning, with a breadth of prices, regions, varietals, and large and small production represented. But wine costs a pretty penny, and the menu is in financial lockstep. This is splurge country, but well worth it.

PELAGIA TRATTORIA $$$

International Plaza, 2223 N. Westshore Blvd., Tampa, 813/313-3235, www.pelagiatrattoria.com
HOURS: Daily 6:30-10:30 A.M., 11:30 A.M.-3 P.M., and 5:30-10 P.M.

This swanky hotel eatery has turned a lot of heads. The bold Mediterranean palate in the dining room is echoed in Chef Andrew Basch's lush cuisine. At breakfast, this means waffles with cappuccino mousse and walnuts; at lunch, crunchy fried olives stuffed with three meats or mussels braised with merguez; and for dinner, the stylish crowd enthuses about the rack of lamb with fig-port sauce. It's the prettiest hotel restaurant in all of Tampa, located on the main level in the Renaissance Tampa Hotel, Bay Street.

MEXICAN

MEKENITA MEXICAN GRILLE $

17623 N. Dale Mabry Hwy., Lutz, 813/264-1212, www.mekenitamexicangrille.com
HOURS: Mon.-Sat. 11 A.M.-9 P.M.

Rand Packer, the celebrated former chef of Roy's, went out on his own a few years back with Mekenita. It's an order-at-the-counter, funky, and affordable outpost of regional Mexican cuisine—cooking from Oaxaca, the land of seven moles. Best dishes are the *sopes* (fried masa topped with vegetables and meat) and the smoked pork tacos.

PACIFIC RIM

ROY'S $$$

4342 W. Boy Scout Blvd., Tampa, 813/873-7697, www.roysrestaurant.com
HOURS: Sun.-Thurs. 5:30-10 P.M., Fri.-Sat. 5:30-10:30 P.M.

The Tampa dining cognoscenti has embraced the lively and über-stylish Hawaiian-fusion cuisine of celebrity chef Roy Yamaguchi. Even on a Monday night, Roy's has got the kind of buzz that could cover a whole bunch of power tools in action. Not that the sleek interior needs any touch-ups. Expanses of richly buffed wood and sea grass are punctuated by blown-glass sconces and Asian-inspired wrought-iron fixtures. About the prettiest dining room in Tampa, it seems only fitting that the clientele is a mix of the beautiful, the affluent, and the preternaturally suave. The nightly-changing menu always features some of "Roy's classics," such as the justifiably famous miso-charred

Pelagia Trattoria

butterfish with its zingy kimchee-lime infusion. Don't miss the macadamia tart or the oozy chocolate soufflé.

PAN-ASIAN

ZEN BISTRO GRILL + SUSHI 💲💲

International Plaza, 2223 N. Westshore Blvd., Tampa, 813/443-0732, www.zenbistrotampa.com

HOURS: Mon.-Wed. 11 A.M.-midnight, Thurs.-Sat. 11 A.M.-3 A.M., Sun. 11 A.M.-10 P.M.

Hoang Le's Zen Bistro Grill has been a resoundingly popular Westchase Pan-Asian hot spot since 2006. Le took over the Bay Street unit that housed Cafe Japon, overhauling the space, including work on the floors, ceilings, and restrooms, plus the addition of a distinctive exterior facade that makes it stand out. He has wisely chosen to pare his menu, offering a range of "greatest hits" dishes from Thailand, Vietnam, and Japan. Pairing deftly with the menu's bold flavors, the drinks (great signature infusions) show off the smart work that general manager and chief mixologist Natalie Haney has done with a full liquor license.

SOUTHERN

WIMAUMA 💲💲

4205 S. MacDill Ave., Tampa, 813/793-1687, www.wimaumafoods.com

HOURS: Mon.-Fri. 11 A.M.-3 P.M. and 5-10 P.M., Sat.-Sun. 10:30 A.M.-3 P.M. and 5-10 P.M.

Chef Gary Moran and his wife, Amy, unveiled Wimauma at the end of 2011 in the space vacated by Delizie Bakery. Moran, who spent time as executive chef at Datz and has a long resume of prestigious kitchen jobs in New York, focuses on giving Southern comfort foods a little polish. There's some exciting stuff here, things Tampa hasn't seen much of before. For example, perfectly fried Florida oysters set on dollops of lush guacamole and paired with dabs of smoked tomato jam. Or pickled golden raisins lurking in the bottom of a balanced carrot/ginger/coconut milk soup.

RESTAURANTS

STEAKHOUSE
CHARLEY'S STEAKHOUSE $$$
4444 W. Cypress St., Tampa, 813/353-9706,
www.talkofthetownrestaurants.com
HOURS: Sun.-Thurs. 5-10 P.M., Fri.-Sat. 5-11 P.M.
Part of a small, family-owned, Florida-based
chain of steakhouses of the same name,
Charley's is all about fat, grilled steaks, and
sturdy California cabs, served in a warren
of formal but a little tired-looking rooms. It
started in 1974 and is one of Tampa's original men's clubs for 1,100-degree seared steaks
(three-inch-thick filet mignon, 32-ounce porterhouse, 18-ounce boneless New York strip).
The signature dish is the ultimate surf and
turf: a 50-ounce filet mignon paired with a
two-pound Australian lobster tail. 'Nuff said.

COUNCIL OAK $$$
5223 N. Orient Rd., Tampa, 813/627-7628,
www.seminolehardrocktampa.com
HOURS: Sun.-Thurs. 5-10 P.M., Fri.-Sat. 5 P.M.-midnight
Owned by the Seminole tribe (as is the restaurant of the same name in Hollywood), Council
Oak is a contender in the great American steakhouse wars. It has a similar masculine vibe to
other famous steakhouses, and an à la carte
approach to steaks and chops. It opened with
much fanfare as part of the Seminole Hard
Rock Hotel & Casino, Tampa's big expansion

a few years back. Smack in the center of the
gaming pandemonium, it's an elegant bastion
of luxe seafood followed by big red meat, all ca-
pably prepared for the most part and presided
over by a remarkably knowledgeable waitstaff.

THE PALM $$$
205 Westshore Plaza, Tampa, 813/849-7256,
www.thepalm.com
HOURS: Mon.-Fri. 11:30 A.M.-11 P.M., Sat. 5-11 P.M., Sun.
5-10 P.M.
One of 30 in the chain, The Palm features
prime Angus steaks and caricatures of Bay Area
politicos and luminaries on the wall. All the
usual steakhouse bells and whistles (creamed
spinach, potatoes au gratin, fried asparagus) are
offered à la carte.

SHULA'S $$$
InterContinental Tampa, 4860 W. Kennedy Blvd.,
Tampa, 813/286-4366, www.donshula.com
HOURS: Mon.-Thurs. 11:30 A.M.-2 P.M. and
5:30-10 P.M., Fri. 11:30 A.M.-2 P.M. and 5:30-10:30 P.M., Sat.
5:30-10:30 P.M., Sun. 5:30-9:30 P.M.
Not surprisingly given coach Don Shula's hand
in it, Shula's features decor that is all in tribute
to the Miami Dolphins. It's the kind of steakhouse where they parade the meat in front
of you before you select your slab (48-ounce
porterhouse?!).

Downtown St. Petersburg   Map 6

AMERICAN
THE AVENUE $
330 1st Ave. S., 727/851-9531, www.theavenuedtsp.com
HOURS: Sun.-Thurs. 11:30 A.M.-midnight, Fri.-Sat.
11:30 A.M.-3 A.M.
The Avenue's upscale burgers, a notch above
nearby Five Guys, aim to compete with
Tampa's Square 1 Burgers or Burger 21. But
more importantly, it aims to feed the hungry beer drinkers at next door World of Beer

(WOB). They will deliver a burger or wrap directly to your bar stool at WOB, but there's
plenty to entice WOBblers to take the 20 steps
east on 1st Avenue. On weekends, The Avenue
serves a late-night burger menu all the way
until 3 A.M., with some very crafty breakfast
burritos and scrambled-egg bowls thrown into
the mix. There's live music on weekends, $0.25
wings and $2 Bud Light drafts on Mondays,
and $5 build-a-burger nights on Wednesdays.

CASSIS AMERICAN BRASSERIE $$

170 Beach Dr. NE, 727/827-2927, http://cassisab.com

HOURS: Daily 8 A.M.-11 P.M.

Anchoring Beach Drive's increasingly glamorous Restaurant Row, Cassis opened a few years back at the base of the Ovation tower on the downtown waterfront. It has yellow walls and unimpeded sightlines across the generously portioned restaurant to the lovely bar and out to the umbrella-shaded sidewalk tables. A black-and-white checkered floor has that Parisian je ne sais quoi. Born in Macon, France, executive chef Jeremy Duclut worked in Philadelphia with George Perrier from Le Bec Fin for 12 years. His culinary approach at Cassis is classic French brasserie staples with a handful of American comfort foods thrown into the mix.

Z GRILLE $$

104 2nd St. S., 727/822-9600, www.zgrille.net

HOURS: Mon.-Thurs. 11:30 A.M.-3 P.M. and 5-10 P.M., Fri. 11:30 A.M.-3 P.M. and 5-11 P.M., Sat. 11 A.M.-3 P.M. and 5-11 P.M.

Zack Gross is among the very few local chefs who can boast a James Beard nomination. He's audacious, opinionated, and in a perpetual state of self-reinvention. Even his restaurant, Z Grille, at the bottom of Signature Place, has personality. The edgy decor is dominated by a 10-foot bamboo half-pipe with artwork from local tattoo artist Evil Don. It's playful yet still sophisticated, and that's the way the food is, too. Think Dr Pepper fried ribs, deviled eggs that come revved up with crab meat or avocado and bacon, or a bacon-lettuce-avocado-seared-sea-scallop tomato composed salad called the B.L.A.S.T. Chef Zach's flavors are assertive but suave: Slices of chipotle barbecue pork tenderloin are overshadowed by a lush jalapeno goat cheese creamed corn. The wine list features a number of splurgy by-the-glass offerings, most from California, that pair beautifully with the menu.

BRITISH PUB
MOON UNDER WATER $$

332 Beach Dr. NE, 727/896-6160, www.themoonunderwater.com

HOURS: Sun.-Thurs. 11:30 A.M.-11 P.M., Fri.-Sat. 11:30 A.M.-midnight

Since 1996, the calling card for the comfy British pub Moon Under Water has been a loose, ethnically diverse array of pub grub, all able accompaniments to a delicious, foam-capped black and tan. The signature dish, chicken curry, is something of a party, arriving with a hot metal bowl of saffron-yellow basmati; another of dusky curry; a crisp, peppery pappadam; an oblong of warm naan; and little bowls of mango chutney, onion pickle, and cuke-spiked yogurt. Perhaps reflecting Britain's other colonial interests, the menu features quite a number of Middle Eastern dishes, but you'll also find laudable fish and chips.

GASTROPUB
TRYST GASTRO LOUNGE $$

240 Beach Dr. NE, 727/821-4567, http://trystgastrolounge.com

HOURS: Mon.-Fri. 4 P.M.-3 A.M., Sat.-Sun. 11:30 A.M.-3 A.M.

Tryst is about as stylish a place as we've seen in these parts. It has walk-up indoor-outdoor counter seating and low-slung sidewalk seats (dog-friendly), an attractive staff, and faux alligator chairs that you just can't stop running your fingers over. The beer list is thoughtful and shows enough breadth to accommodate most tastes (a lot of IPAs), and the cocktail list features a number of unusual signature drinks, many involving muddled fruit. The dinner menu is geared around shareable nibbles that support the drinks menu, whereas the lunch menu is a fairly pricy business-appropriate lineup of salads and sandwiches.

RESTAURANTS

TOP DOGS

When a Chicago-style hot dog is packed to capacity with the traditional fixings—yellow mustard, alarmingly neon green relish, a dill pickle spear, tomato slices, chopped onion, "sport peppers" (hot little babies packed in vinegar), and a couple shakes of celery salt—you call it "dragged through the garden." A Chicago bun is flecked with poppy seeds; the dog itself is all-beef and pretty darned salty.

For a Coney Island dog with its full complement of bells and whistles, you want it "all the way." Except, confusingly, there are two kinds of Coney Island dogs, the New York beef franks made famous by Nathan's, et al., but also a style of dog in Michigan that is topped with all-meat chili, yellow mustard, and diced yellow onion.

Tampa dog aficionados have been crowding into **Mel's Hot Dogs** (4136 E. Busch Blvd., Tampa, 813/985-8000, www.melshotdogs. com) since 1973. It's a fine dog, the house special, packed with sauerkraut, onion, mustard, relish, and pickle. Still, the Polish sausage is a fat, juicy choice, accessorized with brown mustard and grilled onions.

On the Pinellas side, the alpha dog is clearly **Coney Island** (250 Dr. Martin Luther King Jr. St. N., St. Petersburg, 727/822-4493), which goes all the way back to 1926. The coin of the realm is the Michigan-style chili dog (the topping is technically called Coney sauce), eaten swiftly atop a stool at the counter, washed down with an impossibly thick chocolate shake. Septuagenarian **Dairy Inn** (1201 Dr. Martin Luther

King Jr. St. N., St. Petersburg, 727/822-6971, www.dairyinn.com) also serves up a dandy dog, but it is sometimes eclipsed by the Coney Island chili or the homemade root beer.

The exuberant orange-and-yellow signage can be distracting, but head for the basic Chicago dog at **Bruce's Chicago Grill and Dog House** (7733 Ulmerton Rd., Largo, 727/524-1146). There's a good snap on the dog when you bite into it. Bruce's has lots of other enticing possibilities, like the Reuben dog with a drizzle of Russian dressing and mantle of molten Swiss.

Frankies of Tampa (909 W. Kennedy Blvd., Tampa, 813/425-3647, www.frankiestampa. com) is a fabled dog chain in Connecticut; the four-year-old Tampa location is the only foray into Florida. Get the Frankies plain foot-long and stand before the relish bar, where you can choose from sauerkraut and the hot relish they ship in from New York. For a little more money they have specialty dogs: there's a bacon dog, and one topped with New York-style onions (they're fried and then blushed with a little marinara).

Then there's **Yummy's** (2914 Beach Blvd. S., Gulfport, 727/321-9869, www.yummysgulfport. com), which opened a couple of years ago in an adorable house on the main drag in Gulfport. The Yummy dog is textbook, the snappy tube steak hunkered under the sweet relish and sport peppers. The place itself has a high funk factor (yard sale tchotchkes function as decor and impulse buys), and the owners could not be more friendly.

ITALIAN

🍷 BELLA BRAVA ❸❸❸

204 Beach Dr. NE, 727/895-5515, www.bellabrava.net
HOURS: Sun.-Thurs. 11:30 A.M.-2:30 P.M. and 5-10 P.M.,
Fri. 11:30 A.M.-2:30 P.M. and 5-11 P.M., Sat. 5-11 P.M.

What makes a place Italian? The presence of pasta? A marked propensity for checked tablecloths and candles in Chianti bottles? Maybe molten mantles of mozzarella cheese oozing over some unsuspecting eggplant or chicken? It's more nebulous than that; it's about the vibe. Take Bella Brava: In a tony corner spot on the

Restaurant Row of Beach Drive, it could be any cuisine, with a breezy, stylish indoor-outdoor space. Yet there are the bruschetta, risotti, and antipasti that new generations of Tampa Bay Area residents are being weaned on, all served at fairly reasonable prices.

GRATZZI ITALIAN GRILLE ❸❸

211 2nd St. S., 727/623-9037, http://gratzzigrille.com
HOURS: Mon.-Thurs. 11 A.M.-10 P.M., Fri.-Sat.
11 A.M.-11 P.M., Sun. 4-10 P.M.

The longtime go-to Italian restaurant Gratzzi

features the three Ps: paninis, pizza, and pastas, but with loads of nice touches like some tableside service (check out the Cavatelli Bada Bing) and a deep wine list. The menu will be familiar, but the kitchen exhibits a steady hand.

MEDITERRANEAN
CAFÉ ALMA ❸❸
260 1st Ave. S., 727/502-5002, www.cafealma.com

HOURS: Mon.-Wed. 11 A.M.-3 P.M. and 5-10 P.M., Thurs.-Fri. 11 A.M.-3 P.M. and 5-midnight, Sat. 5-midnight, Sun. 10:30 A.M.-3 P.M.

Downtown St. Petersburg owes a bit of its recent hipness to trendy downtown gathering spots like Café Alma, one of its originals. Open from lunch to late night, the atmosphere sets the mood for the stimulating yet charmingly straightforward Mediterranean-inspired dishes. Entrées include Spanish-inflected paella alongside traditional French bouillabaisse and peppercorn-crusted Hudson Valley duck breast served atop a sweet corn pancake. While lunchtime brings business diners, at night the vibe is decidedly more festive.

MARCHAND'S BAR & GRILL ❸❸❸
Renaissance Vinoy Resort, 501 5th Ave. NE, 727/894-1000, www.marchandsbarandgrill.com

HOURS: Daily 11:30 A.M.-2:30 P.M. and 5:30-10 P.M.

In keeping with the glamour of the historic Vinoy, its restaurant, Marchand's, sparkles with opulent appointments and an equally opulent clientele. The restaurant has undergone some major changes in recent years. Its entrance now shows off the central Vinoy Bar; heavy armchairs in sumptuous velvet have been added; and a small wine cellar room provides an enviably intimate dining space for four. But perhaps the biggest change is the chef and the dining concept: One side used to be Marchand's, with a Mediterranean menu; the other the Terrace Room, with seafood-heavy American cuisine. Now it's all called Marchand's. The kitchen has wisely kept the

seafood focus, but dishes reflect a more stylish and still loosely Mediterranean sensibility with saucing and garniture.

NEW AMERICAN
MFA CAFÉ ❸❸
255 Beach Dr. NE, 727/822-1032, https://fine-arts.org/visit/mfa-cafe

HOURS: Mon.-Sat. 11 A.M.-3 P.M., occasional Sunday brunch

Unveiled along with the lovely new Hazel Hough Wing, the MFA Café, is really a cordoned-off section of the soaring atrium at the museum's center, where light streams in from floor-to-ceiling windows. It's a prime locale for special parties and glamorous soirees. During the day it's given over to some of the most sophisticated lunches around: soups (a stunning creamy smoked tomato), salads (think smoked duck paired with citrus-dressed frisée, crisp apple, and toasted walnut), and a burger that alone justifies paying the museum admission price.

PARKSHORE GRILL ❸❸❸
300 Beach Dr. NE, 727/896-9463, www.parkshoregrill.com

HOURS: Sun.-Thurs. 11 A.M.-10 P.M., Fri.-Sat. 11 A.M.-11 P.M.

With its outside patio within eyesight of the Museum of Fine Arts, Parkshore is a place to linger. The bar is lively but elegant, and the menu leans to very smart spins on contemporary American cuisine (pan-seared scallops, lobster pasta, great martinis). Chef Tyson Grant is a huge advocate for sustainably-sourced seafood.

PIZZA
WOOD FIRED PIZZA ❸❸
344 1st Ave. S, 727/282-1888, www.wood-firedpizza.com

HOURS: Sun.-Tues. 11:30 A.M.-midnight, Wed.-Sat. 11:30 A.M.-3 A.M.

Peter Taylor opened his first pizzeria in New

Tampa on Bearss Avenue in 2009. In 2012 he opened a much more ambitious venture in St. Petersburg, a bigger Wood Fired Pizza with a massive outdoor deck, tucked between the new World of Beer and the Avenue. He figures, with a denser concentration of foodies and a robust number of late-night revelers, he could clean up with both pizza aficionados and those looking for a quick nosh (his pizzas take two minutes to make and two minutes to bake). They are super-thin crusted, offered in 10-inch or 12-inch rounds. What makes Wood Fired different is the prominence of the crust. It is not lost under an avalanche of sauce and cheese. It is chewy verging on crunchy, the topping ingredients usually spare. But they are good, often novel ingredients.

SUSHI

ROLLBOTTO SUSHI ⑤
221 1st St. NE, 727/487-2681, http://rollbotto.com

HOURS: Mon.-Thurs. 11 A.M.-11 P.M., Fri.-Sat. 11 A.M.-2 A.M., Sun. noon-11 P.M.

Rollbotto brings St. Petersburg the first taste of a new trend sweeping Japan: robot chefs. Rollbotto's robots don't look exactly like something from *Lost in Space*. In an industrial room shiny with chrome, Rollbotto is an order-at-the-counter, pick-your-own-ingredient sushi bar. At one end is a big square robot box that, in the blink of an eye, spreads the sushi rice on the nori. Then humans do the filling and rolling and another robot box finishes things up by neatly slicing the long rolls into 10 perfect futomaki (those are the fat rolls) slices. Sushi is the way to go here (other items like miso soup and pot stickers are forgettable), either from the lineup of signature rolls or those of your own devising. Bins a la Subway pack the nuts and bolts, from proteins like grilled eel and sweet tofu to veggies like spring mix and asparagus.

Parkshore Grill

VEGETARIAN

MEZE 119 ⑤

119 2nd St. N., 727/498-8627, www.meze119.com

HOURS: Mon.-Thurs. 11 A.M.-9 P.M., Fri.-Sat. 11 A.M.-midnight, Sun. 10 A.M.-2 P.M.

Billed as "authentic Middle Eastern food with modern flair," Meze is actually 100 percent vegetarian. It's not that owner Dean Hershkowitz is being coy. It's as he says: "A lot of the food we're making is inherently vegetarian. The fact that it's vegetarian is secondary." Meze 119 cooks up exciting and inexpensive spins on traditional Turkish, Lebanese, Syrian, and Israeli dishes in a light, airy space, with lots of colorful pillows and a funky tree mural on one wall. Servers are warm and helpful, and the prevailing vibe is hip and upbeat.

VIETNAMESE

LA V ⑤

441 Central Ave., 727/820-3500, www.lavfusion.com

HOURS: Mon.-Sat. 10 A.M.-10 P.M., Sun. 11 A.M.-10 P.M.

The second restaurant for Thuy Le, La V fills a real void, bringing a cuisine that is nearly absent among downtown St. Petersburg's several dozen restaurants. And the cuisine fits the time and place, ably catering to workers at lunchtime, as well as partiers by night, with a menu that is fresh, affordable, and quick. Le could give lessons to other aspiring restaurateurs in how to make guests feel special, how to exude warmth, and how to explain food that might be a little exotic for some. Le's got 60 smoothies and boba teas (those teas with the fat straws and lurking balls of tapioca at the bottom), in flavors ranging from durian to fresh avocado. And foodwise, there are really four choices at V: noodles, soups, rice dishes, or banh mi sandwiches. The last is the acme of French-Vietnamese collaboration, a crusty baguette packed with pickled carrot and daikon, fresh herbs, jalapeno rounds, and a choice of protein. Le has paired her short menu with a thoughtful lineup of beers and wines that marry suavely with the lively flavors of the food.

St. Pete Beach Map 7

AMERICAN

THE HURRICANE ⑤

807 Gulf Way, 727/360-9558, www.thehurricane.com

HOURS: Sun.-Thurs. 11 A.M.-9:30 P.M., Fri.-Sat. 11 A.M.-10 P.M.

If you can go to just one place in the St. Pete Beach area, go to The Hurricane on Pass-A-Grille Beach for the blackened grouper sandwich. The place may seem a little touristy; but order that sweet white fish, amped with red and black pepper and lots of salt, add in some tomato, lettuce, and a big swath of mayo, all on a pretty, soft roll, and you're set. It's as good as it gets in Pinellas County. There's a nice bar adjacent to the restaurant and a rooftop sundeck up top for sunset scrutiny.

BARBECUE

PCI BAR & GRILL ⑤⑤

Postcard Inn, 6300 Gulf Blvd., 727/369-4950, http://postcardinn.com

HOURS: Sun.-Thurs. 11:30 A.M.-10 P.M., Fri.-Sat. 11:30 A.M.-11 P.M.

PCI has a number of dishes that help explain why Postcard Inn has become party central (well, there's also the beach access, the funky-cool decor, and the beach volleyball). A generous platter of nachos comes packed with smoky chili, slender pickled jalapenos, molten cheddar, and all the fixings, and the St. Louis ribs are shellacked with a balanced sweet-tangy sauce and pink with slow smoke.

RESTAURANTS

CONTINENTAL
MARITANA GRILLE AT THE DON CESAR ❸❸❸

3400 Gulf Blvd., 727/360-1881, www.doncesar.com

HOURS: Sun.-Thurs. 5:30-10 P.M., Fri.-Sat. 5:30-11 P.M.

Located in St. Pete Beach's iconic pink hotel, Maritana has "special occasion" written all over it. There's a great chef's table for groups up to eight, at which executive chef Kenny Hunsberger is put through his Floribbean-cuisine paces, from marmalade-roasted Gulf red snapper served with pea vines to grilled filet mignon with truffled mashed potatoes and candied shallots. The restaurant's interior is lovely: Patrons are surrounded by 1,500 gallons of saltwater aquariums and indigenous Florida fish.

ITALIAN
VERDUCCI PIZZERIA & TRATTORIA ❸❸

7736 Blind Pass Rd., 727/363-7900

HOURS: Mon.-Thurs. noon-3 P.M. and 4-10 P.M., Fri. noon-3 P.M. and 4-11 P.M., Sat. 4-11 P.M., Sun. 4-10 P.M.

Bustling, intimate, without unnecessary razzle-dazzle, and with just plain good homemade Italian pizzas and pastas, Verducci has been discovered by snowbirds and winter tourists at the beach. With no shortage of places to eat along Blind Pass or Gulf Boulevard, what stands out here is a commitment to making food from scratch. There's the dense almond chocolate tart and the lighter ricotta cheesecake; buttery garlic knots and calzones lush with ricotta, mozzarella, and parmesan; even the creamy balsamic dressing on the included side salad is clearly made in-house.

MEXICAN
AGAVE RESTAURANT ❸❸

6400 Gulf Blvd., 727/367-3448

HOURS: Mon.-Thurs. noon-9 P.M., Fri.-Sat. noon-9:30 P.M., Sun. noon-8:30 P.M.

Nina and Richard Madison's tiny three-year-old (it stood a block away for three years before

The Hurricane

COURTESY OF VISITSTPETECLEARWATER.COM

that) restaurant Agave is about as warm and fun as it gets in St. Pete Beach. Grab a seat at the bar and listen to the 'rita shaker banging out a rhythm while you wait for a table. A basket of chips comes with a trio of sauces—hot, hotter, hottest—and a bigger cup of mild salsa cruda. The menu ranges far afield, from straightforward Mexican staples (tacos, tostadas, enchiladas) to more sophisticated "new Mexican" fare culled from Nina's family recipes from the Laguna region. This means you'll find the likes of shredded pork in tomatillo sauce, lively Baja-style fish tacos, and mole poblano. And if you're a tequila lover, you'll want to pay a visit. Agave has 90 varieties.

SEAFOOD
DOCKSIDE DAVE'S ❸

7141 Gulf Blvd., 727/360-4200, www.docksidedavesgrill.com

HOURS: Mon.-Sat. 11 A.M.-10 P.M., Sun. noon-10 P.M.

Dockside Dave's is no longer in its original,

divey location in Madiera Beach (condos forced it out). Still, it's beloved as one of the local fish sandwich superstars, with onion rings on the side. The decor isn't much, but it's a good place to try one of the local specialties, smoked amberjack spread. Though, this is perhaps an acquired taste.

MAD FISH ❸❸❸
5200 Gulf Blvd., 727/360-9200,
www.madfishonline.com
HOURS: Sun.-Thurs. 4-10 P.M., Fri.-Sat. 4-11 P.M.

Set in a blue neon and gleaming chrome diner, the inside of Mad Fish has been wrapped in lustrous African mahogany. Reminiscent of the dining cars on vintage trains, it's elegant, with an extensive wine bar and an emphasis on fresh fish. According to owner Dan Casey, Mad Fish services nearby convention and hotel business. Look for the signature shrimp Guanajuato, a tomato-based shrimp cocktail enlivened by Mexican orange soda, and a dessert caddy of still-warm cookies served with glasses of banana milk shake.

Gulfport   Map 7

CUBAN
HABANA CAFÉ ❸❸
5404 Gulfport Blvd. S., 727/321-8855,
www.habanacafe-usa.com
HOURS: Mon.-Sat. 11 A.M.-9 P.M.
Habana Café has a little upstairs art gallery and its own cigars and smoking room. Recently owner Jo Hastings has added in plucky Cuban classics like *boliche* (slow-simmered eye of round stuffed with sausage), *ropa vieja,* and tostones (little fried plantain flying saucers).

ITALIAN
PIA'S TRATTORIA ❸❸
3054 Beach Blvd. S., 727/327-2190,
www.piastrattoria.com
HOURS: Mon.-Sat. 11:30 A.M.-2:30 P.M. and 5-9:30 P.M.
Pia's is the kind of sweetly earnest restaurant that you'd like to think unfurls fully realized from the ground, with good basic ingredients and a healthy inoculation of Italian culinary know-how nurtured by sweat and love. Its

setting is a teeny bit foyer and mostly outdoor patio covered with a chickee thatch and populated by a hodgepodge of picnic tables. The menu is short, the same at lunch and dinner, and weighted to crusty pressed panini and pastas topped with one of a handful of simple sauces.

SEAFOOD
BACKFIN BLUE CAFÉ ❸❸
2913 Beach Blvd. S., 727/343-2583,
www.backfinbluecafe.com
HOURS: Wed.-Mon. 4-9:30 P.M.
Nestled in a 1920s-era pink-and-green cottage, Backfin has the kind of front porch that's easy to settle into and hard to leave. It's renowned locally for its crab cakes, corn and crab soup, slow-roasted prime rib, and bacon-wrapped shrimp, and it makes most publications' annual list of top restaurants. Despite the erudition in the kitchen, it's got an Old Florida vibe that's especially charming to out-of-towners.

Clearwater and Clearwater Beach — Map 8

AMERICAN
HOOTERS ⑤
2800 Gulf-To-Bay Blvd., 727/797-4008,
www.hooters.com
HOURS: Sun.-Thurs. 11 A.M.-11 P.M., Fri.-Sat. 11 A.M.-
midnight

Really, you owe it to yourself and owl fans everywhere to go to the original Hooters. Now 25 years old and recently massively remodeled, the original, pleasant, ramshackle sports-oriented joint has spawned an international empire and short-lived airline. It's a family restaurant, really, with good chicken wings (order them not breaded, with the really hot sauce, but a little dry so they don't come all goopy). Only, it's a family restaurant in which all waitresses are wildly pneumatic and wear those flesh-colored pantyhose from the 1970s under orange nylon short-shorts. There is also a new Hooters location, which opened in 2012 in Clearwater Beach (381 Mandalay Ave., 727/443-7263, www.hooters.com).

BREAKFAST
LENNY'S RESTAURANT ⑤
21220 U.S. 19 N., 727/799-0402
HOURS: Daily 6 A.M.-3 P.M.

Lenny's has long been the hands-down winner for breakfast, especially for the Jewish staples of blintzes, knishes, and latkes. You can get an omelet here, too, if you want to look like a goy. Many of the extremely affordable breakfast combos are named for members of the owner's family. Lenny's kids run the joint these days, but it still has personality (goofy jokes on the ceiling, garage-sale knickknacks in lieu of decor) and if you're not afraid of carbs, the potato pancakes with sour cream eat like a meal. (Phillies phans: This is where spring training players and fans go to mingle over breakfast.)

JAPANESE
KIKU JAPANESE FINE DINING ⑤⑤
Pelican Walk Plaza, 483 Mandalay Ave., 727/461-2633,
www.clearwaterbeachkiku.com
HOURS: Mon.-Thurs. 11:30 A.M.-2 P.M. and 5-10 P.M., Fri. 11:30 A.M.-2 P.M. and 5-11 P.M., Sat. 5-11 P.M.

When you're ready to declare *omakase* (essentially, "let it rip, Chef, I'm putty in your hands"), the man behind the sushi counter at Kiku is one to trust for the freshest fish flown in from Hawaii, Seattle, Boston, California, and New York. Tatami rooms are available for when you want privacy for a small party (they can accommodate 2–8 people).

MEXICAN
BESA GRILL ⑤⑤
2542 N. McMullen Booth Rd., 727/400-6900,
www.besagrill.com
HOURS: Mon.-Thurs. 11:30 A.M.-10 P.M., Fri.-Sat. 11:30 A.M.-11 P.M., Sun. 11:30 A.M.-9 P.M.

Besa Grill is Latin-inspired, not Mexican exactly, with stylish, nightclubby decor that telegraphs nothing about the food. It's a place suitable for a little black dress, but is equally jeans-friendly. The vibe is warm, with friendly young servers and bartenders who seem eager to share their mad mixology. The booze focus is tequila, with some really sophisticated margaritas, from cucumber-cilantro to blackberry mint. These aren't goofy slushy versions. Sweetness is reined in and excellent tequilas employed.

NEW AMERICAN
CARETTA ON THE GULF ⑤⑤⑤
Sandpearl Resort, 500 Mandalay Ave., 727/441-2425,
www.sandpearl.com
HOURS: Sun.-Thurs. 7 A.M.-3 P.M. and 5:30-10 P.M., Fri.-Sat. 7 A.M.-3 P.M. and 5:30-11 P.M.

Sandpearl Resort, the first new resort to be

built on Clearwater Beach in 25 years, does not suffer from the hotel-dining blahs. It contains a nice poolside café and a coffee shop, but the major accomplishment is Caretta on the Gulf. Named for a species of loggerhead turtle, the restaurant has all the elements that make for success: sleek and knowledgeable service, a gorgeous beach view, stunning decor, plus tasty and fairly priced food and drink. A lovely raw bar near the restaurant entrance sets the tone: ceviche, oysters on the half shell, spiny lobster and spicy tuna sushi rolls. Then the rosy glow and crackle of a wood-burning oven sends out roasted fishes, chicken, and meats that for the most part are paired with thoughtful, unusual side dishes and sauces.

PIZZA
CRISTINO'S COAL OVEN PIZZA ❸❸
1101 S. Fort Harrison Ave., 727/443-4900,
www.cristinospizzeria.com
HOURS: Mon.-Thurs. 11 A.M.-9 P.M., Fri.-Sat. 11 A.M.-10 P.M.
Three Italian brothers, Lenny, Marco, and Joe Cristino, opened Cristino's Coal Oven Pizza a few years back just south of downtown Clearwater. It's not anything fancy—a dozen or so tables done up casually, with food display cases anchoring the room. Service is friendly and unfussy; the drink list is just a handful of unspecified vinos and a few familiar beers. The big coal oven is unobtrusive, but it's the source of exactly half of the excitement here.

The good stuff comes in the form of four basic pies: margherita, marinara, bianca, and quattro formaggi. Keep 'em simple and you're in for a delicious, thin-crust pizza. The other half of the excitement at Cristino's? The house gelatos are spectacular, from the vanilla stracciatella to the chocolatey-hazelnut swirl.

SEAFOOD
SHOR AMERICAN SEAFOOD GRILL ❸❸❸
301 S. Gulfview Blvd., 727/373-4780,
www.shorclearwater.com
HOURS: Daily 6:30 A.M.-10 P.M.
The main restaurant in the fairly new Hyatt Regency Clearwater Beach Resort & Spa, SHOR has bragging rights to a supremely great sunset-viewing vantage. The dining room is spare and open, half the seats with an unobstructed view of the gulf, half the seats with an unobstructed view of one of the area's prettiest exhibition kitchens. The menu allows you to build your own: Pick a protein, seasoning, sauce, and side. Or leave the decisions to the kitchen: Tiny French lentils get a zippy vinaigrette with a touch of tarragon, atop which just-blanched ribbons of zucchini peek out from beneath a fillet of crisp-skinned pan-seared black grouper. In toto, it's food that is visually pretty and with a great breadth of flavors and a commitment to sourcing locally and sustainably.

RESTAURANTS

Dunedin   Map 8

CHINESE
IVORY MANDARIN BISTRO ❸❸
2192 Main St., 727/734-3998, www.ivorybistro.com
HOURS: Sun.-Thurs. 11 A.M.-9:30 P.M., Fri.-Sat. 11 A.M.-10 P.M.
Around since 1993 in Dunedin, the old-timer Ivory Mandarin Bistro has slowly accrued a wall's worth of accolades and Best Of awards

along with its devoted, largely non-Chinese clientele. Crisp linens, Chinese floral prints, and sprays of silk orchids lend a dash of formality to the proceedings, but the menu reads like a greatest-hits list of Cantonese-American dishes. That means a workhorse hot and sour soup, juicy pork spare ribs, sweet-tangy orange beef, and nurturing pan-fried chow fun noodles.

ECLECTIC

KELLY'S ❸❸

319 Main St., 727/736-5284, www.kellyschicaboom.com

HOURS: Sun.-Thurs. 8 A.M.-10 P.M., Fri.-Sat. 8 A.M.-11 P.M.

An ad description of Kelly's, "For just about... Anything!" isn't hyperbole, really. Super family-friendly, Kelly's has the kind of far-reaching, comfort-food menu that rivals Tolstoy for reader stamina, leaving no stone unturned, from eggplant-portobello-tomato Napoleons to butternut squash ravioli. It's a kids' kind of joint, very affable and accommodating. Its **Chic-a-Boom Room** (727/736-0206) next door is more serious evidence that Dunedin has one of the most lighthearted, fun-loving communities around.

ITALIAN

BASCETTI'S ITALIAN GRILLE ❸❸

1568 Main St., 727/738-2808

HOURS: Tues.-Thurs. 4-10 P.M., Fri.-Sat. 4-11 P.M., Sun. 4-9 P.M.

Longtime Dunedin restaurateur Jimmy Stewart, owner of Spoto's Steakjoint 2, opened the intimate Bascetti's in a strip mall in Dunedin. Turns out, Stewart's always wanted to do an authentic Italian restaurant as well, one with homemade pastas and simple, gutsy pizzas and salads. The restaurant space itself is pleasant and inviting, nothing super fancy, but with generous booths and white-clothed tables and with a separate barroom featuring a long, marble-topped bar and comfy leather bar stools. Service is similarly warm and not too formal.

MEDITERRANEAN

BASQUE ❸❸

28910 U.S. 19 N., 727/330-7712,

www.basqueexperience.com

HOURS: Tues.-Thurs. 4-10 P.M., Fri.-Sat. 4-11 P.M., Sun. 4-9 P.M.

Basque is a huge, nightclub-like space, one that has been warmed with water features, lush greenery, and an earth tone color scheme. The gastronomic palette isn't drawn strictly from the Basque region: It's more of a romp around Spain, from the seafood dishes in the north to the paellas in the east and the roasted meats and stews of Central Spain. Then there's stuff the average Spaniard might eye suspiciously (lobster tater tots?! ahi tuna tempura with ponzu sauce?). Then, after grazing, guests can linger to listen to music and dance.

MEZZE ON MAIN ❸❸

680 Main St., 727/216-6222

HOURS: Tues.-Thurs. 4-10 P.M., Fri. 4 P.M.-midnight, Sat. 11:30 A.M.-midnight, Sun. 11:30 A.M.-10 P.M.

In this charming house that was briefly the Living Room and then Dunedin Smokehouse, Mezze is slightly away from Main Street's main drag. It's a free-standing house with an inviting deep porch and an indoors with one long wall of bookshelves, warm lighting, and lots of wood. Food draws inspiration broadly from the Mediterranean, with moderately priced Italian brick-oven pizzas as well as Moroccan tagines and the odd Greek or Israeli dish. Breads replace the fork: olive oil-lush focaccia, crunchy crostini, chewy pizzas, and Israeli-style bourekas provide the platform.

MEXICAN

CASA TINA ❸❸

365 Main St., 727/734-9226, www.casatinas.com

HOURS: Sun.-Thurs. 11 A.M.-10 P.M., Fri.-Sat. 11 A.M.-11 P.M.

Downtown Dunedin has been charmingly reinvigorated with restaurants and cafés in recent years. At Casa Tina, shimmery orange and teal curtains pick up the dappled light from punched tin star lanterns and an altarlike candelabrum at the entrance. Rough-hewn wooden chairs, a wood-and-concrete floor, and an open kitchen pass-through inform your expectations: casual, affordable, fun, and Mexican. Bingo on all counts, but Casa Tina has a few tricks up its sleeves. Rice, beans, and all sauces are

PURE KITSCH

The following restaurants are some of the area's kitschy, homey Old Florida spots.

Beak's St. Pete (2451 Central Ave., St. Petersburg, 727/321-9100, www.beaksoldflorida. com): On a pleasant stretch of St. Petersburg's Grand Central District, Beaks St. Pete doesn't so much have decor as an astounding accretion of yard-sale castoffs. The culinary focus is dishes like crab corndogs and smashed tamale soufflé. It's a grownups-only place at night.

Kelly's (319 Main St., Dunedin, 727/736-5284, www.kellyschicaboom.com): At Kelly's, the day's fun could start with Butterfinger muffins or French toast with chocolate and Cognac, drift through lunch of banana pancakes or Hellburgers, and head into dinner of duck breast, Emeril's escolar, and house-smoked pork chops. Virgel Kelly and pals always add an extra smile and a kick, like gazpacho butter or chili onions, and the wildest silly-tinis served outdoors and in the adjoining Chic-a-Boom Room. It's the kind of far-reaching comfort food menu that leaves no stone unturned, from eggplant-portobello-tomato Napoleons to butternut squash ravioli. Kids are welcome at this very friendly and accommodating joint.

Fourth Street Shrimp Store (1006 Fourth St. N., St. Petersburg, 727/822-0325, www.theshrimpstore.com): Festooned with murals and paraphernalia of all types (vaguely nautical, with a naked maidenhead heavy on the Gasparilla beads), this funky shack is casual and fun, at a fair price. Pass the seafood counter at the entrance and grab a seat. Next task: order the thick clam chowder, fried oysters, a little catfish, or, when available, grouper, the local pride and joy. A wraparound porch provides limited extra seating and a full bar adds to the festivity.

Rick's on the River (2305 North Willow Ave., Tampa, 813/251-0369, www.ricksontheriver.com): Some come by boat and others by kayak or inner tube to Rick's. And what they come for are the views of the Hillsborough River and the downtown skyline, the raucous roadhouse feel, and the kind of loud live bands on the weekend that make lip reading a handy skill. The outdoor patio at Rick's has been a boaters' weekend hangout for the past 18 years on the basis of its fish sandwich and the oysters Rick-afellar and fish spread. Boaters find easy mooring along several floating docks that can accommodate up to 70 boats, free of charge to diners (overnight dockage is $1 per foot).

vegetarian, and virtually all entrées are offered in vegetarian and vegan versions that are far from perfunctory. The carnivore has the full complement of options, but it's the vegetarian or pescatarian who is most ably served. Next door they own **Pan y Vino** (369 Main St., 727/734-7700, www.panyvino.com), a pizza parlor and wine bar.

SEAFOOD
THE BLACK PEARL ⑤⑤⑤
315 Main St., 727/734-3463,
www.theblackpearlofdunedin.com
HOURS: Daily 5-9:30 P.M.

A little bit of a splurge, special-occasion restaurant, The Black Pearl has been here for more than 20 years with a tiny, intimate dining room that never fails to charm. Try the cedar-planked salmon or the crab imperial. It's one of those rarefied places that embody the outré word "nouvelle," meaning fairly steep prices and aesthetic aspirations, and fairly low quantity on each plate. It works for us; you be the judge.

BON APPETIT ⑤⑤⑤
150 Marina Plaza, 727/733-2151,
www.bonappetitrestaurant.com
HOURS: Mon.-Thurs. 11:30 A.M.-9 P.M., Fri.-Sat.
11:30 A.M.-10 P.M., Sun. 11 A.M.-8:30 P.M.

Bon Appetit is attached to the Best Western Yacht Harbor Inn and Suites, so there's a certain amount of that holdover Continental cuisine fanciness one associates with hotel restaurants. Owners Peter Kreuziger and

TAMPA BAY SEAFOOD

Water, water all around. The upshot? Seafood. Rivers, bays, and the Gulf of Mexico provide a smorgasbord of fish and shellfish, which you can sample at fancy emporiums of haute cuisine, scruffy-around-the-edges fish shacks, or in the raw at area sushi and Asian restaurants.

FINE DINING

Oystercatchers (Grand Hyatt Tampa Bay, 2900 Bayport Dr., Tampa, 813/207-6815, http://hyatt.com/gallery/oystercatchers): Fish is the main attraction for dinner, with many entrées offered simply grilled or sautéed (sides are separate, steakhouse-style, but they're seafood-friendly sides: braised bok choy with sesame oil or caramelized fennel). There's variety, from meaty, mild grilled black grouper to more assertive pompano in parchment. Both are excellent. Food and beverage director Brooke Burnett has pared the wine list to include a thoughtful number of bottles and something for everyone by the glass in terms of price and varietal. A menu of house cocktails, including the Floridian martini and mango mojito, make Oystercatchers a great place to just hang out with friends.

Mystic Fish (3253 Tampa Rd., Palm Harbor, 727/324-2754, www.3bestchefs.com/mystic): Mystic Fish's interior telegraphs the kitchen's focus: shimmery rows of abalone shells, aquariums filled with darting tropical fish, and chandeliers that resemble swarms of luminous sea eels. It's seafood, front and center. Owners Eugene Fuhrmann and Doug Bebell each spent years at other fabled seafood houses in these parts and they know what they're doing. This translates to grouper piccata, kona-seared Atlantic salmon, and blackened Chilean sea bass with ginger-soy Hijiki sauce. Still, even the vegetarian is ably served: soy-glazed edamame and snow peas; matchstick carrots with apricot curry; tandoori grilled onions and zucchini; kona-grilled asparagus; and ajillo artichoke hearts.

FISH SHACKS

Wild Blue Crab and Shrimp Company (2005 Central Ave., St. Petersburg, 727/209-0813): The order-at-the-window little shack/store, fronting the Haslam's bookstore parking lot, has an immense funk factor. Its location is no accident, situated a little more than half a mile from Bama Sea Products, its chief purveyor and muse. The owners have built their concept around the small, sweet wild gulf shrimp. They come crumb-battered and deep-fried, paired with horseradish-powered cocktail sauce, or they come in gumbo, jambalaya, or packed into a po' boy.

Dockside Dave's Grill (14701 Gulf Blvd., Madeira Beach, 727/392-9399, http://docksidedavesgrill.com): The fish sandwiches here are king of the beach. It's not rocket science, but the combination of snowy white, locally caught grouper, battered and fried, and drippy red tomato, crisp lettuce, a few rounds of white onion, and a fairly soft roll indeed approaches genius. Add in a funky waterside setting and a remarkably edible smoked amberjack spread, and you're definitely in Mensa territory. Fishphobes can try Buffalo's own beef on 'weck and a sassy order of onion rings.

Frenchy's Saltwater Café (419 Poinsettia Ave., Clearwater Beach, 727/461-6295, http://frenchysonline.com): This cozy, hole-in-the-wall favorite on Clearwater Beach serves up seafood fresh from the boat at bargain prices. Food is served with cold beer, good humor, modest fixings, plus great desserts. The specialty here is a grouper Reuben. It's also a major heavy hitter in the local traffic of stone crabs. The original Frenchy's Café opened in 1981 and many subsequent Frenchy's have dotted the landscape in Clearwater Beach, all fueled by their own fleet of commercial fishing boats.

Karl Heinz Riedl manage to add a definite panache to the seafood-heavy menu, whether it's a passel of garlic-heady mussels steamed in herbaceous sauvignon blanc or the season's freshest stone crabs adorned with only a squeeze of lemon and a pool of clarified butter. The thing is, you don't have to get all uppity and pay the big prices—guests can watch the dolphins play as the sun sets out on the water and not spend a bushel if they dine at the Marine Café adjacent to the restaurant. It's a different menu than the fancier sibling, but a single sheet of signature dishes from the main restaurant is available outside.

STEAKHOUSE
SPOTOS STEAKJOINT 2 $$$
1280 Main St., 727/734-0008,
www.spotossteakjoint2.com
HOURS: Sun.-Thurs. 4-10 P.M., Fri.-Sat. 4-11 P.M.

Spotos Steakjoint sends out ably aged and prepared steaks. But get this, from a recent menu: filet of Burmese python. That's not a joke. Owner Jimmy Stewart has gotten interested in wild game, importing a range of exciting options (rattlesnake, for example) and holding occasional wine and game dinners. Stewart sets a feverish pace for coming up with new dishes and packing in happy hour specials; he's constantly in a state of reinvention, not content to stick with just the steaks.

Greater Pinellas County   Map 9

ASIAN
ALÉSIA RESTAURANT $
7204 Central Ave., St. Petersburg, 727/345-9701,
www.alesiarestaurant.com
HOURS: Tues.-Fri. 11:30 A.M.-2:30 P.M. and 5:30-9 P.M.,
Sat. 10 A.M.-2:30 P.M. and 5:30-9 P.M.

Off the beaten path in St. Petersburg, Alésia is all charm, with an oh-so-Parisian French-Vietnamese fusion bent, at prices that make it an everyday option, with a gooey croque-monsieur one day and a pho or lemongrass-inflected vermicelli bowl the next. Unpolished concrete floors, big windows, and fresh white paint provide a clean backdrop for rough-hewn wooden tables and chairs, while an umbrella-covered courtyard off the back fills with the whisper of several fountains.

BREAKFAST
SKYWAY JACK'S RESTAURANT $
2795 34th St. S., St. Petersburg, 727/867-1907
HOURS: Daily 5 A.M.-3 P.M.

Skyway Jack's Restaurant has been a kitschy classic around here for more than a quarter century. It moved once because it was on the approach to the Skyway Bridge and got pushed out to make room for more lanes. It sells items like scrambled pork brains served with eggs, potatoes, and grits. Stick with regular breakfast food (orange-pecan French toast or the creamed chipped beef on toast) or the smoked mullet if you're feeling bold.

GERMAN
CAFE VIENNA $$
5625 4th St. N., St. Petersburg, 727/527-6404,
www.caffevienna.com
HOURS: Tues.-Fri. 11:30 A.M.-2 P.M. and 5-9 P.M., Sat.
and Sun. 5-10 P.M.

Look around the pretty, forest green dining room of Cafe Vienna, flanked at the front by a bar lined with personalized beer mugs and wine glasses, and it's clear: This place has devoted regulars. They find their mug, have it filled with a Spaten pilsner or Franzikaner weissbier, and then consider if they're in the mood for a bratwurst and sauerkraut, or maybe stroganoff over thick squiggles of spaetzle, the

RESTAURANTS

RIPE FOR THE PICKING

Most of us are so far removed from where our food comes from that it's hard to even envision its provenance. If we concentrate, we may conjure long, symmetrical rows of green leaves fringing the tops of loamy soil hillocks, farmhands parting the thicket to extract jewel-tone strawberries or giving a little yank to unearth a young carrot.

That's part of the picture, but taking a field trip to local pick-your-own farms reveals 21st century farms that look nothing like this. New technology is changing the way farmers coax their crop into being. Many of these farms are hydroponic, the advantages for the consumer being that the hydro-stacker pots rotate, much like a spinning sunglass display in a drugstore, making it easier for pickers to find what's ripe and obviating the need for any kneeling or squatting.

While prices fluctuate, they still are invariably lower than that at the grocery store, making picking your own a natural match for the thrifty shopper.

Interested shoppers can visit the following local farms:

- **Hydro Harvest Farms** (1101 Shell Point Rd. E., Ruskin, 941/915-7208, www.hydroharvestfarms.com): hydroponic vegetables and strawberries; year-round Monday–Saturday 10 A.M.–5 P.M., Sunday 10 A.M.–4 P.M.

- **Parke Hydro Farms** (3715 Tanner Rd., Dover, 813/927-4049, www.parkehydro. com): hydroponic vegetables and strawberries; year-round Tuesday–Saturday 9 A.M.–5 P.M.

- **Wheeler Farms** (14801 Balm Rd., Balm, southern Hillsborough County, 813/634-1868): beans and peas; May and June.

- **Lee Vineyards** (10251 McIntosh Rd., Dover, 813/335-1865): tropical and exotic fruits, grapes; summer.

- **Favorite Farms** (10070 McIntosh Rd., Dover, 813/986-3949, www.favoritefarms. net): strawberries; only open for pick-your-own after the commercial season, late March–early April.

- **Glover's Blueberry Farm** (5615 W.O. Griffin Rd., Plant City, 813/245-6818): blueberries; only open for pick-your-own after the commercial season, mid-May–June 1.

- **Hunsader Farms** (5500 County Road 675, Bradenton, 941/331-1212, www. hunsaderfarms.com): strawberries, rhubarb, cauliflower, broccoli, onions, and other vegetables; year-round Monday–Saturday 8 A.M.–4 P.M.

unlikely love children of fettuccine and dumplings. Beate Klobucar, who hails originally from Stuttgart, Germany, has presided over several German restaurants in St. Petersburg, including the current location since 2006, with a menu that is homey, flavorful, ample, and a change of pace.

MEXICAN
CASITA TAQUERIA 🟢

2706 4th St. N., St. Petersburg, 727/820-4365, www.casitatacos.com

HOURS: Mon.-Wed. 11 A.M.-9 P.M., Thurs.-Sat. 11 A.M.-10 P.M.

Adorable, with a blue-and-purple-and-loud color scheme outside and lively Día de los Muertos decor within, Casita Taqueria opened late in 2011. Newlywed owners Don and Gwen Arvin have traveled widely, enjoying the taquerias of Southern California. Largely mom-and-pop holes in the wall, these serve simple, fresh, uncomplicated dishes without a lot of sauce or molten cheese or sour cream. No crunchy shells, no avalanche of lettuce and tomato, no ground beef with "taco seasoning." The tacos they craved were straightforward handmade corn masa soft tortillas, hot from the griddle, furnished sparsely with meat (braised beef, shredded chicken), and topped with maybe a little crunchy cabbage or pico de gallo, a spritz of lime juice, and a ruffle of cilantro. And now St. Petersburg can enjoy just that, with a glass of sangria or an icy Negro Modelo.

CARMELITA'S ❸

5042 E. Bay Dr., Clearwater, 727/524-8226, www.carmelitas.net
HOURS: Sun.-Thurs. 11 A.M.-9:30 P.M., Fri.-Sat. 11 A.M.-10 P.M.

Like each of the legendary locations, the Clearwater Carmelita's serves up luscious, zingy-spicy green enchiladas to dispatch with a potent margarita. It's the kind of extra-cheese, refried-bean, gooey saturated-fat smorgasbord that somehow tastes just right after a long night. The digs are comfy and family-friendly but don't go if you're looking for cutting-edge regional Mexican fare. There is also a location in St. Petersburg (5211 Park St. N., St. Petersburg, 727/545-2956).

NEW AMERICAN
❿ CAFE PONTE ❸❸❸

13505 Icot Blvd., off Ulmerton Rd. in the Icot Center, Clearwater, 727/538-5768, www.cafeponte.com
HOURS: Mon. 11:30 A.M.-2 P.M., Tues.-Thurs. 11:30 A.M.-2 P.M. and 5:30-10 P.M., Fri. 11:30 A.M.-2 P.M. and 5:30-11 P.M., Sat. 5:30-11 P.M.

In foodie circles, Cafe Ponte may be the top dog. Chef Chris Ponte trained at Taillevent in Paris and studied at Johnson & Wales and the Cordon Bleu; his sophisticated restaurant in the Icot Center is a proper showcase for his luxurious palette. (The strip mall setting may confound would-be diners, but a single meal will set them straight.) The food is smart but luxurious: rich mushroom soup with a dollop of truffle cream; crispy whole snapper with mango, mint, and macadamia nuts over a ginger-vanilla rum sauce; and a supremely comforting yet vaguely exotic braised short rib tagine. Duo of duck brings braised thigh and pan-roasted breast with a heady Asian spice, paired with seared foie gras, a gingered sweet potato pancake, and an orange-Szechuan peppercorn sauce.

SEAFOOD
E & E STAKEOUT GRILL ❸❸❸

100 Indian Rocks Rd. N., Belleair Bluffs, 727/585-6399, www.3bestchefs.com
HOURS: Mon.-Thurs. 11:30 A.M.-10 P.M., Fri.-Sat. 11:30 A.M.-10:30 P.M., Sun. 11:30 A.M.-9 P.M.

After 26 years in the same location, E & E Stakeout has done a major renovation. The kitchen received the bulk of chef Erwin Scheuringer's attention, with a complete gut and rebuild, but the rest of the building got new plumbing, air-conditioning, carpeting, banquette upholstery, and other nice touches. Since its reopening, E & E gets chugging at 4 P.M. with an older, early-dinner crowd. The tables turn again for the 7-ish crew, and even as these people depart there's a trickle of new blood coming in. This place does some serious business. People come for its vast menu, with a new lineup of small plates, loads of steak options, and a ton of seafood. A tip: Unlike a lot of places, the evening specials are among the greatest deals.

RESTAURANTS

NIGHTLIFE

Why do white-sand beaches seem to call out for cold beer? A question for the ages, one that can be adequately pondered in Pinellas County. Along the Gulf side of the peninsula, beach bars abound in just about every community, most sporting a grouper sandwich, a Jimmy Buffet–inspired band, or a facsimile of either one. We've listed the biggies, but the truth is there are dozens of little ramshackle, sandy-floored watering holes you may just stumble into (or maybe the stumbling comes later). And downtown St. Petersburg has undergone a massive nightlife overhaul since 2010, with dozens of bars, clubs, and craft beer houses popping up.

Tampa is trickier. Although better than it used to be, the downtown tends to roll up the sidewalk at night. Still, there are new bars and craft cocktail emporiums worth exploring. Hyde Park has its fair share of nightspots, but Ybor City is the city's nightlife district, drawing 40,000 visitors on weekends. It's where people step out. During the week there are few bars with throbbing music oozing out onto the street; then it's more about sedate dining. Forget date night on the weekend; then it's a place you rove with buddies, scaring up trouble. Beyond Ybor, there are pockets of irrational exuberance near the USF campus and at Channelside and International Plaza.

But whether you rave or rhumba, after-hours entertainment in the Tampa Bay area runs the

HIGHLIGHTS

LOOK FOR **C** TO FIND RECOMMENDED NIGHTLIFE.

C Best Tropical Brain-Freeze Cocktail: Part pick-up bar, part waterside watering hole, **Bahama Breeze** offers island-themed tropical drinks that are sure to please (page 85).

C Top Place to Play Pool Shark: It's not called **The Rack** for nothing. South Tampa's favorite pool hall serves decent sushi, too (page 88).

C Best Bar to Kick You into Vacation Mode: Shephard's Beach Resort is a big, shambling, fruity-drink-serving beach bar of conga lines and paper wristbands (page 90).

C Hottest Spots for Gay Nightlife: Ybor City has sprouted a whole new crop of gay-friendly establishments in recent years, with sister properties **G. Bar** and **The Honey Pot** two of the most magnetic draws (page 92).

C Best Bar in which to Sing "Danny Boy": On Thursday, Friday, and Saturday nights, **MacDinton's Irish Pub & Restaurant** in Hyde Park has lines up to a couple hundred strong. These aren't all folks of Irish descent, but they seem to know their way around a Guinness (page 93).

C Best Place to See Big Names in a Small Venue: From hip-hop to alt-country, **Jannus Live** hosts visiting superstars in an indoor-outdoor tree-shaded nightclub (page 94).

gamut from pulsing house music to demure coffeehouse poetry readings. By and large, dress is casual (dress codes are usually posted outside establishments or on websites), cover charges are generally low or nonexistent, and show prices slide well below those in bigger metro areas. Beach bars may lean a little heavily on the Jimmy Buffet oeuvre, but with a little effort all musical tastes can be accommodated at local nightspots. And who is tops in liquid refreshment? Neat, on the rocks, shaken not stirred-Tampa Bay's best cocktails are spread far and wide, with numerous places thronged most nights with aperitif aficionados.

NIGHTLIFE

Bars

C BAHAMA BREEZE

3045 N. Rocky Point Dr. E., Tampa, 813/289-7922, www.bahamabreeze.com
HOURS: Daily 4 P.M.-2 A.M.
COST: No cover
Map 5

Located out on the Courtney Campbell Causeway in the Rocky Point area, Bahama Breeze is a froufrou tropical-drink singles hangout with a huge waterside deck on which you can occasionally see Rays players and Buccaneers. Island-theme playground that it is, it gets top honors for the tropical drinks. Their frozen piña colada comes with swirls of strawberry ice and a float of Myers's dark rum.

BAR LOUIE

International Plaza, 2223 N. Westshore Blvd., Tampa, 813/874-1919, www.barlouieamerica.com
HOURS: Daily 11 A.M.-2 A.M.
COST: No cover
Map 5

Bar Louie has got more taps going than a Savion Glover show. More than 40 beer taps line the long bar, as does a broad age range of sophisticated shoppers and partiers. An urban industrial vibe makes you feel far from the ritzy shopping of International Plaza mall. The encyclopedic array of beers can make you feel just about zippo in no time. It's a huge and echoey space, at its best when the after-work professionals swarm in for a casual nosh and a fancy brew or two. The chichi martinis seem to be the purview of the well-heeled female patrons, many of whom are surrounded by shopping bags from the day's prey.

BEAKS ST. PETE

2451 Central Ave., St. Petersburg, 727/321-9100, www.beaksoldflorida.com

HOURS: Tues.-Sun. 4-11 P.M.

COST: No cover

Map 9

Beaks doesn't so much have decor as an astounding accretion of stuff. It's a more-is-more motif whereby, if 1 plastic parrot is good, 20 plastic parrots are great. A long row of 1970s rococo chandeliers illuminates the tomato soup–red bar; fake tropical plants are everywhere; carved decoys, plastic bamboo fountains, and birdcages imprisoning fake jailbirds of a variety of species crowd in at the bar with the customers, themselves mostly attired in a cacophony of Hawaiian shirts. It's the kind of comfortable, good-time neighborhood joint that usually takes decades to create. The funky little bar/restaurant is the brainchild of founders Evelyn Powell and Jamie Farquharson. The culinary focus is bar food with a twist, most of which are improvements upon the originals. Kids are not allowed.

CENTRO CANTINA

Centro Ybor, 1600 E. 8th Ave., 813/241-8588

HOURS: Mon.-Sat. 11 A.M.-2:30 A.M., Sun. noon-2:30 A.M.

COST: No cover

Map 3

Margarita madness and killer karaoke can be found at Centro Cantina. A raucous spring-break-all-year crowd flocks to this lively Centro Ybor tequila-centric watering hole. It's a fun place, right at the pulsing heart of Ybor City, in which to pick your poison and let it rip. Think you can handle a 64-ounce margarita? Feel free to attempt it amongst these consummate 'rita

professionals. Food runs to dips and chips, so the draw is the rustic indoor-outdoor space and abounding good cheer. Smokers are welcome.

CHIC-A-BOOM ROOM

319 Main St., 727/736-0206, http://kellyschicaboom.com

HOURS: Sun.-Thurs. 11 A.M.-2 A.M., Fri.-Sat. 11 A.M.-3 A.M.

COST: No cover

Map 8

A little more glamorous and hip than many bars on the Dunedin scene, Chic-a-Boom Room skews a little young and a little more toward the fancy-martini side. Decor is kitschy-cool 1950s diner. The same owners have Kelly's next door.

COYOTE UGLY

1722 E. 7th Ave., 813/228-8459, www.coyoteuglysaloon.com

HOURS: Tues.-Sat. 5 P.M.-3 A.M.

COST: No cover

Map 3

In the center of all the action, Coyote Ugly aims older, not more mature, and is often just about the biggest party in Ybor City, presided over by the most audacious bartenders to ever wield a shot glass. If you have to ask what a body shot is you're ripe for a hard life lesson from one of Coyote's devilish (and usually gorgeous) bartenders. Just like in the movie (which in turn was based on a bar in New York City), all-female bartenders drag the unsuspecting up on the bar for some raunchy drinking, dancing, and whatever. The barebones room is festooned with discarded brassieres from exuberant all-ages patrons.

THE GARDEN

217 Central Ave., 727/896-3800, http://thegardendtsp.com

HOURS: Daily 11:30 A.M.-2 A.M.

COST: No cover

Map 6

The Garden's namesake garden, under the shade of a banyan, is the choicest seating. It's a cocktail kind of joint, with food largely an afterthought (think ballast, not haute cuisine, but Mediterranean in spirit). The 1880s building has a kind of sophistication imparted by the lovely setting, the cigars sold at the back, and the live jazz.

GULFPORT ON THE ROCKS

5413 Shore Blvd. S., 727/321-8318,
www.gulfportontherocks.com
HOURS: Daily 10 A.M.-2 A.M.
COST: No cover
Map 7

Gulfport isn't beachy, but the comfy staple Gulfport on the Rocks is just across from Williams Pier and Boca Ciega Bay. The thick fog of smoke inside is shorthand for "no food served here." There's usually live music—maybe the Edgewater Band ("back from its tour of Pinellas Park")—ably making its way through "Mustang Sally" and other crowd-pleasers. A beer-and-shots kind of comfy neighborhood bar, it features a nice pool table with straight cues—cheap and seemingly underutilized.

THE HUB

719 N. Franklin St., 813/229-1553,
www.thehubbartampa.com
HOURS: Mon.-Sat. 10 A.M.-3 A.M., Sun. 1 P.M.-3 A.M.
COST: No cover
Map 1

The Hub is dark, it's smoky, it's cash only, and the drinks will grow hair on your chest. And those are all the good qualities. The Hub is a beloved dive bar where no one exactly remembers why they started coming. The drink of choice is the kamikaze, but frankly they aren't particularly good until you've had your third. Under certain circumstances the jukebox is a masterful work of diabolical genius. It reads like a blue-collar bar, but many of the regular constituents are circuit court judges and lawyers lingering downtown for a grungy good

time. For many Tampans, ending an evening here is a tradition.

JIMMY B'S BEACH BAR

6200 Gulf Blvd., 727/367-1902
HOURS: Daily 11 A.M.-2 A.M.
COST: No cover
Map 7

The signature drink at Jimmy B's is something called a Hot Wet Spot, equally embarrassing to order and to drink: a piña colada with a drizzle of blueberry liqueur, all topped with a fluff of whipped cream. Slightly salacious embarrassment seems to be a theme: The menu boasts the "biggest weenie on the beach" among a handful of sandwiches, bar snacks, and pizza. Alas, the kitchen gets backed up on busy nights, so you may end up eyeballing others' jalapeño poppers, grouper fingers, and onion rings. The outdoor deck is gorgeous, with a long, gently illuminated boardwalk down to the beach. Stand on the sand, listening as the band segues from Rush to Pink Floyd, then make your way back out to the front past the girl peddling Jägermeister shots and other bad ideas.

O'KEEFE'S TAVERN AND RESTAURANT

1219 S. Fort Harrison Ave., 727/442-9034,
http://okeefestavernonline.com
HOURS: Daily 11 A.M.-2 A.M.
COST: No cover
Map 8

O'Keefe's is the bar to beat for St. Patrick's Day. A good-times, pint-or-three shambling Irish pub, its history goes back to the 1960s when it was O'Keefe's Tap Room, a history still visible despite the many additions and remodelings. A white brick exterior gives way to a comfortable series of rooms festooned with lots of green accents and Irishobilia. The brogue-required bartenders are fast and furious with the beers (more than 100 offerings) and the all-ages crowd is unified by their affection for the place. Once known for its "seven-course Irish dinner"

NIGHTLIFE

(that's a six pack and a potato), O'Keefe's fare is pretty good.

PCI BEACH BAR

Postcard Inn, 6300 Gulf Blvd., http://postcardinn.com

HOURS: Daily 11:30 A.M.-2 A.M.

COST: No cover

Map 7

A few years back the Postcard Inn took over an old, squatty beachside Travelodge and revamped it, giving it a kicky nostalgic surfboard theme and relaunching with a good barbecue restaurant and one of the best beachside bars around, the PCI Beach Bar, a rough-hewn wooden structure festooned with old license plates. On a weekend evening around dusk it's 10 deep at the bar, most revelers clad in bathing attire and with a serious aim of partying hard. The cocktails are surprisingly good (not just the froufrou tropical frozen kinds), the beers are cold, and the views of beach and water are stunning.

PEABODY'S

15333 Amberly Dr., 813/972-1725,

www.peabodysbilliards.com

HOURS: Daily 11 A.M.-3 A.M.

COST: No cover

Map 4

It may not be the cutting edge in nightlife, but Peabody's has earned a loyal clientele among New Tampa young professionals. Run by the same people who have the more youthful dance club, The Palms Club, next door, Peabody's appeals to a fairly mature New Tampa crowd, but one that appreciates a happy-hour-all-the-time policy (two-for-one and more). Big screen TVs, lots of billiards, electronic darts, and NTN trivia games don't distract from the smiley, nubile staff. It's a sports bar in sheep's clothing, one where the whole family won't mind sharing lively conversations over burgers (but after 9 P.M. it's over 21 only).

◖ THE RACK

1809 W. Platt St., 813/250-1595,

www.therackrestaurant.com

HOURS: Mon.-Fri. 4 P.M.-3 A.M., Sat. and Sun.

noon-3 A.M.

COST: No cover

Map 2

Head to The Rack for eight ball and *tekka maki*—a combo made in yuppie heaven. You don't see the kind of serious players who bring their own spiffy Schon or Predator cues, but there's respectable play at most of the tables in the hip, low-light, leather-couched space. The crowd is young but not too young, cool but not too cool.

SKIP'S

371 Main St., 727/734-9151

HOURS: Mon.-Sat. 4 P.M.-2 A.M.

COST: No cover

Map 8

Why is Skip's worth loving? The music is not too loud, everyone seems willing to chat with each other, and it's smack in the middle of good-times downtown Dunedin. Oh, and you can very easily take command of one of the dart boards. A few picnic tables out front allow you to take in the night air, and Skip himself is a warm and inviting presence in the bar. There is minimal food.

SPLITSVILLE

615 Channelside Dr., 813/514-2695,

www.splitsvillelanes.com

HOURS: Mon.-Thurs. 4 P.M.-1 A.M., Fri.-Sat. 11 A.M.-3 A.M.,

Sun. 11 A.M.-1 A.M.

COST: No cover

Map 1

Spares, strikes, whatever: At Splitsville it's good food, a stunningly whimsical environment, and the coolest bowling shoes ever. Splitsville boasts hottie waiters and equally glam clientele. The decor sets you straight with oversized "bowling pin" columns, red velvet ropes, and 12

COURTESY OF PEABODY'S BILLIARDS & GAMES

Peabody's

pristine lanes. Excellent shareable bar snacks are available laneside: The sliders are deliciously messy and oniony; the bacon skins are crisp and laden with fat three ways—sour cream, bacon, and cheddar. Then, for dessert, order up a Snickertini with Stoli Vanilla, Frangelico, Kahlua, and a splash of cream, garnished with chocolate syrup and cocoa powder. You've never had a more delicious libation while wearing bowling shoes.

UNDERTOW BEACH BAR

3850 Gulf Blvd., 727/368-9000,

www.undertowbeachbar.com

HOURS: Tues.-Sat. noon-2 A.M., Sun. 1 P.M.-midnight

COST: No cover

Map 7

Set back from Gulf Boulevard, Undertow Beach Bar is two buildings and a patio squatting right on the sand. The bar, to the left, is boisterous, with a strange running-water moat inset in the long oval-shaped bar. Cocktail waitresses wear something reminiscent of the Dallas Cowboy cheerleaders' late-1970s glory years, but the bathing-suits-and-flip-flops crowd doesn't bat an eye. The outdoor patio is the place to be, with a weathered plywood table and some tiki thatched options for the sun-averse. Some nights there's live reggae, but others the music is canned. Opt for the very respectable rum runners and an order of wings (a generous 12 for $4).

Dance Clubs

CLUB PRANA

1619 E. 7th Ave., 813/241-4139, www.clubprana.com

HOURS: Thurs.-Sat. 9 P.M.-2 A.M.

COST: $10 cover, $30 bottle service

`Map 3`

Club Prana opened its doors in 2000 and quickly became the velvet-roped crown jewel in the Ybor scene. A couple years later the club expanded to five floors. From the main floor and mezzanine to the exclusive 3rd floor lounge, 4th floor "club level," and 5th floor rooftop "sky bar," the space is attractive brushed stainless steel and hardwood floors. Patrons tend to be young and trendy.

CLUB SKYE

1509 E. 8th Ave., 813/247-6606, www.skyetampa.com

HOURS: Mon.-Sat. 1 P.M.-3 A.M.

COST: Cover varies; Sat. no cover before 11 P.M.

`Map 3`

Club Skye is what's on the horizon for Tampa's party nights. Silky white curtains part to reveal the night's drama as it unfolds. What's it gonna be? Whether you're here for Ultimate Ladies' Night, Tipsy Tuesdays for the LGBT community, or Saturday Night Bomb with Wild 94.1 FM broadcasting live, Skye is the party to beat in Ybor. Although only certain nights are technically Naughty School Girl Nights, every night has a preponderance of slinky, sexy post-collegiate girls, especially notable when the club runs costume nights or competitions.

CZAR VODKA BAR

1420 E. 7th Ave., 813/247-2664, www.czarnation.com

HOURS: Wed., Fri., and Sat. 10 P.M.-3 A.M.

COST: $5 cover

`Map 3`

Czar is located in the atmospheric Pleasuredome/Tracks/El Goya building. Vodka drinks are de rigueur at Czar, with two rooms sporting dance floors, video screens, and nice booths (the side room is called Cyberia); there's also a super swank chill out room. Wednesdays feature "Le Hump" party, Fridays is something called Filthy Richard, and Saturdays are the Peoples' Party.

◖ SHEPHARD'S BEACH RESORT

601-619 S. Gulfview Blvd., 727/441-6875, www.shephards.com

HOURS: Tiki bar Sun.-Thurs. 2-11 P.M., Fri.-Sat. 1 P.M.-2 A.M.; The Wave nightclub Thurs.-Sun. 9 P.M.-2 A.M.; Sunset Lounge daily 9:30 P.M.-2 A.M.

COST: Cover varies for tiki bar and The Wave, usually $10

`Map 8`

Before you even enter the building, you're immersed in the buzz of Shephard's Beach Resort. There's the valet parking, then the cover charge, and accompanying paper wristband. Get the lay of the land, order fruity drinks with names like Shipwrecks and D Cups, heavy on the Midori, and watch the goings-on at the outdoor tiki bar. Live reggae promotes conga lines and other exuberant group dancing. Inside at the Sunset Lounge, a house band slides through R&B numbers for a calmer crowd. Still, the center of festivities at Shephard's can be found at The Wave nightclub, with go-go dancers in big furry boots and bouncers suitably equipped with mammoth biceps and radio headsets. Just at the water's edge, the patio outside sports leather-clad beds—shades of South Beach.

Gay and Lesbian

There are two discrete areas for gay and lesbian revelry: The Grand Central area of St. Petersburg (go west on Central Ave. from downtown) and much of Ybor City (often called GaYbor). Here are some of the biggies in these two neighborhoods and beyond.

BAXTER'S

1519 S. Dale Mabry Hwy., Tampa, 813/258-8830, www.baxterslounge.com

HOURS: Daily noon–3 A.M.
COST: No cover

`Map 5`

Baxter's just keeps closing and popping up somewhere else. A friendly neighborhood meeting place, Baxter's features hot dancers Wednesday–Saturday nights, movies Thursdays, karaoke on Sundays, and more. Dimly lit, with pool table, darts, and plenty of parking, it's been a local go-to since 1982.

CITY SIDE

3703 Henderson Blvd., 813/350-0600, www.clubcityside.com

HOURS: Daily 11 A.M.–3 A.M.
COST: No cover

`Map 2`

In a weird location for a gay club (in a strip mall, next to a sports bar), City Side is an inviting lounge with pool tables, intimate dance floor, and outdoor patio. Far from a frenetic scene, it's appropriate for a little after-work conversation and relaxation.

DETOUR

2612 Central Ave., St. Petersburg, 727/327-8204, www.detourfl.com

HOURS: Daily 2 P.M.–2 A.M.
COST: No cover

`Map 9`

The neighborhood is called the Grand

NIGHTLIFE

COURTESY OF VISIT FLORIDA

Ybor City is home to the hottest nightlife.

Central District, and thus, this three-venue nightclub until recently was Grand Central Station, now Detour. In over 13,000 square feet, it's got two bars, a large dance floor, two stages to support live entertainment and karaoke nearly every night, pool tables, darts, bowling, a wide outdoor patio, Internet café, and lots of free parking.

◖ G. BAR

1401 E. 7th Ave., 813/247-1016, http://yborclubs.com

HOURS: Tues.-Sat. 8 P.M.-2 A.M.

COST: No cover

Map 3

In an historic turn-of-the-century brick building, G. Bar is 8,000 square feet of fun, with a big dance room, video bar, and a stage for concerts and performers like DJ Greg Anderson, Amy Demilo, Alisa Summers, and Arica Love. There's a line out the door most weekends, with celebrity guests amping up the frenzy level. Many nights there are special events-costumes, strip parties, album release wingdings, etc., with lots of drink specials to match. G. Bar is inviting regardless of sexual orientation.

GEORGIE'S ALIBI OF ST. PETE

3100 3rd Ave. N., St. Petersburg, 727/321-2112, www.georgiesalibi.com

HOURS: Daily 11 A.M.-2 A.M.

COST: No cover

Map 9

The sister property to the booming Wilton Manors outpost down in Fort Lauderdale (and another in Palm Springs, CA), Georgie's Alibi

of St. Pete has settled into an unlikely strip mall. Most days it's a relaxed, pleasant place to unwind and meet new people, but some nights it is more energetic dance parties and special events (drag bingo, anyone?).

◖ THE HONEY POT

1507 E. 7th Ave., 813/247-4663

HOURS: Tues.-Sat. 8 P.M.-2 A.M.

COST: No cover

Map 3

Owned by the same people as G. Bar, The Honey Pot is a stunning club, holding the weekly Steam (for men) and Tease (for women) parties on Friday and Saturday night, respectively. It's a multi-million dollar, three-story space with loads of lighting effects, with a balcony overlooking the festivities of Ybor City and a blue room lounge for relaxing in luxurious style. They host female impersonation shows, circuit deejays, singers, TV reality star appearances, nationally recognized porn superstars, and roaming performers.

YBOR CITY SOCIAL CLUB

1909 N. 15th St., 813/242-2717, http://yborclubs.com

HOURS: Daily 10 P.M.-3 A.M.

COST: No cover

Map 3

Right in the middle of the GaYbor district, Ybor City Social Club is an inclusive nightspot with an 18-and-up policy, with different evenings catering to different crowds (ladies night, indie music, college students—check online for details). It's a beautiful and historic space, with the "dungeon" dance floor downstairs.

Irish Pubs

DUBLINER PUB

2307 W. Azeele St., 813/258-2257,
www.thedublineririshpub.com
HOURS: Mon.-Thurs. 3 P.M.-3 A.M., Fri. and Sat.
noon-3 A.M.
COST: No cover
Map 2

There's a lot of Irish zeal on and around Azeele. If you like your music—or your flirting—with a heavy brogue, head to everyone's favorite quaint Irish bar, the Dubliner. It's set in a tiny house with a nice front porch; burgers are solid and the youngish crowd is convivial.

FOUR GREEN FIELDS

205 W. Platt St., 813/254-4444,
www.tampa.fourgreenfields.com
HOURS: Mon.-Wed. 11 A.M.-1 A.M., Thurs.-Sun.
11 A.M.-2 A.M.
COST: No cover
Map 1

Located one block west of the Tampa Bay Convention Center, the thatched-roof cottage of Four Green Fields is an utter anomaly. Order an Irish whiskey or a black and tan from the man with the thick brogue behind the worn wooden bar. There's an outdoor deck set amid palm trees, live Irish folk music most nights, and some say the best pint of Guinness in Tampa. The menu won't win any awards for originality, but the fry basket is piping hot and generous.

HATTRICKS

107 S. Franklin St., 813/225-4288,
www.sportsbartampa.com
HOURS: Daily 11 A.M.-3 A.M.
COST: No cover
Map 1

A stone's throw from the Tampa Bay Times Forum and the convention center, Hattricks gets packed on Tampa Bay Lightning home games, or any time something boisterous is going on at the Forum (alright, not Justin Bieber). It's an historic three-story building that dates to 1907, with a long, generous bar, lots of TVs tuned to the game du jour, and great bucket-o-beer specials.

◖ MACDINTON'S IRISH PUB & RESTAURANT

405 S. Howard Ave., 813/251-8999,
www.macdintons.com
HOURS: Mon.-Sat. 11:30 A.M.-3 A.M., Sun. 5 P.M.-3 A.M.
COST: No cover
Map 2

MacDinton's is another Irish entry with a killer black and tan, a warming Irish coffee, and a fair representation of Irish staples, from rib-sticking, mashed-potato-y shepherd's pie to respectable corned beef and cabbage. This is absolutely the biggest scene in Tampa, with lines down and around the block on weekend nights. Why? Who can say? The beer tastes just the same as it does at other places. A second location opened in 2012 in St. Petersburg (242 1st Ave. N., St. Petersburg, 727/565-0544).

NIGHTLIFE

Live Music

◖ JANNUS LIVE

220 1st Ave. N., 727/896-1244, www.jannuslive.com
HOURS: Vary by performance
COST: Varies by performance
Map 6

A smaller venue for rock and contemporary acts, Jannus is supposedly the oldest outdoor concert venue in Florida. From jam bands like Medeski, Martin, and Wood, to the Wailers, to Lucinda Williams—it all sounds fabu from a spot in the outdoor courtyard. It's bigger than a nightclub, with bigger acts, but there's still a cool club vibe and usually a 30s-and-up crowd. There is no reserved seating.

NEW WORLD BREWERY

1313 E. 8th Ave., 813/248-4969,
http://newworldbrewery.net
HOURS: Daily 3 P.M.-3 A.M.
COST: Most evenings no cover; some bands $3-9
Map 3

New World Brewery is one of Ybor City's oldest and most beloved venues, with a lush tropical courtyard and a range of musical tastes from alt-rock to cool fusion jazz. There are more than 30 microbrews on tap (Magic Hat #9, etc.)—they don't brew their own anymore, but the owners are connoisseurs of other suds excellence and everyone seems to be a regular.

ORPHEUM

1902 Avenida Republica de Cuba, 813/248-9500,
www.theorpheum.com
HOURS: Doors open nightly 7 P.M., show times vary; some shows require 21 and up, some allow all ages
COST: Varies by performance
Map 3

Local acts, regional acts, and national acts take the stage regularly in this club run by the folks at the State Theater. There is often an opener and a headlining act for not too much dough.

It has a great sound system and is a music lover's dream night out. Punk, blues, alt-country, they all plays here to a diverse crowd. Some nights it's just DJs and dancing, which is still fun. Be sure to call ahead—not all shows allow all ages—and be sure to check out the leopard print pool table when you get here.

THE PALLADIUM

253 5th Ave. N., 727/822-3590, www.mypalladium.org
HOURS: Vary by performance
COST: Varies by performance
Map 6

Part of St. Petersburg College, this is a popular venue for visiting groups, whether it's rock, jazz, cabaret, chamber music, or Serbian folk music. The Palladium consists of the mainstage Hough Hall, with a much-lauded sound system, as well as the more intimate Side Door Cabaret. There is no reserved seating.

PEGASUS LOUNGE

10008 N. 30th St., 813/971-1679,
www.pegasusniteclub.com
HOURS: Mon.-Sat. 1 P.M.-3 A.M.
COST: Varies by performance
Map 4

At Pegasus, live bands, familiar tap and bottled beers, big-screen TV, karaoke (and, um, pornaoke, a variant with the singer backed by classic porn films), and darts produce a recipe for collegiate happiness. USF students heft Mich Ultras while watching bands that range from folk to goth—industrial and hard-core—all of it loud. With nearly 30 bands plugging their amps in at the Pegasus every month, this little North Tampa club has become a must-see-and-be-seen for area music lovers. With a large stage, killer sound, a fair amount of seating, and even a decent burger, it's not hard to see why the lounge's reputation has grown. The

The Palladium

beers are the usual suspects, the drinks aren't winning any prizes, but that's no matter to the crowd busy with darts, pool, and even a good jukebox for when the band flags.

THE RITZ YBOR

1503 E. 7th Ave., 813/247-2555, http://ritzybor.com

HOURS: Hours vary by performance

COST: Varies by performance

Map 3

A special-events venue only open for events, concerts, and private parties, The Ritz Ybor has a glorious setting in what was the Rivoli Theatre launched in Tampa in 1917. It was a slightly sketchy nightclub called Masquerade for more than a decade, and only in 2008 did it get revamped as a 17,000-square-foot concert venue. It has hosted a variety of events, from the 2009 Maxim Super Bowl party to the BET Black Carpet Party, as well as concerts from Lady Gaga to the Smashing Pumpkins and Ben Harper.

SKIPPER'S SMOKEHOUSE

910 Skipper Rd., 813/971-0666, www.skipperssmokehouse.com

HOURS: Tues.-Fri. 11 A.M.-11 P.M., Sat. noon-11 P.M., Sun. 1-11 P.M.

COST: Varies by performance

Map 4

Located in northern New Tampa, Skipper's is the city's beloved indoor-outdoor live blues venue. It's Tampa's best live music venue (blues, alt-rock, Tuvan throat singers, the gamut), with concerts held outdoors under the canopy of a huge, moss-festooned live oak. It has a lively 30s-and-up bar scene (a mighty fine mojito), and a ramshackle restaurant serves a wonderful blackened grouper sandwich, gator nuggets, and black beans.

STATE THEATRE

687 Central Ave., 727/895-3045, http://statetheatreconcerts.com

HOURS: Show times vary, generally 9 P.M.-2 A.M.

Tampa Theatre

NIGHTLIFE

COST: $10-15

Map 6

In an historic gutted movie theater shellacked with flat black no-frills paint, State Theatre is where locals get their mosh on. The genres cycle through folk, alt rock, punk, and ska, and thus the audience varies wildly night to night. Regardless of the show, regulars applaud the intimacy of the venue and the "real" (read grungy) quality of the space. There is very limited seating, so it's largely standing-room-only (check out the balcony to take the energy and noise down a notch).

TAMPA THEATRE

711 N. Franklin St., 813/274-8981, www.tampatheatre.org

HOURS: Vary by performance

COST: Varies by performance

Map 1

Built in 1926, Tampa Theatre is a beloved downtown landmark with concerts by the likes of Gordon Lightfoot, Keb Mo, and Bright Eyes, special events, and backstage tours. The creepy/fancy Basque architecture makes it an especially delicious place to see a show, which is almost always a sit-down affair.

Lounges

BLUE MARTINI

International Plaza, 2223 N. Westshore Blvd., Tampa, 813/873-2583, www.bluemartinilounge.com

HOURS: Mon.-Thurs. 4 P.M.-3 A.M., Fri. and Sat. 1 P.M.-3 A.M.

COST: No cover

Map 5

It should come as no surprise that Blue Martini has a bevy of fabulous sillytinis that draw serious devotees. Like, say, the signature Blue Martini, which features Van Gogh Blue Vodka, Cointreau, Blue Curacao, sour mix, and orange juice, served in a big snifter with a glow stick. Silly enough? Still, it's a bar for full-fledged adults, featuring an elevated stage behind the bar on which to see live rock nightly. The menu leans to attractive and contemporary small plates (seared tuna, hummus, and pita chips).

PUSH ULTRA LOUNGE

128 3rd St. S., 727/895-6400, http://pushlounge.com

HOURS: Fri.-Sat. 9 P.M.-3 A.M.

COST: No cover

Map 6

Push, a huge dance club with rooftop bar and outdoor garden patio, heats up the nights in downtown St. Petersburg, not surprisingly at the site of a historic firehouse. Drinks lean to boutique tequilas in a range of stylish margaritas. Celebrities like Paris Hilton have been known to make a showing. A stylish restaurant called Red Mesa Cantina perches coquettishly downstairs to serve revelers duck tacos and such.

Wine Bars

BIANCHI'S ENOTECA

3215 S MacDill Ave., 813/837-2233, http://bianchisenoteca.com

HOURS: Tues.-Wed. 8 A.M.-8 P.M., Thurs.-Sat. until 10 P.M.

COST: No cover

Map 2

About a dozen wines are featured on the chalkboard at Bianchi's Enoteca, all hailing from France, Italy, or Spain. Bianchi's Enoteca leans to Old World wines (but isn't adverse to New): crisp, dry, flinty, even austere quaffs that don't have the superabundance of fruit, sucker-punch of alcohol, or blowsy oak aging you find in so many California wines. This is a space without a full restaurant kitchen: no grill or hood, just a couple of induction burners and a partnership that is gaga over great cheeses and charcuterie.

BOBBY'S BISTRO

447 Mandalay Ave., Clearwater Beach, 727/446-9463, www.bobbysbistro.com

HOURS: Mon.-Tues. 6 A.M.-10 P.M., Wed.-Sun. until midnight

COST: No cover

Map 8

Bob Heilman's Beachcomber has been a beefy *Wine Spectator* award winner for years on the basis of its burgundies, but little sibling Bobby's Bistro is sheer lusciousness for the Oregon and California pinot noir lover. Bobby's draws a mixed clientele, from young professionals to retirees. It opened in 1994, and serves a menu of pizzas and stylish California cuisine that still feels fresh today.

NIGHTLIFE

CARMEL CAFE & WINE BAR

3601 W. Swann Ave., 813/964-6889,
www.carmelcafe.com

HOURS: Mon.-Thurs. 11:30 A.M.-2:30 P.M. and 5-10 P.M.,
Fri. and Sat. until 11 P.M., Sun. until 9 P.M.

COST: No cover

`Map 2`

The newish concept that is Carmel Cafe &
Wine Bar has some key players behind it: Chris
Sullivan, an Outback Steakhouse founder and
its former CEO, and Steve Cook, veteran of
Tampa's Mise en Place, who led the collabora-
tive effort on the menu. It features small plates of
Mediterranean rim cuisine with regional flavors
from Italy, France, Spain, Morocco, and Greece.
It has a 60-label Old and New World wine list
and offers pours of three, six, and nine ounces
facilitated by an iPad ordering system. The
Swann Avenue location has emerged as Tampa's
top spot for girls nights out among the swanky
set. There are also locations in northern Tampa
(14306 N. Dale Mabry Hwy., Tampa, 813/265-
1415) and Clearwater (2548 McMullen-Booth
Rd., Clearwater, 727/724-4228).

CLEARWATER WINE BAR & BISTRO

483 Mandalay Ave., Ste. 113, Clearwater Beach,
727/446-8805, www.clearwaterwinebar.com

HOURS: Tues.-Wed. and Sun. 4-10 P.M., Thurs.-Sat.
11:30 A.M.-11:30 P.M.

COST: No cover

`Map 9`

Tio Pepe, Charley's Steakhouse, the Columbia
restaurant, and Bern's always get major plau-
dits for the breadth of their lists, but often this
amounts to us mere mortals looking wistfully as
we turn the pages of the pricey tome. A fun place
to taste more than 40 eminently affordable wines
by the glass, Clearwater Wine Company is just a
quick walk to the beach. Kristi Lam and her parents orchestrate a casual, living-room atmosphere
on certain Friday nights with live music, offering
tipples from every major wine-producing region
in the world, with deep happy hour discounts

between 5 and 7 P.M. (Oh, and there's a "Yappy
Hour" the last Saturday of the month for the sophisticated dog and his owner.)

CRU CELLARS

2506 S. MacDill Ave., 813/831-1117,
http://crucellarstampa.com

HOURS: Tues.-Sat. 5-10 P.M.

COST: No cover

`Map 2`

Jen Bingham, certified sommelier for Cru
Cellars, focuses on small-production wines
from all the major wine regions, with a real
emphasis on bottles under $50. It's a "hidden
gems" approach that often yields nice surprises.
In addition, Cru offers a menu of sharable small
plates, artisanal cheeses, and a few more substantial dishes, all of which aim to complement
a couple dozen wines by the glass or bottle,
with a handful of provocative flights ("pinot
envy"; a collection of earthy terroir titans called
"down and dirty").

PAN Y VINO WINE BAR

369 Main St., 727/734-7700, http://panyvino.com

HOURS: Tues.-Sat. 5-10 P.M.

COST: No cover

`Map 8`

This little tapas and wine bar was born when
Casa Tina moved to larger digs. Owned by the
same folks, Pan Y Vino Wine Bar offers more
than two dozen wines by the glass, tapas and
small plates that use local or organic ingredients, plus desserts and coffees. More recently it
has added a brick oven for organic pizzas.

TOAST

14921 Bruce B. Downs Blvd., 813/632-3105,
http://toastwineandcafe.com

HOURS: Mon.-Thurs. 11 A.M.-11 P.M., Fri.-Sat. until 1 A.M.,
Sun. until 7 P.M.

COST: No cover

`Map 4`

A certified Level 1 sommelier for Toast, Hector

COURTESY OF CLEARWATER WINE BAR & BISTRO

Clearwater Wine Bar & Bistro

Gonzalez's wine tastes are catholic: Right now his biggest sellers are a silky Mourvèdre, grenache, and Syrah blend from Cline Cellars called Cashmere as well as a crisp-apple Marco Felluga pinot grigio from Friuli-Venezia Giulia. A cedar-planked humidor and private smoking lounge make it a destination for New Tampa's cigar fans of both genders. A retail shop with a welcoming long bar, Toast's kitchen facilities are a bit cramped, so Gonzalez limits himself to a short list of flatbreads and a range of antipasti and nibbles.

WINE EXCHANGE

1609 W. Snow Ave., 813/254-9463,
http://wineexchangetampa.com
HOURS: Mon.-Thurs. 11 A.M.-11 P.M., Fri.-Sat. until 1 A.M., Sun. until 7 P.M.
COST: No cover
Map 2

For nearly two decades, the Wine Exchange has been a defining part of swanky Old Hyde Park Village. In March 2009, the bistro and wine bar relocated to its big, gorgeous digs from a smaller spot around the corner. Order grape by the glass or bottle while scanning the room for Tampa big shots like super attorney Barry Cohen.

WINE MADONNA

111 2nd Ave. NE, Ste. 102, 727/289-7257,
http://winemadonna.com
HOURS: Daily 3-11 P.M.
COST: No cover
Map 6

Opened in 2011, Wine Madonna shares a courtyard with the Ale & the Witch. Owners Kris Radish (a novelist and former newspaper journalist) and Madonna Metcalf (a certified sommelier) work in tandem with the craftbrew tap house, with live music in the courtyard most nights providing an atmospheric backdrop for tippling of either the grape or hops variety. The wine-tasting lounge offers about 65 wines, 45 by the glass, running the gamut from New World to Old World wines at every price point: "We don't want to intimidate anyone. Our working motto is 'seek happiness.'"

NIGHTLIFE

ARTS AND LEISURE

While it was the first state to be settled by Europeans, Florida might be the last state to have entered fully into modernity. It remained more or less a frontier until the 20th century, with the first paved road not until 1920. It was really World War II that changed things in the state, prompting a period of sustained growth that lasted more than 50 years.

Because of its relative youth, the Tampa Bay area has not had enough time to cultivate long-standing arts traditions and venerable cultural institutions like other American cities. Located an hour to the south of the Tampa Bay area, Sarasota has been the undisputed arts capital of the Gulf Coast, having had circus impresario John Ringling lavish his adopted home town with visual and performing arts venues and concerns.

St. Petersburg and Tampa don't quite reach the same heights, but downtown St. Petersburg has, since the turn of the 21st century, made major strides and now competes with the city to the east for per capita arts organizations. All along the waterfront and St. Petersburg's east-west avenues, fanning out from Central, you'll find more than a dozen arts and historical museums, galleries, and local theaters. Despite its sophistication in other arenas (like, um, sports arenas), Tampa doesn't quite measure up, with a sparser number of superlative local arts offerings.

In terms of other types of recreation—

HIGHLIGHTS

LOOK FOR ❰ TO FIND
RECOMMENDED ARTS AND ACTIVITIES.

Tropicana Field is home of the Tampa Bay Rays.

❰ **Best Reason to Feel Surreal:** The famous mustachioed Spanish surrealist is honored in St. Petersburg's sleek new **Salvador Dalí Museum,** a tremendous collection of his work and the work of those inspired by him (page 107).

❰ **Best Place to Share Popcorn with a Ghost:** The **Tampa Theatre,** elaborately decorated to resemble an open Mediterranean courtyard, features 1,446 seats, 99 stars in the auditorium ceiling, nearly 1,000 pipes in its mighty Wurlitzer theater organ–and, some say, the ghost of an old projectionist (page 118).

❰ **Top Sandy Splendor:** There are so many wonderful choices for sun and sand. So why settle for just one when you can opt for the double-whammy of **Caladesi Island and Honeymoon Island State Parks,** a pair of white-sand barrier islands (pages 122 and 125)?

❰ **Best Excuse to Get on Two Wheels: Pinellas Trail** is one of the longest linear parks in the southeastern United States, a 15-foot-wide bike path running from St. Petersburg up to the sponge docks of Tarpon Springs (page 130).

❰ **Best Excuse for Peanuts and Cracker Jacks:** Tampa Bay has both the boys of summer and the boys of spring. You can see professional baseball much of the year, with the **New York Yankees Spring Training** in February and March and the **Tampa Bay Rays** during the regular season (pages 135 and 137).

ARTS AND LEISURE

outdoor activities, spectator sports, and other diversions—Hillsborough and Pinellas counties are both an embarrassment of riches. The wealth of beaches and state parks on the Pinellas side allow for sun, sand, fishing, boating, cycling, and more low-key navel contemplation, while Hillsborough has professional and college sports of all kinds. Tampa gets the nod for retail enticements, with two super-high-end malls to its name, while downtown St. Petersburg offers up a quirky afternoon of window-shopping amongst the many independent boutiques and galleries.

The Arts

MUSEUMS

ARMED FORCES HISTORY MUSEUM

2050 34th Way N., Largo, 727/539-8371,
www.armedforcesmuseum.com
HOURS: Tues.-Sat. 10 A.M.-4 P.M., Sun. noon-4 P.M.
COST: $17.95 adult, $14.95 senior, $12.95 child 4-12, free for active or retired military with ID
Map 9

Tucked away in an industrial park close to a residential neighborhood, the nonprofit Armed Forces History Museum is jammed with militaria, uniforms, videos, and dioramas with large-scale reproductions. Represented are about a half-century's worth of acquisitions for all the wars in which U.S. forces were involved, from World War I through Iraq. Beyond the static displays, including some detailed Japanese war ship models from the film *Tora, Tora, Tora,* you can ride around the grounds in an actual WWII armored reconnaissance car, or strap yourself into a simulator (it seats seven) and dial up big-screen experiences from flying over Iwo Jima to driving around a glacier to landing your fighter jet on an aircraft carrier.

BEACH ART CENTER

1515 Bay Palm Blvd., Indian Rocks Beach,
727/596-4331, www.beachartcenter.org
HOURS: Mon.-Thurs. 9 A.M.-4 P.M., Fri. 9 A.M.-noon
COST: Free
Map 9

A sweet nonprofit arts center, Beach Art Center offers classes for locals in fine arts and crafts. It also has two small galleries in the old American Legion Hall to display works by local artists as well as the occasional traveling show.

CHIHULY COLLECTION

400 Beach Dr. NE, 727/822-7872,
www.moreanartscenter.org
HOURS: Mon.-Sat. 10 A.M.-5 P.M., Sun. noon-5 P.M.
COST: $14.95 adult, $13.95 senior, $10.95 student and child, free for children 5 and younger
Map 6

In 2003, the Museum of Fine Arts was displaying a large number of works by master glass artist Dale Chihuly; his associates had overseen the installation. Then in the last week of the popular exhibit's scheduled time, Chihuly showed up, unannounced, walked among his works and the visitors, and was charmed enough that he agreed to provide many more pieces to go on permanent display in their own space. His "Collection" opened in the summer of 2010, almost across the street from the museum, fronted by a 20-foot-tall sculpture. Within the 7,600-square-foot space are nine display spaces for the only permanent showplace of his works away from his Seattle-area studio. Entrance is by timed ticket, and there are docent-led tours every 30 minutes.

CRACKER COUNTRY

Florida State Fairgrounds, 4700 Orient Rd., Tampa,
813/627-4225, www.crackercountry.org
HOURS: Vary; check the website or call 813/627-4225

COURTESY OF VISITSTPETECLEARWATER.COM

Chihuly Collection

COST: $7 adult, $6 senior and student age 6-12, free for children 5 and younger

Map 5

Most Floridians have heard the axiom that the state wasn't hospitable enough to be settled until a doctor in the Panhandle invented a rudimentary air-cooling system in the 1840s. But the fact is, that doctor, his patients, and thousands of other hardy souls were homesteading, fishing, lumberjacking, and wading into other chores well before the 20th century. A well-to-do Tampa area pioneer family decided to display some 19th-century structures on the Florida State Fairgrounds and more than a dozen authentic buildings have been donated to the site. Visitors can watch a blacksmith, take over the butter churn, take a seat in an 1898 train depot, or watch the animatronic teacher and students in a schoolhouse first used in 1912.

DUNEDIN FINE ARTS CENTER & CHILDREN'S ART MUSEUM
1143 Michigan Blvd., Dunedin, 727/298-3322, www.dfac.org
HOURS: Mon.-Fri. 10 A.M.-5 P.M., Sat. 10 A.M.-2 P.M., Sun. 1-4 P.M.
COST: Free

Map 9

The center, opened in 1974, has four galleries, studio classrooms, the David L. Mason Children's Art Museum, the Palm Cafe, and gallery gift shop. The exhibits are often the work of students. The children's museum provides hands-on activities that assist families in understanding and appreciating the work of Florida artists exhibited in the galleries. Even if you spend your time in the art center and not the children's museum, the scale is such that it's not intimidating or boring for kids.

ARTS AND LEISURE

Florida Holocaust Museum

ARTS AND LEISURE

FLORIDA HOLOCAUST MUSEUM

55 5th St. S., 727/820-0100,
www.flholocaustmuseum.org
HOURS: Daily 10 A.M.–5 P.M.
COST: $16 adult, $14 senior, $10 college student,
$8 child 18 and younger
Map 6

The fourth largest of its kind in the United States, the Florida Holocaust Museum has sections devoted to the memory of millions of innocent people who suffered, struggled, and died in the Holocaust. Exhibitions have ranged from Anne Frank to Jackie Robinson, from an examination of the Jehovah's Witnesses persecution during World War II to Pope John Paul II's relationship with the Jewish people and, looking at the broader picture, genocide in Armenia and Rwanda. It also showcases only loosely linked exhibits such as the lush, life-affirming work of Czech artist Charles Pachner (who lost his whole family during the war), or Kaddish in Wood, featuring woodcarvings of French children of the Holocaust created by Dr. Herbert Savel.

FLORIDA INTERNATIONAL MUSEUM

244 2nd St. N., 727/341-7901, www.floridamuseum.org
HOURS: Vary depending on exhibition
COST: $10 adult, $8 senior and military, $5 student 7 and older, free for children 6 and younger
Map 6

Born in 1995 as an ambitious, donor-supported hall to host traveling mega-shows of spectacular artifacts, the museum began life in what had been downtown St. Pete's major department store, closed a few years earlier. The original displays were blockbusters: Treasures of the Kremlin Museums, which focused on the Romanov Dynasty; Egyptian artifacts; recovered items from the Titanic; and one of the world's largest exhibits dealing with Alexander the Great. But the museum was consistently in debt and began to fall back on less-epic displays—on JFK, later The Cuban Missile

Crisis, and Major League Baseball memorabilia. Finally the museum left the original building, though it has stayed downtown. It is now an affiliate of the Smithsonian Institution, displaying artifacts from the Smithsonian and traveling exhibitions, and more often shows exhibits created from a consortium of other museums around the state and country.

FLORIDA MUSEUM OF PHOTOGRAPHIC ARTS

400 N. Ashley Dr., 813/221-2222, http://fmopa.org
HOURS: Tues.-Thurs. 10 A.M.-5 P.M., Fri. 10 A.M.-8 P.M., Sat. 10 A.M.-5 P.M., Sun. noon-5 P.M.
COST: $10 suggested donation, $8 suggested for student and military
Map 1

This small photography museum opened in 2001 and made a spectacular leap forward in 2012, when it relocated to a glass-walled downtown building known as the Cube. Making use of the floor-to-ceiling panes, the museum placed in five of the windows blow-ups of iconic images it has in its collection or that it has displayed in traveling exhibits. The museum collects, preserves, and displays historic and contemporary works by nationally and internationally known artists. Exhibits have included Paris in the 1930s by Brassai, and portraits by Andy Warhol. The museum also offers photographic programs and workshops to the community.

GLAZER CHILDREN'S MUSEUM

110 West Gasparilla Plaza, 813/443-3861, http://glazermuseum.org
HOURS: Mon.-Fri. 10 A.M.-5 P.M., Sat. 10 A.M.-6 P.M., Sun. 1-6 P.M.
COST: $15 adult, $12.50 senior and military, $9.50 child, free child younger than 1
Map 1

For decades, MOSI was *the* place to take the kids. But in the fall of 2010, Glazer Children's Museum, a challenger of sorts, opened on the downtown waterfront, and it has enjoyed instant success. As a matter of fact, Glazer met its original attendance estimate of 200,000 in the first nine months it was opened—without the benefit of the summer vacation period.

Financed by the community-minded Glazer family (owners of the Tampa Bay Bucs football team as well as the acclaimed Manchester United soccer club), this children's museum boasts more than 170 of what are termed "interactivities," aimed at a relatively young crowd, say elementary school and younger.

Kids can learn what X-rays show at the pretend veterinarian's clinic, slide down a mini firefighter's pole at the firehouse, pretend to steer different kinds of commercial ships, or just get creative making sculptures out of damp noodles. There are 12 themed areas on two levels, and a host of special events on weekends and during the summer months.

GREAT EXPLORATIONS CHILDREN'S MUSEUM

1925 4th St. N., St. Petersburg, 727/821-8992, www.greatexplorations.org
HOURS: Mon.-Sat. 10 A.M.-4:30 P.M., Sun. noon-4:30 P.M.
COST: $10 general admission 1-54 years, $9 senior, free child 1 and younger
Map 9

After spending time at Sunken Gardens, give the kids their due next door at Great Explorations, where the mission is to "stimulate learning through creativity, play and exploration." The hands-on science center fills its 24,000 square feet with lots of slick educational exhibits on things like the hydrologic cycle or ecosystem of the estuary. Many of the exhibits are best appreciated by late elementary–aged kids (let's say kids up to about 11), but exhibits such as Gears and the Laser Harp have appeal even to little kids. And most every child can help overcome a fear of the dark by crawling through the 100-foot-long, dark-as-midnight,

ARTS AND LEISURE

Touch Tunnel, passing mini-obstacles, inclines, and differing textures. Great Explorations makes a fun afternoon, especially when capped by an ice cream at Coldstone Creamery, craftily located on the premises.

HENRY B. PLANT MUSEUM

401 W. Kennedy Blvd., 813/254-1891,
www.plantmuseum.com
HOURS: Tues.-Sat. 10 A.M.-5 P.M., Sun. noon-5 P.M.
COST: $10 adult, $7 senior and student, $5 children 4-12
Map 1

Looking regal yet totally out of place with its minarets, keyhole arches, and ornate Moorish revival architecture, the Henry B. Plant Museum is housed in the dramatic hotel that railroad baron Henry B. Plant built in 1891 at a cost of $2.5 million, with an additional $500,000 for furnishings. Its 511 rooms were the first in Florida to be outfitted with electricity. It operated as a hotel until 1930 and now houses the University of Tampa. The museum consists of opulent restored rooms with original furnishings that provide a window on America's Gilded Age, Tampa's history, and the life and work of Henry Plant. The best time to see it is at Christmastime, when the rooms are bedecked for the season with elaborately trimmed trees, lush greenery, antique toys, and Victorian-era ornaments. There is special pricing for the Victorian Christmas Stroll.

HERITAGE VILLAGE

11909 125th St. N., Largo, 727/582-2123,
www.pinellascounty.org
HOURS: Wed.-Sat. 10 A.M.-4 P.M., Sun. 1-4 P.M.
COST: Free
Map 9

The history buff can visit restored pioneer homes and buildings of Heritage Village. It's a living history kind of thing with people roaming around purposefully in period costume, spinning, weaving, and whatnot. There also are permanent and temporary exhibitions of artifacts from the settling days in this area. Most of the 28 structures—houses, stores, a school, a mill—date to the late 19th century, decades before what would become Pinellas County was sliced off Hillsborough to the east. If you go to Heritage Village, make a day of it and visit the work-in-progress Florida Botanical Gardens at Pinewood Cultural Park nearby.

THE MOREAN ARTS CENTER

719 Central Ave., 727/822-7872,
www.moreanartscenter.org
HOURS: Mon.-Sat. 10 A.M.-5 P.M., Sun. noon-5 P.M.
COST: Free
Map 6

The Morean Arts Center has a long-standing focus on work by area artists as well as many out-of-town names, sometimes international. Its 5,000 square feet of gallery space are divided into six small galleries, plus classroom space for ceramics, painting, drawing, digital imaging, photography, printmaking, jewelry-making, metalworking, and sculpture classes. A few years back, new life was breathed into what was then named the Arts Center when a local philanthropist donated $10 million to establish, one mile away, the only permanent exhibition of glass artist Dale Chihuly's works outside his Washington-state studio area. The Morean and Chihuly collection are part of the resulting St. Petersburg Arts Experience, as are studios and display areas for glass and clay artists. A combination ticket includes all these venues.

MOSI

4801 E. Fowler Ave., 813/987-6300, www.mosi.org
HOURS: Mon.-Fri. 9 A.M.-5 P.M., Sat. and Sun. 9 A.M.-6 P.M.
COST: $21.95 adult, $19.95 senior, $17.95 child age 2-12
Map 4

Tampa's Museum of Science & Industry (MOSI) is a wonderful resource for local schools, family vacationers, or local parents when they're just out of clever ideas. It's a sprawling (400,000 square feet), modern structure that contains more than 450 hands-on activities grouped into learning areas. There's some goofy stuff (the Gulf Coast Hurricane Chamber, which really just blows a bunch of loud air), but ignore that and head to the High Wire Bicycle, the longest high-wire bike in a U.S. museum, which allows visitors to pedal while balanced on a one-inch steel cable suspended 30 feet above ground (the bike is counter-balanced so as not to tip, but there is a net below). The exhibit The Amazing You teaches all about the human body. The museum hosts traveling exhibits as well. Part of a sleek squadron of indoor Virtual Reality fighter-jet rides, the two-seater FS2000 Jet Fighter Simulator ($5 in addition to admission price) allows "pilots" to control the sharp banks, sky loops, and screaming dives of pulse-pounding aerial combat. The museum has an IMAX domed screen—way cool—and hosts traveling exhibits as well.

If you time your visit to allow some cooler temperatures, the free-flying butterfly garden is a treat, with microscopes, magnifying glasses, and chemistry stations.

MUSEUM OF FINE ARTS

255 Beach Dr. NE, 727/896-2667, http://fine-arts.org
HOURS: Mon.-Sat. 10 A.M.-5 P.M., Sun. 1-5 P.M.
COST: $17 adult, $15 senior and military with ID, $10 college student and child age 7-18, free for child 6 and younger
Map 6

In 2008, the Museum of Fine Arts unveiled its much-anticipated Hazel Hough Wing. It started with a gangbuster exhibition of works that have been rarely on view or, in some cases, never before displayed at the MFA. Featuring works by such noted artists as Renoir, Leger, Pissarro, Matisse, Faberge, Chuck Close, and James Rosenquist, it showcased just how marvelous the museum's collection is. Right on

the waterfront adjacent to Straub Park, the museum contains the gamut of art from antiquity to the present day. The collection of 4,000 objects includes significant works by Cézanne, Monet, Gauguin, Renoir, Rodin, Henri, Bellows, Steiglitz, and O'Keeffe. Its permanent collection's strength is 17th- and 18th-century European art, and photography. The museum has a lovely garden as well and an underappreciated café.

SALVADOR DALÍ MUSEUM

1 Dali Blvd., 727/823-3767, www.thedali.org
HOURS: Mon.-Wed. and Fri.-Sat. 10 A.M.-5:30 P.M., Thurs. until 8 P.M., Sun. noon-5:30 P.M.
COST: $21 general, $19 senior, $15 student and child age 13-17, $7 child age 6-12, free for child 5 and under
Map 6

Perhaps the most lauded art museum in Pinellas County, it's the world's most comprehensive, private collection of permanent works by the famous Spanish surrealist master, with other exhibits relating to Dalí. The museum has a number of his important surrealist works, what he described as a "spontaneous method of irrational knowledge based on the critical and systematic objectivation of delirious associations and interpretations." Although he's identified strongly with the movement, in 1934 Dalí was formally expelled from the surrealist Group of Paris with a mock trial (some of the reason for his expulsion had to do with an unsavory enthusiasm for Adolf Hitler). But after he came to the United States (a trip paid for by Picasso), he embarked on his classical period, characterized by what he called nuclear mysticism.

In 2011, the collection got a new, $36-million, waterfront home, said to be able to protect the collection of more than 2,400 items from even a Category 5 hurricane. It is a great space, with a double-helix staircase leading to the upper-level galleries. The works are elegantly annotated and curated, though it's smart to latch on to one of the free, docent-led tours. Even the

COURTESY OF VISITSTPETECLEARWATER.COM

Museum of Fine Arts

gift shop is a trip: melting clocks and elephants with spiders' legs are just a few fun items there.

ST. PETERSBURG MUSEUM OF HISTORY
335 2nd Ave. NE, 727/894-1052, www.spmoh.org
HOURS: Tues.-Sat. 10 A.M.-5 P.M., Sun. 1-5 P.M.
COST: $12 general, $9 senior, $6 student and child age 7-17, free for child 6 and younger
Map 6

It is one of the oldest historical museums in the state, with family-friendly displays and exhibits depicting St. Petersburg's past. Recently remodeled and enlarged, the museum displays a Native American dugout canoe, a cannonball fired by Union sailors toward the home of a Confederate resident, a replica of the world's first scheduled commercial airliner (it flew out of St. Petersburg across the Bay to Tampa, with the mayor as a paying passenger), and lots of other cool stuff. Recent exhibits have ranged from the local homefront during World War II to a traveling exhibit of

artifacts of Princess Diana, Queen Elizabeth II, The Queen Mother, the Duke and Duchess of Windsor (King Edward VIII and Mrs. Wallace Simpson), Prince Charles, and other royals. Not sure what that last one had to do with St. Petersburg, but it was still nice.

TAMPA BAY AUTO MUSEUM
3301 Gateway Centre Blvd., Pinellas Park, 727/579-8226, www.tbauto.org
HOURS: Mon. and Wed.-Sat. 10 A.M.-4 P.M., Sun. noon-4 P.M.
COST: $8 adult, $6 senior, $5 student, free for child 6 and younger
Map 9

Opened in 2005, this 12,000-square-foot space showcases a unique collection of vintage cars and vehicles that demonstrate special creativity and imagination in their history and engineering. They include pioneering front-wheel-drive and rear-engine cars from the 1920s and 1930s, with each vehicle chosen

be fairly miserable in high season. There are several other roads that provide alternate routes: **International Drive** parallels I-4 just to the east and is a long strip of hotels, shopping, restaurants, and other attractions. **Highway 192** (known as Irlo Bronson Memorial Highway in parts) runs east/west, from Walt Disney World Resort in the west through Kissimmee and St. Cloud to the east. Several other local roads—Florida's Turnpike, Central Florida Greeneway (Hwy. 417), and Osceola Parkway—are toll roads, so be sure to have cash in the car.

By Air

Orlando International Airport (1 Airport Blvd., Orlando, general information 407/825-2001, parking information 407/825-7275, www.orlandoairports.net) is located nine miles southeast of downtown Orlando, at the junction of Highway 436 (Semoran Blvd.) and Highway 528 (Bee Line/Beach Line Expwy.). Serving more than 35 million passengers annually, with 898 commercial flights each day, it's a big, orderly, easy-to-use airport serving 51 airlines.

The Nature Coast

The Nature Coast is the rebuttal to Orlando's Disney slickness. Civic-minded boosters have tried to sell this area as "Mother Nature's theme park," but that moniker doesn't quite work. Nothing here is marketed, packaged, or sanitized by crackerjack public relations specialists. It's rural, with the majority of the area set aside as parkland, preserves, reserves, and animal refuges.

In the weathered fishing villages along the coast and the quaint little inland towns, you're likely to see a spiffy fishing boat in every driveway, but you're just as apt to see a dead pickup truck up on blocks in the yard. Residents stay for the affordable living, for the area's easy live-and-let-live tolerance, for the unhurried pace, and—for many, the most important reason—the fish. And that's pretty much why visitors come, too. People drive here to see manatees, black bears, and wading birds; to catch fish; and to dive, to kayak, or to simply contemplate the area's wealth of waterways. There are no white-sand beaches crowded with bikini-clad college kids, no swanky nightclubs with throbbing VIP rooms. From north of Clearwater all the way to the Big Bend (where the Florida peninsula tucks west into the Panhandle), there are precious few multiplexes, museums, or high-fallutin' cultural attractions. All that would get in the way of enjoying one of the least developed stretches of Florida's Gulf Coast.

SIGHTS
Tarpon Springs

There are more than 10,000 species of fresh- and saltwater sponges, simple multicellular animals that sit quietly feeding on plankton and warding off enemies with little toxin-tipped spikes. They are not, as recent cartoons may indicate, loud and obnoxious with a weakness for physical comedy. Still, for some reason, since before the birth of Christ we have been hauling them out of the deep and using their skeletons to clean behind our ears or wipe up a mess.

These days Tarpon Springs, a coastal town 15 miles due north of Clearwater, is more about the *idea* of sponges than actual sponges. Since the 1950s and the advent of synthetic sponges, the Greek sponge divers who populated this town have been largely reemployed as fisherfolk, restaurateurs, and tour boat captains.

Sponge diving had been a family business in Greece at the end of the 19th century, with naturally adept swimmers assisted by rubber suits and heavy copper helmets to which air was pumped via hose. John Corcoris brought the

based on the engineering achievements that made it an important part of the evolution of the automobile. Many of the 44 vehicles are from European companies.

TAMPA BAY HISTORY CENTER

801 Old Water St., 813/228-0097,
www.tampabayhistorycenter.org
HOURS: Daily 10 A.M.–5 P.M.
COST: $12 adult, $10 senior and student age 13–17, $7 child age 4–12, free for child 6 and younger
Map 1

The Tampa Bay History Center's recently finished 60,000-square-foot home in the Channelside district was Hillsborough County's $17 million effort to celebrate the Tampa Bay area's history in the larger context. The permanent exhibits explore 500 years of recorded history and 12,000 years of human habitation in the region. Native Americans and Spanish conquistadors, pioneer settlers and cigar workers, immigrants and cowboys, military and sports heroes all get their 15 minutes in the two floors of exhibit space and the lobby-level gallery and theater. Temporary exhibits are on the third floor. The onsite Columbia Café makes a killer Cuban sandwich.

TAMPA MUSEUM OF ART

120 W. Gasparilla Plaza, 813/274-8130,
www.tampamuseum.org
HOURS: Mon.-Thurs. 11 A.M.–7 P.M., Fri. 11 A.M.–8 P.M., Sat.-Sun. 11 A.M.–5 P.M.
COST: $10 adult, $7.50 senior, military, and Florida teacher, $5 student, free for child 5 and younger; free Fri. 4–8 P.M.
Map 1

You wouldn't think a midsized city art museum could spark so much controversy. And it's not the good kind of controversy, an exhibit of Robert Mapplethorpe's provocative photos, say, or Jeff Koons' Cicciolina sculptures, or anything else that used to get Jesse Helms hot under the collar. For years, the Tampa Museum

of Art has been poised to go somewhere and no one could agree on its destination. Several plans were scrapped entirely, but in 2007, after about 10 years of to-ing and fro-ing, there was a breakthrough. Everyone agreed on a site: in the downtown Curtis Hixon Park, adjacent to a parking garage and overlooking the Hillsborough River. And they agreed on an architect: Stanley Saitowitz from San Francisco. And they agreed on a plan: It has 66,000 square feet, including eight galleries totaling 14,000 square feet.

The facility opened in January 2010 to raves. It now has ample space, in a handsome building, to display changing exhibitions ranging from contemporary to classical. It elegantly showcases its own permanent collection of Greek and Roman antiquities, 20th- and 21st-century sculpture, paintings, photography, and works on paper.

TAMPA POLICE MUSEUM

411 N. Franklin St., 813/276-3392
HOURS: Mon.-Fri. 10 A.M.–3 P.M.
COST: Free
Map 1

Located next to the Tampa Police Department headquarters, it's a sweet little museum that honors fallen officers and preserves historically important records, books, uniforms, guns, and other police equipment. It's especially poignant for visiting law enforcement folks, but kids of all stripes will enjoy the on-site police car, motorcycle, and helicopter.

UNIVERSITY OF SOUTH FLORIDA CONTEMPORARY ART MUSEUM

4202 E. Fowler Ave., 813/974-4133, www.usfcam.usf.edu
HOURS: Mon.-Fri. 10 A.M.–5 P.M., Sat. 1–4 P.M.
COST: Free
Map 4

University of South Florida is an enormous institution, casting its imposing shadow on the cultural scene of Tampa. The visitor, however,

ARTS AND LEISURE

may have little reason to walk around the less-than-picturesque campus. A visit to the Contemporary is a good excuse to drive around the university before parking at the small gallery. USFCAM maintains the university's art collection, comprised of more than 5,000 art works. There are exceptional holdings in graphics and sculpture multiples by internationally acclaimed artists, such as Roy Lichtenstein, Robert Rauschenberg, and James Rosenquist, who have worked at USF's acclaimed Graphicstudio, which allows artists to perfect techniques and explore new media. Contemporary photography and African art are also important areas of this museum's collection. The museum also hosts USF student art shows and oversees sight-specific public art projects on campus.

YBOR CITY MUSEUM STATE PARK

1818 E. 9th Ave., 813/247-6323, www.ybormuseum.org
HOURS: Daily 9 A.M.–5 P.M.
COST: $4 general, free for child 5 and younger
Map 3

The Ybor City Museum State Park is a state historic park consisting of the Ybor City Museum, housed in the Ferlita Bakery building (a neighborhood bakery operated by the Ferlita family, Italian immigrants who established the business at that location in 1896), the casita (an old cigar-worker home), and the garden. The park contains permanent exhibits on Vicente Martinez Ybor, a founder of the community, and early history of Ybor City, the cigar industry, the social clubs of the city, and the Ferlita Bakery itself. Watch a cigar-rolling demonstration (Fri.–Sun. 11 A.M.–1 P.M.). Tours of the casita begin every 30 minutes between 10 A.M. and 3 P.M. And there's a new downloadable audio tour (the two dozen narrators are longtime Tampa residents, some going back four generations) as well as a self-guided walking tour with maps that takes you through this neighborhood, a National Historic Landmark District.

GALLERIES

AIA TAMPA BAY

200 N. Tampa St., Ste. 100, 813/229-3411,
www.aiatampabay.com
HOURS: Mon.-Fri. 9 A.M.-5 P.M.
COST: Free
Map 1

The regional chapter of The American Institute of Architects exhibits work by local and regional architects/artists including photography, paintings, sculpture, and furniture. Its aim is to promote awareness, interest, and understanding of the architecture profession in the Bay Area; call to make sure an exhibit is on display. The group also hosts arts events around the city; check the website for listings.

BAISDEN GALLERY

442 W. Grand Central Ave., No. 100, 813/250-1511,
www.baisdengallery.com
HOURS: Tues.-Thurs. noon-4 P.M., Fri. 11 A.M.-3 P.M., Sat. noon-4 P.M.
COST: Free
Map 1

Located right next to Mise en Place, one of the area's nicest restaurants, this 2,000-square-foot space features three galleries of rotating exhibits, focusing most strongly on influential contemporary glass art as well as contemporary paintings and photography.

BLEU ACIER

109 W. Columbus Dr., Tampa, 813/272-9746,
www.bleuacier.com
HOURS: Sat. 1-5 P.M. and by appointment
COST: Free
Map 5

While Bleu Acier exhibits works in all media, it specializes in mid-career European artists and emerging American artists. Owner Erika Greenberg-Schneider has a special interest in intaglio, photogravure, lithography, photolithography, relief, and monotype, acting as a

COURTESY OF THE CRAFTSMAN HOUSE

Craftsman House

publisher to produce limited editions and multiples of artists' work.

CRAFTSMAN HOUSE

2955 Central Ave., St. Petersburg, 727/323-2787, www.craftsmanhousegallery.com

HOURS: Mon.-Sat. 10 A.M.-6 P.M., Sun. 11 A.M.-4 P.M.

COST: Free

Map 9

Set in a charming 1918 arts and crafts bungalow, the gallery features a selection of fine craft and artwork from more than 300 national and local artisans in clay, blown glass, jewelry, and wooden handcrafted furniture. Visitors can observe artists at work in the converted carriage house pottery studio, explore the garden art courtyard, or have a nibble in the café.

FINN GALLERY

176 4th Ave. NE, 727/894-2899, www.finngallery.com

HOURS: Mon.-Fri. 10 A.M.-6 P.M., Sat. 10 A.M.-5 P.M.

COST: Free

Map 6

Located along the waterfront near the Museum of Fine Arts, this gallery shows originals, reproductions, and limited editions of works by former city resident P. Buckley Moss as well as work by several other accomplished artists. White walls and glossy wood floors provide an intimate forum for enjoying Moss's paintings of nature, farm life, and family and friends.

FLORIDA CRAFTSMEN INC.

501 Central Ave., 727/821-7391, www.floridacraftsmen.net

HOURS: Mon.-Sat. 10 A.M.-5:30 P.M.

COST: Free

Map 6

For more than half a century, this has been Florida's only statewide nonprofit organization representing thousands of Florida's established and emerging fine craft artists. It is supported by the state and the city. The gallery in the heart of downtown has about 2,000 square feet

ARTS AND LEISURE

SECOND SATURDAY GALLERY WALK

St. Petersburg Downtown Arts Association, representing more than 30 art galleries and other downtown businesses, hosts a monthly event to give the public the chance to view art (sometimes first showings) after hours and meet with some of the artists. Part of the recent surge in art galleries downtown has been a corresponding increase in classes. Jumping to the front of the line in the past decade is a collection of galleries and studios that are part of the Morean Arts Center. Its major exhibit is the Chihuly Collection of that master artist's works.

But that's just the rose icing on this cake. Also available are studios that can be visited and a variety of lessons for working in clay and even blowing glass. Each has the requisite shop selling those artworks created in the city and immediate area.

The **Morean Center for Clay** (420 22nd St. S., St. Petersburg, 727/821-7162, www.moreanartscenter.org, Tues.-Sat. 10 A.M.-5 P.M., lessons at various times) is part of a larger ceramics beehive that occupies an old railroad warehouse. More than a dozen classes for all skill levels are offered here, pretty much on a weekly basis; prices vary by class.

The **Glass Studio & Hot Shop** (719 Central Ave., St. Petersburg, 727/822-7872, www.moreanartscenter.org, daily noon-5 P.M., classes at various times and prices) provides demonstrations of glassblowing. Visitors can reserve a one-on-one, 30-minute lesson ($75) in creating their own glass object.

---

of space to display works for sale, and a similar amount of room for exhibitions. There are also 18 studios, and the Florida Craftsmen hosts workshops and educational programs. The facility is especially delightful around the winter holidays, with seasonal crafts of all kinds.

SCARFONE/HARTLEY GALLERY AT UNIVERSITY OF TAMPA

310 N. Boulevard, 813/253-6217, www.ut.edu/scarfonehartleygallery
HOURS: Tues.-Fri. 10 A.M.-4 P.M., Sat. 1-4 P.M.
COST: Free
`Map 1`

A university teaching gallery, the Scarfone/Hartley functions as an extension of the classroom in all media. The galleries provide an opportunity to meet artists and view and study original works created by contemporary national, international, and regional artists including students and faculty.

THE STUDIO@620

620 1st Ave. S., 727/895-6620, www.studio620.org/620

HOURS: Tues.-Sat. noon-4 P.M.
COST: Varies by performance
`Map 6`

Brainchild of artistic directors David Ellis and Bob Devin Jones, this tiny yet ambitious space plays host to performance art, visual art exhibitions, theater, music, and special events, including some of the more avant-garde arts happenings in the Tampa Bay area. From spoken-word open-mike nights to socially-conscious documentary films, refugee youth photography exhibits, and shows of local printmakers, the city of St. Petersburg is that much more sophisticated for having 620 in its midst. It's small, but it packs a punch.

THEATER

AMERICAN STAGE THEATRE

163 3rd St. N., 727/823-7529, www.americanstage.org
HOURS: Curtain usually Tues.-Thurs. 7:30 P.M., Fri. and Sat. 8 P.M., weekend matinees 3 P.M.
COST: $35-47
`Map 6`

At the top of the dramatic arts heap in Pinellas County, American Stage is Tampa

American Stage Theatre

Bay's oldest professional theater, with a six-play mainstage season, children's theater, and educational outreach.

In its 29th year in 2007, American Stage announced that it had entered into a partnership with St. Petersburg College to build a brand new state-of-the-art building in the heart of downtown St. Petersburg, facing Williams Park. The new American Stage Theatre Company at the Raymond James Theatre opened its season in 2009 and has scored record ticket sales to match its usually positive reviews. American Stage presents its Mainstage Series (reaching from the Tony Award-winning *Wit,* to *The Vagina Monologues* and Shakespeare's works) in the 182-seat Raymond James Theatre year round and the annual American Stage in the Park each spring. The theater's other programming includes: "After Hours" series, school tour, and camps and classes for children.

CATHERINE HICKMAN THEATER

5501 27th Ave. S., 727/893-1070,
http://gulfportcommunityplayers.homestead.com
HOURS: Vary by performance
COST: Varies by performance
Map 7

In the little town of Gulfport on Boca Ciega Bay, the 178-seat Catherine Hickman Theater, owned by the city of Gulfport, hosts Gulfport Community Players community theater productions and Pinellas Park Civic Orchestra concerts. While the theater is not gorgeous to look at from the outside, it's an intimate size with sloped flooring for better viewing and an interior courtyard that's a lovely place to while away intermission.

DAVID A. STRAZ JR. CENTER FOR THE PERFORMING ARTS

1010 N. MacInnes Pl., 813/229-7827 or 800/955-1045,
www.strazcenter.org

ARTS AND LEISURE

HOURS: Vary by performance
COST: Varies by performance
Map 1

Just about the only game in town for performing arts, it's a huge arts complex housing four distinct theaters, in which audiences can see Opera Tampa (the resident company), the Florida Orchestra, comedies, dramas, cabaret, dance, music, alternative theater, children's theater, and an annual Broadway series. Most local arts series and events find a home at the performing arts center—Tampa Bay's Festival of Latin American art, Patel Conservatory's Tampa Bay Youth Orchestra Spring Concert. You name it, the curtain goes up here.

DAVID FALK THEATRE

428 W. Kennedy Blvd., 813/253-6243
HOURS: Vary by performance
COST: $17-30
Map 1

Operated by the University of Tampa, this facility is the site of student theatrical productions. The theater, built in 1928, is fully equipped and seats 1,000. There is no seniority; freshmen are allowed to audition for all productions in their first semester, so there's no telling what might happen. Recent productions have ranged from *Into the Woods* to *Schoolhouse Rock*.

FRANCIS WILSON PLAYHOUSE

302 Seminole St., 727/446-1360,
www.franciswilsonplayhouse.org
HOURS: Curtain 8 P.M. and matinees 2 P.M.
COST: Musicals $13-26, nonmusicals $11-21
Map 8

Francis Wilson Playhouse is a more venerable community playhouse, having opened in 1930. The intimate, 182-seat theater showcases eight comedies and musicals *(Plaza Suite, Pippin)* per season and a family-oriented program in December.

David A. Straz Jr. Center for the Performing Arts

THE PALLADIUM

253 5th Ave., N., 727/822-3590, www.mypalladium.org
HOURS: Vary by performance
COST: Varies by performance
Map 6

Located in what once was a church built in 1925 in the Romanesque revival style and now providing a range of community theater offerings, it's under the umbrella of St. Petersburg College. It hosts college functions but also acts as a community theater, with St. Petersburg Opera Company and other local performing arts agencies using the space. It's also used for musical acts from rock to jazz, chamber music to cabaret, the occasional stand-up comic, Elvis impersonator, and even a medium. There is no reserved seating.

© ROB/HARRIS PRODUCTIONS.

ARTS AND LEISURE

PROGRESS ENERGY CENTER FOR THE ARTS–THE MAHAFFEY

400 1st St. S., 727/892-5798, www.themahaffey.com

HOURS: Vary by performance

COST: Varies by performance

`Map 6`

The Mahaffey changed entirely in 2004 when it was determined that its Bayfront Center Arena was no longer viable in the marketplace. The arena, which had hosted Ringling Bros. Barnum and Bailey season-opening shows, minor league ice hockey, and indoor pro soccer, was demolished, opening up space for the current Mahaffey Theater renovation. The $20 million project more than doubled lobby size, adding guest amenities and expanding ballroom capacity and versatility. The signature component of the renovated theater is a three-story glass curtain wall and glass enclosed atrium that overlooks the beautiful downtown waterfront. A lovely 2,031-seat theater, it hosts touring Broadway shows, many performances of the Florida Orchestra, jazz, ballet, opera, and contemporary performers as well. Another $2 million touch-up was completed in November 2011. The Mahaffey is directly on the waterfront, within walking distance of its new neighbor the Dalí Museum, as well as shopping, fine restaurants, and many of the downtown's other museums.

RUTH ECKERD HALL

1111 N. McMullen Booth Rd., 727/791-7000, www.rutheckerdhall.com

HOURS: Vary by performance

COST: Varies by performance

`Map 8`

Ruth Eckerd Hall is the locus for much of the area's lively arts activity. The 2,200-seat space was designed by the Frank Lloyd Wright Foundation about 30 years ago and the space still looks fresh, the sound still full and lush (acoustically, it had an overhaul not long ago). It's home to the **Florida Orchestra** (mailing address 244 2nd Ave. N., #421, St.

COURTESY OF RUTH ECKERD HALL

Ruth Eckerd Hall

Petersburg, 813/286-2403), which is the top regional orchestra, performing more than 130 concerts annually here, at the Mahaffey Theater in downtown St. Petersburg, and elsewhere. Beyond symphonic music, Ruth Eckerd hosts pop and revival musical acts, stand-up artists such as Jerry Seinfeld and Bill Maher, visiting theater, and other performing arts. (Its educational wing, the Marcia P. Hoffman Performing Arts Institute, features a 182-seat Murray Studio Theatre for more intimate performances, three studio classrooms, four private teaching studios, a dance studio and rehearsal space, and an arts resource library.) Ruth Eckerd has joined with the City of Clearwater to raise funds to renovate the Capitol Theater, which opened in 1921 as a vaudeville and movie house, and still hosts occasional live performances and films.

ST. PETERSBURG CITY THEATRE
4025 31st St. S., 727/866-1973, www.splt.org
HOURS: Curtain 8 P.M. and matinees 2 P.M.
COST: $20 adult, $10 student and child
Map 7

Throughout its 88 (!) years as Florida's oldest continuously operating community theater, St. Petersburg City (formerly, Little) Theatre presents seven community productions per season, split fairly evenly between musicals, comedies, and dramas. They usually put on crowd-pleasers such as *A Streetcar Named Desire* or *Hairspray*.

CONCERT VENUES

COLISEUM
535 4th Ave. N., 727/892-5202,
www.stpete.org/coliseum
HOURS: Vary by performance
COST: Varies by performance; nominal fee for parking area
Map 6

The historic Coliseum was built in 1924 and purchased by the city of St. Petersburg in 1989.

They've gussied up the gorgeous space and reopened it as a multiuse facility, hosting a range of things from Florida Orchestra pops concerts to the Toronto All Star Big Band to an exotic bird show. It can hold 2,000 for a concert, 2,000 for a dance.

LIVE NATION AMPHITHEATRE AT THE FLORIDA STATE FAIRGROUNDS
4802 U.S. 301 N., Tampa, 813/740-2446
HOURS: Vary by performance
COST: Varies by performance
Map 5

A decade ago, Tampa welcomed the Ford Amphitheatre, a state-of-the-art venue for 30–40 big-league music concerts a year. At an expense of $23 million, the outdoor open-air theater was constructed with huge video screens, a 7,200-square-foot stage, 9,900 reserved seats, and room for 10,500 more on the lawn. It's gorgeous, like a huge circus tent mated with the *Millennium Falcon.* There are enough bathrooms and lots of fairly tasty food options.

The idea was that the amphitheater would host the myriad big-ticket acts that travel around the U.S. each year, but the problem is that all those big acts gear up to do outdoor shows in the summer. You do not want to go to an all-day show in Tampa in the middle of July. You could hurt something, or at the very least sweat through everything. The venue literature assures that the plastic cover on top shields the amphitheater from the sun and keeps it cool. No dice. Get 10,000 sweaty bodies grooving in 90°F heat at 90 percent humidity, and someone could pass out.

USF SUN DOME
4202 E. Fowler Ave., Tampa, 813/974-3111,
www.sundomearena.com
HOURS: Vary by performance
COST: Varies by performance
Map 4

This 55,000-square-foot multipurpose

entertainment/sports facility on the campus of the University of South Florida hosts 300 events each year, many of them USF Bulls men's and women's basketball and volleyball teams, but also lectures and political rallies (Desmond Tutu, John Kerry, Ron Paul—not all on the same bill), rock concerts (Elton John, Florence + the Machine), tae kwon do and MMA tournaments, garden shows, and more. The 10,000-seat facility underwent a $35 million update in 2011–2012.

CINEMA
AMC VETERANS 24
9302 Anderson Rd., Tampa, 888/262-4386, www.amctheatres.com
HOURS: Vary by show
COST: Varies by show and age of customer
Map 5

Most AMC Theater locations feature mainstream first-run movies served up in clean multiplexes with acceptable popcorn. The Veterans location occasionally shows more cerebral, art-house movies. For more mainstream film options try AMC's other locations at **AMC West Shore 14** (210 Westshore Plaza, Tampa, 888/262-4386) and **AMC Tri-City Plaza 8** (5140 East Bay Dr., Largo, 727/531-5796). Tickets can be purchased in advance via AMC's website.

BEACH THEATRE
315 Corey Ave., 727/360-6697, www.beachtheatre.com
HOURS: Vary by show
COST: Varies by show
Map 7

The St. Pete Beach Theatre is a historic landmark built in 1939 for about $50,000 by Boston financier Stephen Girard. Since then, it's operated continuously under a succession of owners (except briefly when German U-boats were spotted off the nearby Gulf coast and a blackout was ordered that shut down the theater for about 18 months), most recently screenwriter

Michael France. Continuing financial problems make the theater's future uncertain.

MUVICO THEATERS
Muvico Centro Ybor 20, 1600 E. 8th Ave., 813/242-0664, www.muvico.com
HOURS: Vary by show
COST: Varies by show and age of customer
Map 3

Muvico Theaters offer mainstream first-run movies served up in clean multiplexes with acceptable popcorn. Tickets can be purchased in advance via the website. Other locations include the **Starlight 20** (18002 Highwood Preserve Pkwy., Tampa, 813/558-9755) and the **BayWalk 20 and IMAX** (151 2nd Ave. N., St. Petersburg, 727/502-0965).

TAMPA PITCHER SHOW AND THE TAKE 2 LOUNGE
14416 N. Dale Mabry Hwy., Tampa, 813/963-0578, www.tampapitchershow.net
HOURS: Vary by show
COST: $7 adult, $6 child
Map 5

The idea is superb. Eat real food—as opposed to Milk Duds and Jordan Almonds—in the dark while watching a first-run movie. With craft beers, wine, or even hard cider. It's like what we do at home but with a few improvements: a) you don't have to shop, prepare, serve, or clean up the food, and b) the screen is much bigger. Still, the Tampa Pitcher Show has logistical problems. First off, if you're seated at a normal round or square table, someone is facing away from the screen. You have to sit in a line, but then the table isn't equally accessible for all. Really, you need those individual TV trays to make it all work. Second, you know how when you spill your M&Ms the whole floor at the movies is filled with a satisfying pinging noise and then a little crunchiness underfoot? Doesn't work as well with steak or mashed potatoes. The cinema, now about 30 years old, was on the brink of closure, but has been newly renovated and an upscale lounge with full liquor and dining service added. And in addition to the regular flicks, it has such niche offerings as a combo drag queen/bingo night, *Rocky Horror Picture Show,* stand-up comics, and audience participation in a live murder-mystery version of Clue.

◖ TAMPA THEATRE
711 N. Franklin St., 813/274-8981,
http://tampatheatre.org
HOURS: Vary by show
COST: $8
Map 1

Tampa has its share of multiplexes, but eschew the 20-screeners in favor of two hours in the dark at the Tampa Theatre. Built in 1926, it's a beloved downtown landmark with an acclaimed film series, concerts, special events, and backstage tours. They say the grand movie palace's decor is something called Florida Mediterranean, but it reads more vintage creepy rococo, with statues and gargoyles and intricately carved doors. Many believe that the theater is haunted by the ghost of Foster Finley, who spent 20 years as the theater's projectionist. So if you feel a hand in your popcorn, it may not be your seatmate's. Sometimes the films shown are classics, accompanied by the 1,400 pipes of the theater's Mighty Wurlitzer; other times they're more indie. Theater concessions include excellent popcorn, sophisticated candies, and beer and wine. Tampa Theatre was the first public building in Tampa to be equipped with air-conditioning.

Festivals and Events

WINTER
FLORIDA STATE FAIR
4800 U.S. 301 N., Tampa, 813/621-7821,
www.floridastatefair.com
Map 5

The Florida State Fair is a 12-days-in-February salute to the state's best in agriculture, industry, entertainment, and foods on a stick. Or any fried food, actually. It's been going strong since 1904, with more than 100 rides and shows spread across a 325-acre site. Recent additions include a ridiculously campy Las Vegas–style review, deep-fried fudge, something called a walking taco (um, really nacho chips in a bag with all the gunk tossed in), and an interactive livestock show called "Ag Venture." That's all fine and good, but the real draw is the nostalgic feel of 4-H youngsters showing off their prized chickens and such, or maybe the Elvis impersonation contest. Or the racing pigs. Or the grand line-up of country singers. Or...Shoot, there's something for most everyone.

FLORIDA STRAWBERRY FESTIVAL
2202 West Reynolds St., Plant City, 813/752-9194,
www.flstrawberryfestival.com
Map 5

February and March are busy months and are also the time for the county fair–like Florida Strawberry Festival, with a huge midway, national country acts, and lots of strawberry cook-offs. Plant City is known as the "Winter Strawberry Capital of the World," and these sweet babies are delicious. More than 5,000 acres of strawberries are planted annually. With an annual value of more than $400 million, Hillsborough County is one of the largest agricultural counties in the nation, producing—beyond strawberries—citrus, tomatoes, cucumbers, eggplant, squash, okra, peppers, beans, dairy products, eggs, ornamental horticulture, tropical fish, beef cattle, swine, and more. The Strawberry Festival is so grand it goes for 10 days, 12 hours a day. A real highlight is the strong line-up of country musical acts, often with matinees.

GASPARILLA FILM FESTIVAL

Ybor City, 813/514-9962, www.gasparillafilmfestival.com

Map 2

What passes for the dead of winter in Florida is a great time for the well-received Gasparilla Film Festival. It launched in 2006, and over a four-day weekend in early spring 2012 the festival drew more that 10,000 moviegoers. Tampa's always had its share of wonderful, smaller film festivals—Tampa International Gay and Lesbian Film Festival in October, the Independent Film Festival in September, even the Ybor Festival of the Moving Image—but Tampa remained the largest city in the country without a big annual film festival. Now the Gasparilla Festival, named for the beloved fictional pirate who is the focus of several outdoor parades and a flotilla "assault" each spring, takes place at venues in Ybor City, downtown Tampa, and elsewhere. In 2012, more than 120 films of various lengths were screened in a variety of genres: what they are calling Latin Panorama (films with a Latin twist); New Horizons (films that directly focus on the arts); Fun and Fear (a mix of comedies and horrors); short films; and special screenings of featured American indie films. Then spice it all up with a handful of industry panel discussions, VIP parties, glamorous dinners, and B-list celebrity sightings.

GASPARILLA PIRATE FEST

Ybor City and Downtown Tampa, 813/251-8844, www.gasparillapiratefest.com

Map 1

The biggest party in Tampa comes at the end of January and beginning of February with the Gasparilla Pirate Fest, a kooky celebration more than 100 years old. It honors legendary but fictional pirate José Gaspar, "last of the Buccaneers," who his supporters say terrorized the coastal waters of West Florida during the late 18th and early 19th centuries. The weekend festivities get underway when about 1,000 ersatz pirates sail into downtown on a fully rigged pirate ship, a replica of an 18th-century craft that is 165 feet long by 35 feet across the beam, with three masts standing 100 feet tall. The ship is met by a flotilla of hundreds of pleasure crafts intent on "defending the city," but there's enough grog being served everywhere that the little boats wind up as more a salutary flotilla. The upshot is that pirates take over Tampa for a while. After the mayor surrenders the city, there is an invasion brunch (which probably didn't really happen anywhere in Pirate Land). And then, like Mardi Gras only with more "argh, me matey" and eye patches, there is a long parade of floats and the mandatory bead-tossing. There is also a kiddies' parade on a different day. The length of Bayshore Boulevard is lined with bleachers for the occasion, musical acts sprout on stages all over town, and there's general merriment and carousing.

HOLIDAY BOAT PARADE

Downtown St. Petersburg, 727/821-6464, www.stpeteboatparade.org

Map 9

For a quarter of a century on the first or second weekend in December, boats from around Pinellas put on the dog, or at least the strings of lights. Come out to the North Straub Park, Vinoy Park, or the Pier on the downtown waterfront for a view of this annual illuminated festival. Boat owners assemble around the Harborage Marina, south of downtown, then motor through Bayboro Harbor and on to the Vinoy Yacht Basin. Events begin before noon, with children's activities, live music, and in the afternoon a chili challenge contested by about a dozen local restaurants.

The Honda Grand Prix of St. Petersburg takes place on a 1.8-mile, 14-turn course through downtown streets.

SPRING

BAY AREA RENAISSANCE FESTIVAL

11315 N. 46th St., Tampa, 800/966-8215,
www.bayarearenaissancefest.com
COST: $19 adult, $15 senior, $11 child age 5-12
Map 9

Jugglers, jousters, sorcerers, and turkey legs: In mid-February through early April, the annual Renaissance fair gives people ample time to celebrate in costumes before hot weather sets in. As a way to bring the Renaissance into step with current fads, there are theme weekends, such as Buccaneer Beer Fest; Wine, Chocolate, and Romance; and German Invasion: Halfway to Oktoberfest! Whatever stitches your tapestry.

HONDA GRAND PRIX OF ST. PETERSBURG

Downtown St. Petersburg, 727/898-4639,
www.gpstpete.com
Map 6

At the end of March or beginning of April, live concerts, family events, and a variety of sports exhibitions complement this open-wheel road race through the streets of St. Petersburg. Typically the St. Pete Grand Prix is the opening event for the IZOD IndyCar Series. Bring your earplugs or, better yet, your headphones tuned to the car-to-pit transmissions.

MAINSAIL ARTS FESTIVAL

Vinoy Park, 727/892-5885,
www.mainsailartsfestival.org
Map 6

Along the waterfront of downtown St. Petersburg, one of the most respected arts festivals in the country is held on a weekend in the second half of April, with participants from all over the country exhibiting their work. They compete, in all media, for about $50,000 in prize money.

SUMMER

ST. PETE PRIDE STREET FESTIVAL & PROMENADE

Downtown St. Petersburg, 727/279-5428, www.stpetepride.com

`Map 6`

Each year since 1993, the LGBT community and their supporters celebrate gay and lesbian pride and commemorate the bravery of the Stonewall rioters with a parade on the last Saturday of June. The St. Pete Pride has grown into one of the largest Pride events in the southeast and is the largest one in the state of Florida, with nearly 100,000 people taking to the streets. Local restaurants and bars follow suit with big celebrations, an excuse for nearly all of St. Pete to come out in support.

FALL

AIRFEST AT MACDILL AIR FORCE BASE

8415 Bayshore Blvd., Tampa, 813/828-7469, www.macdill-airfest.com

`Map 5`

One of the largest air shows in the Department of Defense, AirFest, usually held in November, features the U.S. Air Force Air Demonstration Squadron (the Thunderbirds) performing aerial maneuvers in their F-16 Fighting Falcons, plus flyovers and aerobatics by WWII planes, early and current fighter jets, and helicopters and precision drop-ins by military parachute teams. The event and parking are free. Although wildly popular with civilians, at times tension in the world has cancelled the show because MacDill is home to Central Command, the administrative office for the wars in Iraq and Afghanistan.

CLEARWATER JAZZ HOLIDAY

Coachman Park, 727/461-5200, www.clearwaterjazz.com

`Map 8`

Each year more than 50,000 visitors come to Coachman Park in downtown Clearwater during the third week of October to enjoy four days and nights of free jazz by some of today's greats. Now in its 30th year, the festival started as a 10-day music jam held in the back of a flatbed truck.

GUAVAWEEN

Ybor City, 813/241-8838, www.ybor.org

`Map 3`

Tampa's second biggest party is not unlike Gasparilla for its focus on wild costumes and wilder revelry. Guavaween is the city's Cuban-style Halloween celebration, held on the Saturday closest to that holiday. Riffing on the fact that Tampa was nicknamed "The Big Guava," the celebration features the Mama Guava, who has sworn to take the "bore" out of Ybor (EE-bore) City. Really, after the Mama Guava Stumble, a night parade, is over, revelers use it as a big excuse to drink too much and wander the streets of Ybor City in preposterous attire. Live music, costume contests...and did we mention drinking?

STONE CRAB FESTIVAL

Frenchy's Restaurants, 727/449-2729, http://frenchysonline.com

`Map 8`

Stone crab season opens mid-October, celebrated each year with a Stone Crab weekend in which visitors and locals plow through 10,000 pounds of claws (you eat only one of each beast's claws because fisherfolk haul 'em up, yank off one claw, and throw the crabs back to grow another). Eat the claws like the locals: chilled (it's gauche to ask for them hot) with mustard sauce. The venerable Frenchy's restaurants now number four, and the festival is celebrated at all.

Recreation

BEACHES

◀ CALADESI ISLAND STATE PARK

Directly to the south of Honeymoon Island, accessible only by boat, 727/469-5918; ferry 727/734-1501, www.floridastateparks.org/caladesiisland

HOURS: Daily 8 A.M.-sunset

COST: $6 per boat for up to eight people, $2 per kayaker; ferry $14 adult, $7 child age 6-12

Map 9

Of Honeymoon and Caladesi, Caladesi is the wilder of the two islands. There's the state park marina and swim beach right near where the ferry lets you off, but the rest of the island remains undeveloped. The Gulf side of the island has three miles of white-sand beach (this is the part that always makes the top rankings of beaches), and the bay side has a mangrove shoreline and sea grass flats. So, Gulf side for swimming and beach lolling, the bay side for birding and wildlife watching. You'll see lots of beautiful creatures, but the most entertaining are the armadillos, which are so myopic they may walk right over your shoe if you're very still, like a bunch of befuddled, yet armored, Mr. Magoos.

If you're a strong kayaker or sailor, there are kayak and sailboat rentals on the causeway near Honeymoon Island. Once on Caladesi, there's a 3.5-mile canoe trail starting and ending at the south end of the marina that leads paddlers through mangrove canals and tunnels and along sea grass flats on the bay side of the island.

Two cautions about Caladesi: Don't miss the last ferry or you'll be in a real pickle. And if you have brought a dog over to the dog beach at Honeymoon, it's a shame but Caladesi doesn't allow pets on the ferry (if you go by private boat, pets are invited on leash).

CLEARWATER BEACH

West on Hwy. 60, www.clearwater-fl.com/info/about/ geography/beaches.asp

HOURS: Year-round lifeguards daily 9:30 A.M.-4:30 P.M.

COST: Free; metered parking

Map 8

When you conjure in your mind a Florida Gulf Coast beach, it's Clearwater you're imagining. These are textbook stretches of white sand and clear, warm, Gulf water, with lots of comfy beachside hotels and waterside amenities for families. The area is home to a couple of world-class beach destinations, the kinds of places that often make the annual Top 10 list issued by Dr. Stephen Leatherman ("Dr. Beach" has been ranking America's beaches for about 15 years).

A fairly urban city beach, Clearwater Beach is the only Pinellas County beach with year-round lifeguards. It is a miles-long, wide stretch offering showers, restrooms, concessions, cabanas, umbrella rentals, volleyball, and metered parking. **Pier 60,** where the beach meets the causeway, is the locus of lots of local revelry and activity; during the day, it's a heavily trafficked fishing pier, while at night the focus is Sunsets at Pier 60, a festival that runs nightly two hours before sunset to two hours past sunset, with crafts, magicians, and musicians all vying for your attention with the ostentatious sunset display over the Gulf of Mexico. Pier 60 also contains a covered playground for the little ones, who will also like catching the bright red Jolley Trolley ($4.50 unlimited daily pass) from Clearwater Beach and heading back to your hotel, downtown, or to Sand Key.

Clearwater Beach has a few rules to follow: No alcohol on the beach. Swim within the "safe bathing limit" area, extending 300 feet west of the high water line and clearly marked by

Clearwater Beach

buoys or pilings. Jet Skis and boats are not allowed within this line. Clearwater Beach is a good beach if you just have a couple of hours to spend; many of the area's other best beaches require more of a commitment and are more of a full-day adventure.

EGMONT KEY STATE PARK

At the mouth of Tampa Bay, southwest of Fort de Soto Beach, St. Petersburg, 727/893-2627, www.floridastateparks.org/egmontkey

HOURS: Daily 8 A.M.-sunset

COST: Free

`Map 9`

Accessible only by ferry or private boat, Egmont Key makes a great day trip. There aren't a lot of facilities on the island, which is wild except for the ruins of historic Fort Dade and brick paths that remain from when it was an active military post with 300 residents. You'll see the 150-year-old working lighthouse (constructed in 1858 to "withstand any storm" after a first

one was savaged by two hurricanes in 1848 and 1852), gun batteries built in 1898, a pretty stretch of beach, and lots of gopher tortoises and hummingbirds. There is no camping on Egmont Key.

FORT DE SOTO STATE PARK

3500 Pinellas Bayway S., Tierra Verde, 727/552-1862, www.fortdesoto.com

HOURS: Daily sunrise-sunset

COST: $5 parking

`Map 9`

South of St. Petersburg, Fort De Soto Park is an embarrassment of riches, with 1,136 unspoiled acres, seven miles of beaches, two fishing piers, picnic and camping areas, a small history museum, and a 2,000-foot barrier-free nature trail for guests with disabilities, set on five little, interconnected islands. The fort itself is in the southwest corner of Mullet Key. The islands were once inhabited by the Tocobaga and were visited by Spanish explorers in the 1500s. It was surveyed by Robert E. Lee before the Civil War, and during the war, Union troops had a detachment on both Egmont and Mullet Keys. The fort was built in 1898 to protect Tampa Bay during the Spanish-American War and is listed on the National Register of Historic Places. And during World War II, the island was used for bombing practice by the pilot who dropped the bomb on Hiroshima. But you thought we were talking about beaches, right?

Well, exploring the old fort is part of what makes this experience special (hey, it was named top beach by TripAdvisor in 2009 and a few years earlier by Dr. Beach), drawing more than 2.7 million visitors annually. After fondling the four massive seacoast rifled mortars (the only ones of their kind in the United States), head on to one of the two swim centers, the better of which is the North Beach Swim Center (it has concessions). At the beach, you're likely to see laughing gulls, ibis, and ospreys, as well as beach sunflowers and beach morning glories peeking out from the sea oats. Fishing enthusiasts can choose between the 500-foot-long pier on the Tampa Bay side or the 1,000-foot-long pier on the Gulf side. Each has a food and bait concession.

Once in the park, take a right at the stop sign, go one mile, and on the right look for **Topwater Kayak** (3500 Pinellas Bayway S., Tierra Verde, 727/864-1991, daily 9 A.M.–6 P.M., last rental at 3:30 P.M., single kayak $23/one hour, $29/two hours; canoes $30/one hour, $40/two hours; bike rentals are available inside the park, $6/hour, $20/day, cash only). It also issues maps of the area. Numbered signs along the shore mark a 2.25-mile kayak trail through Mullet Key Bayou.

Fort de Soto Park has the best camping in the area, with campsites ($34/night, RV spots $40) directly on the Gulf. There are 236 sites. But here's the rub for visitors. Most of the 236

Fort De Soto State Park

campsites require reservations, which can be made six months in advance. There are a handful of walk-in campsites available, but they are hot commodities. All sites have water and electrical hookups, and there are modern restrooms, dump stations, a camp store, washers/dryers, and grills. Pets are allowed in Area 2 and some of the spots are directly on the water. Be advised: the resident raccoons are more dexterous than most, able to pick cooler locks and unwrap lunch meat with aplomb.

◖ HONEYMOON ISLAND STATE PARK
1 Causeway Blvd., west end of Hwy. 586, Dunedin, 727/469-5942
HOURS: Daily 8 A.M.–sunset
COST: $8 for up to eight people per car, $4 single occupant, $2 pedestrian and bicyclist
Map 9

Honeymoon Island and Caladesi Island are perfectly suited for visiting back to back. In fact, the two islands were once part of a single larger barrier island, which was split in half during a savage hurricane in 1921. Together, these state parks offer nearly 1,000 acres of mostly undeveloped land, not too changed from how it looked when Spanish explorers surveyed the coast in the mid-1500s.

The Tocobaga were the first known residents of Honeymoon Island. First known as Sand Island, then more inelegantly as Hog Island, Honeymoon got its current name in the early 1940s when marketing folks tried to pitch it as a retreat for newlyweds, with little palm-thatched bungalows and cottages. It didn't quite take, stymied also by World War II, and the island went through several ownership changes before becoming a state park.

Honeymoon Island offers visitors all kinds of fun activities. The fishing is especially good—you're likely to catch flounder, snook, trout, redfish, snapper, whiting, sheepshead, and, occasionally, tarpon. The island is home to 208 species of plants and a wealth of shore

and wading birds, including a few endangered bird species.

The pet beach is also recommended, for those who've brought their pets with them.

PASS-A-GRILLE BEACH
1000 Pass-a-Grille Way, 727/363-9247
HOURS: Always open
COST: Metered parking $1.25 per hour or $5 per day
Map 7

Pass-A-Grille Beach is at the southern end of the string of barrier islands, at the tip of the beach communities. It was one of the first public beaches on Florida's west coast and the area's first resort, dating from the late 1800s. It's still considered one of the loveliest, with more than a hint of the bohemian amongst the locals. Small shops, snack bars, and restaurants are located along the coast, making this a pleasant place to catch some rays and have a refreshing drink in the shade when the sun gets too hot. From here there's shuttle service out to unspoiled Shell Key. You can also get a free ride in a sort of golf-cart-on-steroids; just tip the driver when you're at your destination.

ST. PETE BEACH
Gulf Blvd.
HOURS: Daily 24 hours
COST: Metered parking
Map 7

St. Pete Beach has a livelier vibe than many Gulf Coast beaches, but not quite a spring break magnitude of sybaritic indulgers; that's more likely at Clearwater Beach. The beach is long and re-nourished, sand-wise. There are concessions, picnic tables, lots of parking, showers, and restrooms. In all, it's a very nice day at the beach.

To the north of St. Pete Beach along Gulf Boulevard, there are a number of other good beaches along the barrier island of **Sand Key,** which contains the eight communities between St. Pete Beach and Clearwater Pass. **John's**

ARTS AND LEISURE

Pass Beach, at the southern end of Sand Key and running north for a couple of miles into **Madeira Beach,** has beautiful sand and good fishing. Going north, the beaches in **Redington Beach** have limited public access but are pretty. Still farther north, **Indian Rocks Beach** has good public access and a party vibe (lively beach bars). Bypass the beaches in **Belleair,** as access and amenities are very limited, in favor of an afternoon at **Sand Key County Park** (1060 Gulf Blvd., this is the north end, at Clearwater Pass), which has lifeguards (Mar.–Sept.), playgrounds, cabana rentals, and lots of wide, white-sand beach.

PARKS

ANCLOTE KEY PRESERVE STATE PARK
1 Causeway Blvd., Dunedin, 727/469-5942
HOURS: Daily 8 A.M.–sunset
COST: Free
`Map 9`

You've got to want it, but this set of four small islands, accessible only by private boat or ferry, is a treat. More than 43 species of birds call it home, or at least temporary asylum, and there's a lovely 1887 lighthouse still standing on the southern end of the island, not doing much of anything, sort of like the human visitors. Camping overnight is free, there are grilling and picnic facilities, and the fish (snook, sea trout, and mullet) in these waters seem eager to please. For ferry service, contact **SunLine Cruises** (Tarpon Springs, 727/944-4468) or **Sponge-O-Rama** (Tarpon Springs, 727/943-2164).

BOYD HILL NATURE PRESERVE
1101 Country Club Way S., St. Petersburg, 727/893-7326, www.stpete.org/boyd
HOURS: Tues.–Fri. and Sun., 9 A.M.–7 P.M., Sat. 7 A.M.–7 P.M.
COST: $3 adult, $1.50 child age 3-16; $2 tram tour
`Map 9`

It's about 245 acres of pristine Florida wilderness, with five distinct ecosystems: hardwood hammocks, sand pine scrub, pine flatwoods, willow marsh, and the Lake Maggiore shoreline. This city park is a favorite, as it is incredibly convenient, just minutes from downtown, but it nonetheless feels far from the madding crowds. Precious green space in an urban landscape, it is an important stopover on the Atlantic flyway: 165 bird species have been observed here. You can cycle or stroll miles of paths, camp, and wander through the small educational center with its exhibits on the five ecosystems and a living history settlement demonstrating the hard life of Floridians in the late 19th century. One of those hardships still thrives in Lake Maggiore: You're practically guaranteed to see gators gliding in the water or sunning on the banks. Please observe them from a distance, and if there are little gators near the mama, leave quickly. She is super-protective of her hatchlings.

BROOKER CREEK PRESERVE
3940 Keystone Rd., Tarpon Springs, 727/453-6800, www.friendsofbrookercreekpreserve.org
HOURS: Trails: daily 7 A.M.–about one hour before sundown
COST: Free
`Map 9`

For a rough-and-ready nature experience, drive up to Brooker Creek Preserve, an 8,500-acre wilderness in the northern section of the county near Tarpon Springs. Currently, its environmental education center offers four miles of self-guided hiking trails at the southern end of Lora Lane off of Keystone Road, about 0.5 miles east of East Lake Road. The preserve also offers two-hour guided hikes every Saturday (reservation required, 727/453-6800), and it hosts the annual **Run in the Woods** in April, the area's only walk/run that is completely cross-country through beautiful backwood pinelands and prairies. This land is the habitat for deer, otter, wild turkey, bobcat, coyote, a variety of orchids, birds, and butterflies.

Brooker Creek Preserve is an 8,500-acre wilderness area northeast of Clearwater.

HILLSBOROUGH RIVER STATE PARK

15402 U.S. 301 N., Thonotosassa, 813/987-6771,
www.floridastateparks.org/hillsboroughriver

HOURS: Daily 8 A.M.–sunset

COST: $6 for up to eight people per car, $4 single
occupant, $2 pedestrian and cyclist; $24 camping

Map 5

One of Florida's original state parks, built
in 1938 by the Civilian Conservation Corp,
the park is home to Fort Foster, a replica of
a Second Seminole War fort; it is open for
guided tours on Saturdays and Sundays ($2
fee). The Fort Foster Visitor Station houses a
display of artifacts from that period and re-
counts the operation of the fort. The park's
Rapids Nature Trail meanders through oak
hammocks to the edge of the Hillsborough
River at the point where an outcropping of
limestone rocks has created rapids, a popular spot for photographers. The park rents canoes and offers 112 campsites, picnic areas,
an accessible swimming pool, pavilions, and
the Hillsborough Park Pool Side Café and
Gift Shop.

LETTUCE LAKE REGIONAL PARK

6920 E. Fletcher Ave., 813/987-6204

HOURS: Daily 8 A.M.–7:30 P.M. in spring and summer,
daily 8 A.M.–5:30 P.M. in fall and winter

COST: $2 per vehicle, with up to eight occupants

Map 4

For a bit of unmediated nature that's close to
civilization, head to Lettuce Lake Regional
Park, just northeast of the University of South
Tampa. It's a stone's throw from urban sprawl,
but don't hold that against the park. The
dense wilderness shelters a 3,500-foot-long
raised boardwalk and a tower overlooking the
Hillsborough River, a perfect place from which
to spy on tall wading birds, gators lurking
amongst cypress knees in the swamp, or even
delicate orchids and other epiphytes nestled in
the trees' crooks. Rent a canoe for a closer look
at the creatures that call this tannin-tinged

ARTS AND LEISURE

COURTESY OF VISITSTPETECLEARWATER.COM

WALKING AND OTHER ON-LAND TOURS

Get spooked during **Downtown St. Petersburg Ghost Tours** (300 Beach Dr., in front of the Hooker Tea Co. and Café, St. Petersburg, 727/894-4678, www.ghosttour.net, daily 8 P.M., $15 adult, $10 child age 4-12), a 75- to 90-minute, candlelit walking tour of the city's most haunted places, led by a guide in a creepy, Halloween-appropriate costume.

Bayside Tours (at the St. Petersburg Museum of History, 335 2nd Ave. NE, St. Petersburg, 727/896-3640, www.gyroglides.com, $30-50) offers 60- and 90-minute tours of the city on Segways. With speeds of up to 12 mph, they can be used in pedestrian areas and are a perfect way to cover serious ground at a pace slow enough to really appreciate things. Headgear and a lesson are provided.

You can rent a bicycle, tricycle, or other stylin' wheeled vehicle for a jaunt around downtown St. Petersburg from **Wheel Fun Rentals** (800 2nd Ave. NE, St. Petersburg, 727/820-0375, www.wheelfunrentals.com, daily). Guided tours are also available.

Sawgrass sees thousands of birds migrate through the 333-acre park during the fall and spring. A one-mile elevated boardwalk winds through a maple swamp and oak hammock. There are also a half-mile, graded, dirt trail through drier land and a great two-story observation tower offering views of the swamps, canals, and lake, where you're likely to see wood storks, herons, egrets, and ibis, in addition to gators, turtles, and the occasional snake. The park has naturalist-led nature tours and field trips, and its Anderson Environmental Center contains a large freshwater aquarium and exhibits on the area. Note that during the wet months it can get a bit flooded in this park.

If you find an injured bird in your wandering, call **Suncoast Seabird Sanctuary** (18328 Gulf Blvd., Indian Shores, 727/391-6211, www.seabirdsanctuary.com, daily 9 A.M.–sundown, free), one of the country's largest nonprofit hospitals for wild birds. With a relatively new medical facility, the sanctuary rescues and releases hundreds of birds each year into the wild. The sanctuary, founded in 1971, offers a free tour every Wednesday and Sunday at 2 P.M., meeting at the beachfront deck.

water home, hike the fully accessible boardwalk or dirt trails (no dogs on the boardwalks), then settle in for a picnic at one of the waterfront shelters, equipped with barbecues. A children's playground, restrooms, and water fountains make this swath of nature very civilized indeed.

SAWGRASS LAKE PARK

7400 25th St. N., west of I-275, St. Petersburg, 727/217-7256, environmental center 727/526-3020, www.pinellascounty.org/park/16_sawgrass.htm
HOURS: Daily 7 A.M.–sunset
COST: Free
Map 9

A spot on the Great Florida Birding Trail, also lauded by the National Audubon Society,

SNEAD ISLAND AND EMERSON POINT PARK

5801 17th St. W., Palmetto, 941/776-2295
HOURS: Daily 7 A.M.–sunset
COST: Free
Map 9

Owned by the State of Florida and maintained by the Manatee County Conservation Lands Management team, Snead Island is just east of Egmont Key (south of Pinellas County), a good excuse to tramp around in nature. Fifteen miles of it borders shoreline along the Gulf and the lovely Manatee River. The park is favored by hikers because of its variety of trails and loops, with occasional boardwalks hugging the waterways.

BALLOONING

Up, up, and away in a beautiful hot-air balloon, and all you have to bring is a camera and your loved ones. Meet before dawn at a restaurant on the commerce strip of Dale Mabry, whereupon you are whisked into the **Big Red Balloon Sightseeing Adventures** (8710 W. Hillsborough Ave.; meeting place Mimi's Café, 11702 N. Dale Mabry, 813/969-1518, www.bigredballoon.com, 6-10 A.M. daily, year-round by reservation only, weather permitting, $185 adult, $160 child) van and taken to your agreed-upon launch site (there are more than 30 in the greater Tampa area from which to choose). Once inflated, the various red balloons rise to between six and eight stories tall—the largest one is the biggest balloon in the Southeast. The balloons, which accommodate 4-10 passengers, take a one-hour sunrise flight at up to 1,000 feet, drifting over New Tampa, southeast Pasco County, Lutz, and Land O' Lakes. A champagne toast followed by a hearty breakfast back at Mimi's is included in the price.

During the champagne toast in the landing field, the pilot recites a traditional balloonist prayer, "The winds have welcomed you with softness, the sun has left you with warm hands, you have flown so high, and so well, that God has joined you in your laughter, and set you gently back again into the loving arms of Mother Earth." Feel free to join in.

Snead Island is home to Emerson Point Park, which is worth tacking on to your adventure: The park's 365 acres of salt marshes, beaches, mangrove swamp, lagoons, grass flats, hardwood hammocks, and semi-upland wooded areas are viewable from a well-maintained eight-foot-wide shell path, as well as more rustic walking and biking paths. Manatee County has poured money into this park in recent years such that master gardeners convene here regularly for guided walking tours of the varied plant and animal life. Call 941/722-4524 to find out the tour schedule.

Of special note to Native American historians, Emerson Point Park is home to the **Portavant Temple Mound** (east end of 17th St. W.), an impressive mound complex. Walkways and boardwalks take you over and around a huge, 150-foot, flattop temple mound and several horseshoe-shaped shell middens. Interpretive markers explicate the site.

WEEDON ISLAND PRESERVE CULTURAL AND NATURAL HISTORY CENTER

1800 Weedon Dr., St. Petersburg, 727/453-6500, www.weedonislandpreserve.org
HOURS: Preserve open daily 7 A.M.-15 minutes before sunset; cultural center open Thurs.-Sat. 9 A.M.-4 P.M.
COST: Free
Map 9

Extending along the west side of Tampa Bay in Pinellas County, Weedon Island Preserve is an odd bird, an attraction hard to classify exactly. It's more than 3,700 acres on a group of low-lying islands in north St. Petersburg that, as long as 10,000 years or so ago, was home to Timucuans and Manasotas. The largest estuarine preserve in the county, it is also home to a large shell midden and burial mound complex. Visitors to the cultural center can see artifacts excavated from the site by the Smithsonian in the 1920s in exhibits designed collaboratively by anthropologists, historians, and Native Americans.

But you can't spend all your time at the cultural center watching videos about the art and history of the early peoples of Weedon Island, nor even information on the area's brief use as a movie studio in the early part of the 20th century (the sunlight was mandatory for good cinematography in those days). The park has six miles of canoe trails (watch for manatees, dolphins, wading birds, and—yikes!—sharks). On land there are almost two

ARTS AND LEISURE

SCALING NEW HEIGHTS

John Gill is said to be the father of modern bouldering. It used to be that serious rock climbers would, on occasion, undertake a climb without a rope. Considered more a mental exercise in problem solving, this ropes-free style of climbing gained purchase in the 1950s, legitimized as a sport by Gill and others. As the name implies, these climbs might be practiced on large boulders or rock faces, but can be done just as easily indoors at a climbing center. These kinds of climbs are often referred to as "problems."

So then you could say that **Vertical Ventures** (5402 Pioneer Park Blvd., Ste. E, Tampa, 813/884-7625, www.verticalventures. com, Tues.-Thurs. noon-10 P.M., Fri. noon-midnight, Sat.-Sun. 10 A.M.-6 P.M.) is here to help you solve your problems.

"People are into minimalist things these days, so bouldering is the rage now," says Christian Tartaglia, co-owner of Florida's first climbing gym and Tampa's only indoor rock-climbing facility. "Bouldering tends to be a more gymnastic or dynamic style of climbing. There are no ropes or gear, so even the beginner can start off bouldering. It doesn't go quite as high."

The 6,000 square feet of professionally designed climbing surface focuses on both of the two main kinds of climbing: bouldering and "top roping," a two-person climbing system that includes a belayer on the ground who holds the safety rope around the climber.

Either style can be quickly understood by the rookie climber. Both bouldering and top roping require shoes ($5 rentals) and chalk ($2), while top ropers will also need a harness ($4 rentals).

For the newcomer, a beginning belay class ($35) teaches the basics: knots, tying in to the rope, and belaying a climber. You'll learn climbing commands necessary for top-roped climbing and basic climbing techniques. Then you're on your own for climb time: you, your partner, ropes, and a whole lot of wall.

---

miles of handicapped-accessible boardwalk and paved path (no bikes allowed), a 45-foot-tall observation tower, a fishing pier (snook, redfish, spotted trout), and waterfront picnic facilities. Weedon Island Preserve Center offers guided nature hikes every Saturday and regularly scheduled guided canoe excursions (for registration, call 727/453-6506).

BIKING
FLATWOODS PARK
14302 Morris Bridge Rd., 813/987-6211
HOURS: Daily sunrise–sunset
COST: Suggested donation $1
Map 4

Flatwoods is an 11-mile paved loop that takes riders near baby feral pigs, armadillos, sidewinding snakes, big red grasshoppers with carapaces like lobsters, and sometimes suave blue birds that we think are indigo buntings. If you don't have a bike, you can walk it, hike it, or skate it. This 5,400-acre pine flatwoods

and cypress swamp make up one of the five parks that comprise the Wilderness Park system (the others are Trout Creek, Dead River, Morris Bridge, and John B. Sargeant Memorial Park). For more great rides in Tampa, visit oliverscycles.com—it's a local bike shop that unfortunately doesn't rent bikes.

PINELLAS TRAIL
1st Ave. S. and 1st St., park ranger 727/582-2100, www.pinellascounty.org
HOURS: Daily sunrise–sunset
COST: Free
Map 9

The 37-mile-long Pinellas Trail is one of the longest linear parks in the southeastern United States, running essentially from Tampa Bay in downtown St. Petersburg up to the sponge docks of Tarpon Springs. A rails-to-trails kind of deal, the original rail track was home to the first Orange Belt Railroad train in 1888, and is now a well-maintained, 15-foot-wide trail through parks and coastal areas for bikers, in-line skaters, and joggers. There is a free guide to the Pinellas Trail available at the trail office, area libraries, and the Pinellas County Courthouse Information Desk (it can also be downloaded online). It lists rest stops, service stations, restaurants, pay phones, bike shops, and park areas along the trail. The trail is not illuminated and should only be used during daylight hours.

Now you just need to rent a bike. **Chainwheel Drive** (1770 Drew St., Clearwater, 727/441-2444; and 32796 U.S. 19 N., in Palm Lake Plaza, Palm Harbor, 727/786-3883, Mon.–Fri. 10 A.M.–7 P.M., Sat. 10 A.M.–5 P.M., Sun. 11 A.M.–5 P.M., $24 for four hours for hybrids, $40 for a full day with a road bike), with two locations, will rent you bikes, and a rack so you can load them up.

CANOEING

CANOE ESCAPE
12702 U.S. 301, Thonotosassa, 813/986-2067, www.canoeescape.com
COST: Self-guided rentals $46–69
Map 5

You want to see big gators? Great blue herons the size of the Wright brothers' first plane? River otters, turtles, families of wild pigs? Paddle down the gently flowing Hillsborough River in a 16,000-acre wildlife preserve called Wilderness Park. You can rent canoes or kayaks and head out on your own, choosing from six day-trip combos. All paddling adventures start at Canoe Escape. Whether you go on a guided tour or on your own, call ahead, then drive to their building. Staff will equip you, give you maps and paddling pointers, then take you over to your debarkation point (all paddles are downstream), and establish a pickup time.

The Sargeant Park to Morris Bridge Park is a two-hour paddle, 4.5 miles long, with 70 percent shade and alternating sun and shade. Morris Bridge Park to Trout Creek Park is a two-hour, four-mile paddle, with 80 percent shade and a little full sun at the end. From Trout Creek Park to Rotary Park it's 5 miles of full-sun paddling, about two hours, whereas Sargeant Park to Trout Creek Park is a longer, 8.5-mile paddle with the first 75 percent in the shade. Morris Bridge Park to Rotary Park is a long, 9-mile route, and Sargeant Park to Rotary Park is for experienced paddlers only, with 14 miles of river to paddle.

If solo paddling seems daunting, Canoe Escape offers a 4.5-mile interpreted guided tour ($50 pp for two-person canoe, $75 pp for solo kayak). This is recommended for the newcomer to the area because the guides' vast knowledge of the local flora and fauna enrich the trip immeasurably. Rental prices include shuttle fee, paddles, and life vests.

FISHING

SUNSHINE SKYWAY FISHING PIERS
South on I-275 toward Bradenton; North Pier, 727/865-0668, South Pier, 941/729-0117, www.skywaypiers.com
HOURS: Daily 24 hours
COST: $4 per vehicle, plus $4 per adult (12 years and older), $2 for child age 6–11, free for child 5 and younger; sightseeing fee $3/hour
Map 9

In 1990, Hardaway Constructors of Tampa and a demolition team from Baltimore joined forces to perform the largest bridge demolition in Florida history. They were doing away with the old Sunshine Skyway Bridge, which had opened in 1954 as a 15-mile crossing from St. Petersburg to Bradenton. From a long causeway on both sides, the steel bridge had a steep cantilever truss, 750 feet wide and with 150 feet of clearance above the water.

It wasn't enough clearance.

There had been some indication of this: At least five freighters or barges were roughed up by this bridge, most of them with minor damage. But it was during a violent storm on May 9,

1980, that empty phosphate freighter *Summit Venture* slammed into the No. 2 south pier of the southbound span. It knocked 1,261 feet out of the center span, the cantilever, and part of the roadway into Tampa Bay. Thirty-five people on the bridge at the time perished. The only victim who survived had his truck fortuitously land on the deck of the *Summit Venture*.

One of the worst bridge disasters in U.S. history, it prompted the design, funding, and building of the new Sunshine Skyway Bridge. At a cost of $245 million, it's the world's longest

BOATING AND FISHING TOURS

Scurvy Steve, Barracuda Brandi, Gangplank Gary, and the other pirates will greet you with an "argh, me matey" on the deck of **Captain Memo's Original Pirate Cruise** (25 Causeway Blvd., Dock 3, Clearwater Beach, 727/446-2587, daily 10 A.M., 2 P.M., and sunset cruises, hours vary seasonally, $36 adult, $31 senior and child age 13-17, $26 child age 3-12, $11 child 2 and younger), a two-hour voyage on a fancy bright red pirate ship. In a similar vein, another pirate ship sails from **John's Pass Village & Boardwalk** (12901 Gulf Blvd. E., between Madeira Beach and Treasure Island, 727/423-7824, www.thepirateshipatjohnspass. com, Mon.-Sat. 2 P.M. and sunset, call for Sun. departures, $35 general, $30 senior, $25 child age 2-10, $10 child 1 and younger). The Royal Conquest offers a **Pirates at the Pass** cruise on a fully kitted out pirate ship. You'll engage in water pistol battles and treasure hunts and listen to pirate stories. Prices for both ships include wine, beer, and soft drinks.

Families also seem to enjoy the dolphin tours out of John's Pass and into scenic Boca Ciega Bay. **Hubbard's Sea Adventures** (departs from 150 John's Pass boardwalk, 727/393-1947, www.hubbardsmarina.com, daily 1 P.M., 3 P.M., and 5 P.M., $16.82 adult, $8.41 child age 3-11, free for child 2 and younger) brings you face-to-face with the bay's breadth of wildlife.

Farther south, **Dolphin Landings** (4737 Gulf Blvd., behind the Dolphin Village Shopping Center, St. Pete Beach, 727/360-7411, www. charterboatescape.com, sailing times vary, $35) conducts 2-hour dolphin-watch cruises and longer 3-4-hour trips to Shell Key, an undeveloped barrier island. The scheduled trips and private charters are conducted on one of 40 locally owned sailboats, pontoon boats, and deep-sea fishing yachts.

Dolphin Queen (800 2nd Ave. NE, St. Petersburg, 727/647-1538, www.stpetepier.com/ adventure.asp, 11:30 A.M., 1 P.M., 3 P.M., and 5 P.M., Feb.-Aug.; 1 P.M., 3 P.M., and 4:30 P.M., Sept.-Jan.; $25 adult, $19 military and senior, $14 child age 3-12, free for child 2 and younger) offers 90-minute cruises of Tampa Bay on a 44-foot catamaran.

Shell Key Shuttle (Merry Pier, 801 Pass-a-Grille Way, St. Pete Beach, 727/360-1348, www. shellkeyshuttle.com, $22 adult, $12.50 child 12 and younger) leads low-impact ecotours on the unspoiled small barrier island preserve on Shell Key. Guests enjoy shelling, sunbathing, swimming, and bird- and dolphin-watching. Take a picnic lunch and rent beach umbrellas and snorkel gear. There are three departure and return times.

Sweetwater Kayaks (6331 39th St. N., Pinellas Park, 727/570-4844, $55 with rental) does full-day wildlife tours via kayak. Scoot through mangrove tunnels right by big lurking gators. Sweetwater also arranges custom adventure tours for groups and multiday outings.

Offshore Sailing School (The Harborage at Bayboro, 1110 3rd St. S., St. Petersburg, 800/221-4326, www.offshoresailing.com, starts at $1,295) is a tremendous amount of fun: three days on the water with an instructor and three other students, plus hours of classroom time learning all the sailing jargon, parts of the boat, and points of sail. At the end of the class you take a fairly difficult 80-question test, then get out and show your sailing chops to your teacher, complete with man-overboard demonstrations and doing a quick stop-by "shooting" into the wind. You learn on a midsize day sailer, a Colgate 26, designed specifically for training and chosen by the U.S. Naval Academy to replace their training fleet. Courses are for beginners, racers, and cruisers; there's also a basic keelboating class.

cable-stayed bridge, with a main span of 1,200 feet and a vertical clearance of 193 feet. The four-mile bridge opened for business in April 1987, equipped with a bridge protection system built to withstand an impact from rogue freighters and tankers.

After the construction of the new bridge, the old bridge spans were demolished, except for portions of it that were preserved as fishing piers.

Since the original bridge span was built, fisherfolk have been bragging about the variety of game they catch: shark, tarpon, goliath grouper, kingfish, Spanish mackerel, grouper, snapper, and sea bass. Usually you have to be in a boat in order to have water deep enough for many of these species. Anglers have even caught 1,000-pound tiger sharks from the bridge. With the artificial reefs adding extra enticement, the Sunshine Skyway Fishing Piers are killer fishing spots.

There's a 0.75-mile-long North Pier and a 1.5-mile-long South Pier, together said to be the world's longest fishing pier. You can drive your car onto the pier and park it right next to your fishing spot. There are restrooms on both piers, and bait shops sell live and frozen bait, tackle, drinks, and snacks. They also rent rods. The North Pier has a large picnic area next to the bait shop. You don't need a fishing license to fish off the piers.

FISHING CHARTERS
Map 9

Inshore trips may yield snook, tarpon, Spanish mackerel, king mackerel, cobia, sheepshead, red snapper, and others. Offshore, you're more likely to catch gag or black grouper, amberjack, sea bass, triggerfish, red snapper, and gray snapper. Offshore, bottom, inshore, or even surf-casting: There are lots of people around here with enormous experience willing to take you

COURTESY OF VISITSTPETECLEARWATER.COM

ARTS AND LEISURE

fishing in the waters of Pinellas County

SMOKIN'

Here's a tricky scenario. You're on a great Gulf Coast vacation, the weather's perfect, you're feeling relaxed, so you decide to do a little charter fishing. You're out on the boat, you feel a yank, and there's a 40-pound greater amberjack on your line. You work a while and haul in a couple more of those and a whole mess of 20-inch Spanish mackerel. What a great day. But now what? Are you going to take that fish cooler back to your hotel and stink up the joint?

Here's what to do. Go to **Ted Peters Famous Smoked Fish** (1350 Pasadena Ave. S., South Pasadena, 727/381-7931, Wed.-Mon. 11:30 A.M.-7:30 P.M., $10-20, no credit cards) and they'll smoke the fish for you for $1.50 per pound. They can even make kingfish taste good, and that's saying something. They fillet them, throw them over a smoldering red oak fire in the smokehouse, then package them up for you to take. (The smoked fish keeps for 4-5 days in the fridge.)

out on a saltwater charter or just hook you up with gear. Oh, and the area's rivers offer decent freshwater fishing for catfish, bass, and bream. And many restaurants in the area are amenable to cooking your fresh catch.

The price of a private charter averages $150–165 per hour (inflated gas prices are hiking that up) for up to six people. Many boats only accommodate six people, so make clear how many people are in your party. You can also sign up for a group charter, pooling with other people who are looking to go out (the prices are the same, you just split it between all the people on the boat). Obviously, you have to find others who are simpatico in terms of what they're fishing for and how long they want to be out. Rod, reel, bait, and fishing license are usually included, but bring your own drinks and lunch.

Hubbards's Marina (150 John's Pass, Boardwalk, Madeira Beach, 727/393-1947,

www.hubbardsmarina.com, from $50 pp) is one of the old-time, reliable companies, offering daily half- and full-day deep-sea charters, with a meal ticket option available. Reservations are required. For something much more low key **The Pier Baithouse** (800 2nd Ave. N., on The Pier, St. Petersburg, 727/821-3750, Sun.–Thurs. 9 A.M.–8 P.M., Fri.–Sat. 9 A.M.–9 P.M.) rents poles, bait, and buckets for fishing from The Pier. The staff can also arrange private fishing charters.

SHUFFLEBOARD
ST. PETERSBURG SHUFFLEBOARD CLUB
559 Mirror Lake Dr. N., 727/822-2083,
http://stpeteshuffle.com
HOURS: Fri. 7–11 P.M.
COST: Free; membership $21.40
Map 6

Shuffleboard used to be so popular that St. Pete boasted 150 clubs. It may have the reputation for being aimed at an older crowd, but you could be in elementary school or college and find peers at the venerable St. Petersburg Shuffleboard Club. Closing out its ninth decade, the club is a throwback to slow-paced fun. Consider: It predates not just iPods but talking movies. You can BYOB, but imbibe responsibly.

BETTING AND DOG RACING
DERBY LANE
10490 Gandy Blvd., St. Petersburg, 727/812-3339,
www.derbylane.com
HOURS: Mon.-Sat. 6:30 P.M., Wed. and Sun. 11:30 A.M. for greyhound racing
COST: Free
Map 9

This is the oldest greyhound track in the country, opened in 1925. With year-round live greyhound racing, daily simulcast racing, a poker room (which recently underwent a $2.5 million renovation), and dining buffet, this is one-stop shopping for those who court Lady Luck. The track is said to be one of the fastest in the country, made up of sand, with a stretch that is 458 feet long. The restaurant and lounge are open Friday and Saturday evenings.

TAMPA GREYHOUND TRACK

8300 N. Nebraska Ave., 813/932-4313, www.tampadogs.com
HOURS: Daily noon-midnight
COST: $2-4
Map 4

Tampa lost its dogs in 2007. Half the year, greyhounds used to thunder around the track after that elusive little bunny. These days it's a slightly seedy place to see simulcasting and to wager on thoroughbreds, trotters, jai-alai, and lots of stuff that capitalizes on the country's protracted mania for Texas Hold 'Em and other poker games.

SPECTATOR SPORTS

❰ NEW YORK YANKEES SPRING TRAINING

Legends Field, 1 Steinbrenner Dr., off N. Dale Mabry Hwy., Tampa, 813/673-3055, www.steinbrennerfield.com
HOURS: Vary by game
COST: Varies by game for N.Y. Yankees, $4-6 for Tampa Yankees
Map 5

Along much of the Gulf Coast, the Grapefruit League's spring training is a serious draw for sports fans each March. Since 1988, the New York Yankees have based their minor league operation, spring training, and year-round headquarters for player development in Tampa. Modeled after the original Yankee Stadium in the Bronx, Legends Field has been the Yankees' home since 1996. The complex houses a 10,000-seat stadium with 13 swanky luxury suites, a community-use field, and a major league practice field. It's also the home of the Florida State League Tampa Yankees (New York Yankees–Florida State League Single "A"

Affiliate) and the Hillsborough Community College Hawks baseball team.

PHILADELPHIA PHILLIES SPRING TRAINING

Bright House Field, 601 N. Old Coachman Rd., 727/712-4504, http://philadelphia.phillies.mlb.com
HOURS: Game days vary, times usually 1:05 or 7:05 P.M.
COST: Varies by game for Phillies, $5-9.50 for Clearwater Threshers
Map 8

The Philadelphia Phillies have been training in Clearwater since 1948. The excellent Bright House Networks Field was opened in 2004 and seats 8,500, though its popular food and drink venues, especially the tiki hut–style bar down the leftfield line, and the berms draw hundreds out of their seats. It also has a kids' play area, group picnic areas, party suites, and club seats. The Phillies' Florida State League Clearwater Threshers make this their summer home and offer constant promotions such as Thirsty Thursdays, when both the seats and the drinks are 2-for-1.

TAMPA BAY BUCCANEERS

Raymond James Stadium, 4201 N. Dale Mabry Hwy., Tampa, 813/870-2700, www.buccaneers.com
HOURS: Vary by game
COST: Single game tickets $30-400
Map 5

Raymond James (RayJay for short) is a wonderful venue in which to see Tampa's Buccaneers or the University of South Florida Bulls play. The Stadium, completed in 1998, holds more than 66,000 fans, 52,000 in general seating, but tickets can sell out for the Bucs' season opener and games featuring the NFL elite teams. Tickets for individual games are sold in person at TicketMaster outlets (813/287-8844, www.ticketmaster.com), not at the stadium or the Bucs' ticket office. The $168.5-million stadium features Buccaneer Cove, a 20,000-square-foot replica of an early 1800s seaport village, complete with a 103-foot-long, 43-ton pirate ship that blasts its cannons (confetti and foam footballs) every time the Bucs score. Well, six times for a touchdown, once for an extra point, twice for a safety or two-point conversion, and three times for a field goal.

Raymond James Stadium also plays host every New Year's Day to the **Outback Bowl** (813/287-8844, 1 P.M. kickoff, $75). The game matches the third-pick team from the SEC and the third-pick team from the Big Ten Conference and is the culmination of a week-long festival in Tampa.

TAMPA BAY LIGHTNING

Tampa Bay Times Forum, 401 Channelside Dr., 813/301-6600, http://lightning.nhl.com

HOURS: Vary by game

COST: $21.75-216

Map 1

The 21,000-seat Forum, on Tampa's downtown waterfront, is home to Tampa's

---

TEE TIME

GOLFING IN TAMPA

Tampa has a couple dozen public and semiprivate courses for the visitor to try. Many of them are located in Tampa's swankier northeast residential developments. Here are a handful of the area's top public courses (par and yardage from the men's tees, rates for the summer):

Babe Zaharias Golf Club (11412 Forest Hills Dr., 813/631-4374, www.babezahariasgc.com): 18 holes, 6,244 yards, par 70, course rating 68.9, slope 121, greens fee $15-42.

Heritage Isles Golf & Country Club (10630 Plantation Bay Dr., 813/907-7447): 18 holes, 6,236 yards, par 72, course rating 70.4, slope 133, greens fees $19-37.

Rocky Point Golf Course (4151 Dana Shores Dr., 813/673-4316, www.rockypointgc.com): 18 holes, 6,444 yards, par 71, course rating 72, slope 122, greens fee $16-23.

Rogers Park Golf Course (7911 N. Willie Black Dr., 813/356-1670, www.rogersparkgc.com): 18 holes, 6,802 yards, par 71, course rating 72.2, slope 121, greens fee $15-42.

TPC Tampa Bay (5300 West Lutz Lake Fern Rd., Lutz, 813/949-0090): 18 holes, par 71, 6,610 yards, course rating 73.6, slope 135, greens fees $59-159.

University of South Florida Golf Course ("The Claw," 13801 N. 46th St., 813/632-6893, www.theclawatusfgolf.com): 18 holes, 6,288 yards, par 71, course rating 72.1, slope 137, greens fee $20-30.

Westchase Golf Course (11602 Westchase Golf Dr., 813/854-2331, www.westchasegc.com):

18 holes, par 72, 6,233 yards, course rating 70.6, slope 127, greens fee $21-59.

If you are thinking about picking up the sport, the **Saddlebrook Golf Academy** (5700 Saddlebrook Way, Wesley Chapel, 800/729-8383, www.saddlebrook.com/golf.html) at the Saddlebrook Resort teaches golfers of all skill levels. Classes combine classroom and practice time with course play on surfaces designed to test specific skills. All training packages include accommodations, 18 holes of golf a day, instruction, meals, and use of resort facilities. There are two 18-hole Arnold Palmer-designed championship courses.

About 25 miles south of Tampa, the **Ben Sutton Golf School** (1007 Cypress Village Rd., Ruskin, 800/225-6923, www.golfschool.com) was the first American school devoted to golf instruction. There are two-, three-, four-, and six-day courses, plus three- and six-hour lessons.

GOLFING IN ST. PETERSBURG

Mangrove Bay and **Cypress Links** (875 62nd Ave. NE, St. Petersburg, 727/893-7800, www.stpete.org/golf, pro shop 6:30 A.M.-5 P.M., driving range 6:30 A.M.-7 P.M.) are two city-owned courses that sit right beside each other. Mangrove Bay is the better course, an 18-hole, 6,770-yard, par-72 facility that also includes a lighted practice range, pro shop, and lessons. Cypress Links is a nine-hole, par-three course. Hole lengths vary from 105 to 187 yards. It has its share of challenges, including lots of water.

National Hockey League team, the Tampa Bay Lightning. The team's owner financed a $40-million upgrade to the facility in 2011 to much praise from hockey fans. The Forum is also one of the busiest entertainment venues in North America, typically hosting 150 events a year (including the Republican National Convention in 2012). The Lightning regularly takes the ice to near-capacity crowds. Its season runs October–April.

█ TAMPA BAY RAYS

Tropicana Field, 1 Tropicana Dr., 727/821-9301, http://tampabay.rays.mlb.com
HOURS: Game days vary, times usually 1:10 or 7:10 P.M.
COST: $10.75-216 (includes buffet and beer, wine, soda)
`Map 6`

Tropicana Field is home to the Tampa Bay Rays (formerly the Devil Rays, but old Satan has been summarily excised). Talk of building a new ballpark somewhere in the Bay Area has been a controversial topic for the past few years. The Rays played their first season here in the domed stadium in 1998, and since then it has been named the second most fan-friendly stadium in the major leagues, according to a fan survey by Sports Travel Inc. On the other hand, loads of people grouse about it, especially the lack of traditional baseball aesthetics: As a concession to the summer's climate twins, high temperatures and humidity, the ballpark has a fabric roof (which is lit orange when the Rays win at home) and artificial turf. The dome is held in place by a series of catwalks over the field that figure in the ground rules, because they are hit by batted balls every season. When the Rays are not in the Trop, it hosts other athletic events (it has hosted an NCAA Final Four championship and NHL games), conventions (it was the site of the welcoming evening event for the 2012 Republican National Convention), trade shows, concerts, and other entertainment, with a seating capacity of 60,000. The seating for Rays games is more than 34,000.

Until 2008, for spring training, the Rays played less than two miles away, against Tampa Bay in the minor league **Progress Energy Park, Home of Al Lang Field.** Now they play in Port Charlotte, a dull 90-minute drive south, in the refurbished **Charlotte Sports Park** (2300 El Jobean Rd., Port Charlotte, 941/206-4487). Don't fret, though, because there is other spring training action nearby. Spring training games take place the whole month of March, and tickets usually go on sale January 15.

TAMPA BAY ROWDIES

Al Lang Stadium at Progress Energy Park, 230 1st St. SE, 813/287-1539, www.rowdiessoccer.com
HOURS: Vary by game, game time most often in the evening
COST: Season tickets $165-570, single-game seats $12-22
`Map 6`

Although the area's pro football, baseball, and hockey franchises have a far-greater following, the Rowdies soccer team is the area's oldest major-league team. And they may have the most devoted fans, or "fannies," as they have been cleverly termed since the lads began play in 1975, one year before the NFL's Bucs started. The Rowdies were born in an early effort to get Americans to embrace what was already the world's favorite team sport. The first Rowdies team—they have changed hands and leagues several times—began play in Tampa, in a football stadium that no longer exists. Along the way, the team played indoor soccer, using a dry ice hockey rink close to where they now play, in an outdoor baseball stadium.

TAMPA BAY STORM

Tampa Bay Times Forum, 401 Channelside Dr., 813/301-6600, www.tampabaystorm.com
HOURS: Vary by game

ARTS AND LEISURE

COST: $15-125 (includes buffet, beer, wine, soft drinks)

Map 1

The Tampa Bay Storm arena football team, nine-time ArenaBowl champs, plays at the Forum, adjacent to Channelside. Arena football is played on an indoor, padded, surface 85 feet wide and 50 yards long, with 8-yard end zones. (At the forum, this is atop the NHL rink used by the Tampa Bay Lightning.) There are eight players for each team on the field at a time, and most every player will play both offense and defense; exceptions include each team's kicker and quarterback, plus three "specialists." It's a dynamic game in a more intimate space than outdoor football and the Storm provides a good introduction to the game.

TORONTO BLUE JAYS
SPRING TRAINING

Florida Auto Exchange Stadium, 373 Douglas Ave., 727/733-0429, http://toronto.bluejays.mlb.com

HOURS: Game days vary, starting time usually 1:05 P.M.

COST: $13-24

Map 8

The Toronto Blue Jays also have spring training in the area, playing at the charmingly named Florida Auto Exchange Stadium, formerly Knology Park, formerly Dunedin Stadium. Built in 1990, it's a serviceable little ballpark, seating 5,509 in a fairly residential area (you end up paying almost as much for parking as for your ticket). There are upper and lower sections, the upper section having a slight overhang, which can be cooling during warm day games.

USF BULLS

Raymond James Stadium, 4201 N. Dale Mabry Hwy., 813/974-3002, www.gousfbulls.com

HOURS: Vary by game, both late afternoon and evening games scheduled

COST: $9-50

Map 5

The powers that be at University of South Florida made a judgment call a few years ago: They wanted the university to be big league, no longer a workhorse state school with a preponderance of commuting students. They've thrown money into the effort, constructing state-of-the-art academic buildings and housing, hiring prestigious senior faculty and promising junior profs. But maybe the single biggest indicator is the football team: The USF Bulls have gone from nonexistence to Division I-AA Independent to I-A to Conference USA, and into the Big East Conference. For the spectator, this means real college football is played during the fall at Raymond James Stadium. Nor is the team shy about taking on some heavyweights: In recent years the Bulls have beaten both Florida State and Notre Dame, in away games.

The community has been quick to embrace this shift, amping up attendance drastically. In 2011, when the Bulls had an off season, they averaged more than 44,500 fans per game at Raymond James. The high-water mark came in 2007, when the Bulls sold 67,018 tickets for the USF-West Virginia game, the largest non-Super Bowl football crowd ever for the stadium—even though the Bulls share the RayJay with the NFL's Buccaneers.

SHOPS

The Tampa Bay area has more than its share of shopping malls, from workhorse models like University Mall (Sears, Old Navy) to the fancy-pants types like International Plaza (Henri Bendel, Louis Vuitton). Beyond the malls, Hyde Park Village has historically represented the largest critical mass of noteworthy boutiques in Hillsborough County, but there has been an exodus in the past few years of national names (Talbots, Ann Taylor) as well as independents. By the end of 2012 the outdoor shopping area, centered around a generous plaza, was set to welcome a new crop of shops to inhabit much vacated square footage. Meanwhile, downtown Tampa has recently welcomed the kinds of boutiques, restaurants, and infrastructure required to service the growing number of high-rise condos. For the first time in decades, visitors can walk along downtown streets near the convention center and do a little window-shopping.

In Pinellas County, downtown St. Petersburg boasts the densest concentration of exciting retail. Along the waterfront, Beach Drive houses the more chichi galleries and boutiques; whereas Central Avenue, especially in the 600 block, is the locus of lots of bohemian whimsy and avant-garde dynamism. After several years of empty storefronts, the local community has reinvested itself in promoting entrepreneurial ventures, much of it fashion, jewelry, third-world handicrafts, and

HIGHLIGHTS

COURTESY OF DOWNTOWN DOGS/RENE NEFF

The staff pooch at Downtown Dogs will gladly help you make a selection.

【 **Best Opportunity to Exercise Your Credit Card:** With 20 restaurants and more than 200 specialty stores, **International Plaza** will take you from A (Apple) to Z (Zara) (page 141).

【 **Best Place to Renounce Your E-Reader: Inkwood Books** is Tampa's only full-service independent bookstore, with regular readings and book club events, set in a sweet Victorian cottage (page 146).

【 **Best Reason to Lose All Self-Control:** The handmade artisan chocolates at **William Dean** were featured recently in the *Hunger*

Games film series, and for good reason: They're both visually stunning and sumptuously flavorful (page 147).

【 **Hot Spot for Canine Couture:** Tampa's **Downtown Dogs** traffics in lavish leashes and "awww" accessories for when man's best friend feels like putting on the dog (page 149).

【 **Top Spot to Reuse, Renew, Recycle:** Shop for gently used True Religion Jeans, J Brand, Current Elliott, Citizens of Humanity, Joie, and more at **Revolve Clothing Exchange** (page 151).

gallery space. First Friday St. Pete is the perfect time to peruse the city's retail smorgasbord, with live music, restaurant specials, and extended hours.

Traditional Florida tourist-obilia (you know,

flip-flops, shell-crusted nightlights, plastic flamingoes, and fudge) will be found in the dozens of shops along Gulf Boulevard, Blind Pass Road, and the other streets that hug the Gulf of Mexico's sandy beaches.

Shopping Malls and Centers

BEACH DRIVE NORTHEAST

Beach Dr. from Central Ave. to 5th Ave. N.

HOURS: Vary by store

Map 6

The area across from the Museum of Fine Arts serves up a scenic view of the bay with a side order of trendy boutiques and shops. They are located almost exclusively along the west side of the street, then wrap around slightly onto each avenue. A must is a stop into Paciugo (pa-CHU-go) for fortifying gelato.

CHANNELSIDE BAY PLAZA

615 Channelside Dr., www.channelsidebayplaza.com

HOURS: Vary by store

Map 1

The entertainment center on Tampa's downtown waterfront, adjacent to the Florida Aquarium and the cruise terminal, Channelside Bay Plaza has a few stores worth investigating—Lit Premium Cigar Lounge, Qachbal's Chocolatier, Wine Design Wine Shop—and a couple of galleries.

ELLENTON PREMIUM OUTLETS

5461 Factory Shops Blvd., Ellenton, 941/723-1150, www.premiumoutlets.com

HOURS: Mon.-Sat. 10 A.M.-9 P.M., Sun. noon-7 P.M.

Map 9

If you want to roll up your sleeves and get serious about retail, you need to drive south on I-75 for about 40 minutes until you reach the Premium Outlets in Ellenton, north of Bradenton. There, you'll find about 130 stores, such as Bose, Ann Taylor, Nine West, Coach, Samsonite, DKNY, Brooks Brothers, kate spade, Villeroy & Boch, Nike, Sak's Fifth Avenue Off Fifth, Wilsons Leather, and Polo Ralph Lauren, all offering deep, deep discounts. It's an outdoor shopping center, with enough variety and average food concessions to make for a pleasant, full, day of shopping.

HYDE PARK VILLAGE

W. Swann Ave., S. Dakota Ave., and Snow Ave., 813/251-3500, www.hydeparkvillage.net

HOURS: Vary by store

Map 2

Hyde Park Village, the outdoor shopping area along Hyde Park's West Swann Avenue, South Dakota Avenue, and Snow Avenue is the most appealing shopping destination in town, especially when the weather is nice. There's a large covered parking lot, free to shoppers, and a lovely landscaped plaza at the center. Pottery Barn and Restoration Hardware are among the bigger stores, along with Brooks Brothers, Anthropologie, and Tommy Bahama.

◖ INTERNATIONAL PLAZA

2223 N. Westshore Blvd., 813/342-3790, www.shopinternationalplaza.com

HOURS: Mon.-Sat. 10 A.M.-9 P.M., Sun. 11 A.M.-6 P.M.

Map 5

With anchor stores Neiman Marcus and Nordstrom, International Plaza, opened in 2001, gets the nod for the Bay Area's fanciest shopping. A handful of usual mall stores (J. Crew, Tommy Bahama, Banana Republic) are spiffed up by their proximity to 200 other specialty shops such as Tiffany & Co., Jos. A. Bank, Louis Vuitton, Montblanc, Gucci, and Coach. Really, it's the poshest assembly of stores in any shopping center on the Gulf Coast, served by an open-air village of restaurants called Bay Street, all in a location just minutes from the airport and downtown. In December, the Christmas decorations in the Neiman Marcus store alone are worth the drive.

JOHN'S PASS VILLAGE AND BOARDWALK

150 John's Pass Boardwalk, Madeira Beach, 727/393-8230, www.johnspass.com

HOURS: Vary by store

Map 9

John's Pass Village and Boardwalk is a catch-all, part-touristy shopping/dining destination and part-locus of fishing activity. This is where to hook up with the local fishing fleet, sightseeing boats, boat rentals, parasailing outfits, and Jet Ski rentals. But it's also nice for a stroll and a little window-shopping along the giftware, resort wear, swimsuit stores, and galleries clustered together. More than 100 merchants have set up shop here, most geared toward visitors.

THE PIER

800 2nd Ave. NE, St. Petersburg, 727/821-6443, www.stpetepier.com

HOURS: Mon.-Thurs. 10 A.M.-8 P.M., Fri. and Sat. 10 A.M.-9 P.M., Sun. 11 A.M.-7 P.M.

Map 6

The Pier has been the heart and soul of visitor activity in St. Petersburg for more than three-quarters of a century, but times are changing. In 1973, a landmark building replaced a boom-time-era structure; resembling an inverted pyramid, or the good guys' home base in a sci-fi movie, it contained restaurants, souvenir stands, a bike-rental office, and even a place to grab a rental rod. You could also depart on a sightseeing boat charter, visit a little aquarium, or simply enjoy the lovely waterfront view from the fifth-floor deck. But engineering studies detected significant deterioration of the foundations for the approach road over the water as well as beneath the building, and the city set aside $50 million for demolitions and creation of an all-new, modernistic structure. The Pier was open until the end of May 2013, then closed for the demolition and new construction.

John's Pass Village and Boardwalk

COURTESY OF VISITSTPETECLEARWATER.COM

SATURDAY MORNING MARKET

In its seventh season, St. Petersburg's Saturday Morning Market has moved one block to the Al Lang Stadium parking lot at the corner of 1st Avenue South and 1st Street downtown. It runs 9 A.M.–2 P.M. early October–late May.

The Tampa Bay area has been a little late to the national farmers' market craze, with many of the weekly outdoor markets featuring more prepared food vendors and handicrafts than locally sourced produce. But the weekly Saturday Morning Market is a great way to enjoy nice weather and a vital downtown scene. Your goal should be to eat your way through it.

GREATEST BARGAINS

At the **Fresh Squeezed Juice** concession you can get an enormous cup of just-squeezed juice for under $3, the halved fruit eviscerated while you watch in a bit of Rube Goldbergery, their essence a heady sweet-tart balance. A couple aisles away, **Flat Top Tacos** ($3) will heap a handmade corn tortilla with crunchy shredded cabbage, a scoop of grilled flaky white fish, squiggles of adobo aioli, cilantro, and a wedge of lime. This is major deliciousness, and a little drippy.

MOST SUBTLE SOPHISTICATION

Paciugo, the Beach Drive gelateria, makes a lovely iced coffee ($2.50). You're handed a quenching but intense cup of cold joe, and only halfway through it do you realize those slowly melting ice cubes are, in fact, frozen coffee. Nice touch.

MOST SINFUL SPLURGE

There's a lot of bustle at the **Crepesville** booth: someone making the crepes, someone spreading the goo, someone taking the orders. Tell them you want the banana Nutella ($5) and still another person starts slicing banana while the goo-spreader slathers on the lush hazelnut-chocolate sauce, folds the crepe in quarters, adds a rosette of whipped cream, and hands it over with a flourish. Tricky to eat with a pliable plastic fork, but necessity is the mother of invention when Nutella is involved.

BEST CONSCIENCE BALM

Find the man in the safari-worthy pith helmet hawking something called **Motsapie.** Really South American arepas ($3 each or four for $10), these are four-inch yellow cornmeal disks sandwiching oozy mozzarella and topped with a flurry of powdered sugar. They are tasty but a teeny bit dry, easy to ignore when you know the profits from Motsapie are donated to a migrant support project in Wimauma.

MOST SERIOUS MORNING FOOD

Uhuru Breakfast Oasis does scrambled eggs, omelets, and fat breakfast wraps, all paired with seasoned home fries and a fruit garnish. That'll get your day going full tilt.

BEST TASTE OF A LOCAL DELICACY

Fisher Seafood sells mostly fresh fish, but you'll also find smoked fish spread, something local foodies swear by, eaten most often accompanied by Saltines or similar crackers.

TYRONE SQUARE MALL

6901 Tyrone Square, St. Petersburg, 727/347-3889, www.simon.com

HOURS: Mon.-Sat. 10 A.M.–9 P.M., Sun. 11 A.M.–7 P.M.

Map 9

Tyrone Square Mall is a standard-issue, 130-store/restaurant indoor mall, mostly geared toward serving the local community. Dillards, JC Penney, Sears, and Macy's are the anchors, with all the familiar filler stores (Sunglass Hut, Bath & Body Works, Hollister Co., JoS. A. Bank). The food court has some adequate contenders.

UNIVERSITY MALL

2200 E. Fowler Ave., 813/971-3465, www.universitymalltampa.com

HOURS: Mon.-Thurs. 10:30 A.M.–8:30 P.M., Fri. 10:30 A.M.–9 P.M., Sat. 10 A.M.–9 P.M., Sun. noon–6 P.M.

Map 4

Located across the street from USF (in fact, USF holds some of its large lecture classes here in the movie theater; no word on whether you can order popcorn), University Mall is a garden-variety indoor shopping center, not very well maintained, with teenagers texting vigorously, mostly familiar mall stores, and a fairly decent food court. Its 16-screen movie theater features a restaurant heavy on the pub grub and a full bar.

WESTFIELD SHOPPING TOWN

8021 Citrus Park Town Center, Citrus Park,
813/926-4644, www.westfield.com/citruspark
HOURS: Mon.-Sat. 10 A.M.–9 P.M., Sun. noon–6 P.M.
Map 5

Westfield Malls dot the Florida landscape, most of them pleasant indoor shopping centers with the full gamut (Abercrombie to Williams-Sonoma) of small shops and anchors, mostly serving the local community. Fairly far from where most visitors stay, the Citrus Park location is a nice example of the breed, with a 20-screen Regal Cinema and a BJ's Restaurant and Brewhouse, which proffers decent salads, pizzas, and house beers.

WESTSHORE PLAZA

250 Westshore Plaza, Tampa, 813/286-0790,
www.westshoreplaza.com
HOURS: Mon.-Sat. 10 A.M.–9 P.M., Sun. noon–6 P.M.
Map 5

About three minutes from International Plaza, Westshore features more than 100 similarly fancy specialty shops and four major department stores, including a lovely Saks Fifth Avenue. It contains a 14-screen AMC Theater and restaurants like Maggiano's Little Italy, P.F. Chang's, and The Palm.

St. Petersburg is a destination for antiquing.

7TH AVENUE (LA SEPTIMA)

7th Ave. from 13th to 23rd Sts., 813/241-8838,
www.ybor.org/shopping
HOURS: Vary by store
Map 3

Shopping along 7th Avenue in Ybor City, Tampa's Latin quarter, will yield some interesting finds. It's a little gritty, with a few vintage clothing shops, a fair amount of racy lingerie, and other specialty shops. This is the place to go if you get a hankering for a tattoo or piercing.

Antiques

GAS PLANT ANTIQUE ARCADE

1246 Central Ave., 941/749-1866,
www.gasplantantiquearcade.com
HOURS: Tues.-Sat. 11 A.M.–5 P.M., Sun. noon–5 P.M.
Map 6

Gas Plant Antique Arcade claims to be the largest antiques mall on the Gulf Coast. Whether that's true or not is unclear, but it does have four floors arrayed with the wares of about 150 dealers. It features American and European antiques, memorabilia and collectibles, and worldwide shipping is available.

COURTESY OF VISIT FLORIDA

PATTY & FRIENDS ANTIQUE MALL

1241 9th St. N., 727/822-2106,
www.pattyandfriends.com
HOURS: Mon.-Sat. 10 A.M.-5 P.M., Sun. noon-5 P.M.
Map 6

Fine, Gas Plant can be the largest, but Patty & Friends is the oldest antiques shop in the

state. Really an association representing 60 dealers, its two converted, adjacent houses are located near a number of other antiques outposts. Furniture, silver, porcelain, pottery, and collectibles of every kind are packed into the houses. The shop also accepts consignment and Internet sales.

Books and Music

We Sunshine State dwellers are a literate lot—how else do you explain the half-dozen Barnes & Noble brick-and-mortar outlets in this age of e-readers? And the lure of listening to and questioning live (!) authors has drawn thousands of folks to the annual Tampa Bay Times Festival of Reading for two decades. There's even the chance of bumping into part-time residents Dennis Lehane, Michael Connelly, and Stephen King (he'll be wearing a baseball cap with the red B on it when the Red Sox play the Tampa Bay Rays, in downtown St. Petersburg).

So it's not surprising that independent bookstores on each side of the bay are so popular that regulars drop by just to be sure they aren't missing anything.

BANANAS MUSIC AND MOVIES

2226 16th Ave. N., 800/823-4113, www.musicfinder.com
HOURS: Tues.-Sat. 10 A.M.-5 P.M.
Map 9

In the old days, like when they still made recordings on vinyl only, Hollywood would have cast Jimmy Stewart and June Allyson to star in the movie version recounting the lives of Bananas owners Doug and Michelle Allen. They were book lovers, working at "real" jobs, who opened a bookstore in 1977. When Michelle put a stack of yard-sale vinyl records on a store shelf, every record sold. Cue the next career. Now they have two vast operations in St. Petersburg: The store holds vinyl records, CDs, and movies in its 6,500 square feet. An

11,000-square-foot warehouse holds an estimated three million more LPs and 45s. The Bananas website lists 13 categories of music, plus comedy albums and "other" for everything beyond those genres.

DADDY KOOL RECORDS

666 Central Ave., 727/822-5665, www.daddykool.com
HOURS: Mon.-Sat. 10 A.M.-8 P.M., Sun. noon-5 P.M.
Map 6

Yep, Daddy Kool Records *is* cool enough to spell its name with a K, covering the spectrum from vintage vinyl to digital downloads. Prices on some products can be high, but the store also offers products for just $3 or $4. In business in this area for a quarter-century, Daddy Kool has a knowledgeable sales staff, a real plus for the casual shopper.

HASLAM'S BOOK STORE

2025 Central Ave., 727/822-8616, www.haslams.com
HOURS: Mon.-Sat. 10 A.M.-6:30 P.M., Sun. noon-5 P.M.
Map 6

Florida's largest new and used bookstore, Haslam's Book Store, merits a couple of hours of browsing, especially if the weather is inclement (a rarity). Haslam's, with more than 300,000 volumes, is owned by the third generation of the same family. In a world populated increasingly by Amazon and the aforementioned Barnes & Noble, it's refreshing sometimes to hang out in an independently owned bookstore. Haslam's has a large number of rare books, and they seem

SHOPS

to be really into science fiction, though it's unlikely there is a publishing genre you won't find in this sprawling landmark.

🅒 INKWOOD BOOKS

216 S. Armenia Ave., 813/253-2638,
www.inkwoodbooks.com
HOURS: Mon.-Wed. and Fri.-Sat. 10 A.M.-6 P.M., Thurs. 10 A.M.-9 P.M., Sun. 1-5 P.M.
Map 2

Tampa has its share of mainstream bookstores, but Inkwood is the city's only independent bookstore. Whiling away an afternoon or evening in the little 1920s bungalow of Inkwood Books is a real treat. There's an extensive schedule of readings, author appearances, and book club events. The founders announced in mid-2012 that they were putting their 20-year-old business up for sale. As of press time, it remains open under the original ownership.

SOUND EXCHANGE

14246 N. Nebraska Ave., Tampa, 813/978-9316,
www.soundexchangetampabay.com
HOURS: Mon.-Sat. 11 A.M.-9 P.M., Sun. 11 A.M.-7 P.M.
Map 4

The Tampa location of Sound Exchange is the oldest and largest store, dating back to 1987 (nothing in North Tampa is that old). In addition to CDs and vinyl, it offers classic stereo equipment from the 1950s to the early 1980s, with a staff that can kibbitz about recordings as well as the best ways to enjoy them, plus the occasional band that crams in between the stacks of records for informal concerts. There are also locations in Brandon (805 W. Bloomingdale Ave., Brandon, 813/651-9316, Mon.–Thurs. 11 A.M.–8 P.M., Fri.–Sat. 11 A.M.–9 P.M., Sun. noon–6 P.M.) and Pinellas Park (7688 49th St. N., Pinellas Park, 727/545-0042, Mon.–Thurs. 11 A.M.–8 P.M., Fri.–Sat. 10 A.M.–8 P.M., Sun. noon–6 P.M.).

ZBOOKZ NEW & USED BOOKS

7901 46th Ave. N., St. Petersburg, 727/698-4669,
www.zbookz.com
HOURS: Tues.-Sat. 11 A.M.-7 P.M.
Map 9

Started in 1984, ZbookZ is now more primarily an online resource for rare volumes. But there is a brick-and-mortar store, too, with a fireplace and a comfy reading room. With 2,000–3,000 new titles at any time, it's still most impressive as a used bookstore. The SparkleSpot bead shop is also on-site.

Chocolatiers

CITY STREET SWEETS

1605 Snow Ave., Hyde Park Village, 813/251-6764,
www.citystreetsweets.com
HOURS: Mon.-Thurs. 11 A.M.-9 P.M., Fri.-Sat. 11 A.M.-11 P.M., Sun. 11 A.M.-9 P.M.
Map 2

City Street Sweets's Steven Ashworth went to the Savannah College of Art and Design, but his real education came at a nearby candy shop. After that, he spent 14 years working for Godiva in Georgia and in Florida. The core of his business is a couple dozen artisanal hand-painted and stenciled ganache-filled chocolates in sophisticated flavors (cocoa chai spice or an Aztec truffle with a dash of cinnamon and cayenne), but Ashworth has a number of ways to appeal to candy enthusiasts. A corner of the store is reserved as "candyland," a kid-friendly compendium of colorful candies and nostalgia-inducing classics (Abba-Zaba or Chick-O-Stick, anyone?), and he makes fudges and barks. Be sure to try the bacon bark.

QACHBAL'S CHOCOLATIER

615 Channelside Bay Plaza, 813/223-5919,
http://qachbalschocolatier.com

COURTESY OF WILLIAM DEAN CHOCOLATES

chocolates from William Dean

HOURS: Mon.-Thurs. 11 A.M.-9:30 P.M., Fri-Sat.
11 A.M.-11 P.M., Sun. 7 A.M.-9:30 P.M.

Map 1

Candy and her daughter, Crystal, make about 80 percent of the confections in Qachbal's shop, doing a robust business when the cruise ships come into port. The shop doesn't prepackage anything, so customers can choose from large dessert truffles, cannoli, fudge, chocolate-dipped pretzels, caramel apples, or seasonal specialties like chocolate-dipped strawberries. (Take note: They've also got an extensive array of sugar-free chocolates.)

TOFFEE TO GO
3251 W. Bay to Bay Blvd., 813/831-6247,
www.toffeetogo.com
HOURS: Mon.-Fri. 10 A.M.-6 P.M., Sat. 11 A.M.-4 P.M.

Map 2

Lisa and Jim Schalk opened their first Toffee to Go in 2004. They are located in a spot not far from Pinky's and other Palma Ceia hot spots. They do just a few things, and they do them well: chocolate macadamia nut toffee, milk chocolate almond toffee, and dark chocolate pecan toffee, all from traditional Schalk family recipes. The toffee has a crisp and buttery center enrobed in luscious chocolate and then rolled in nuts; the overall effect is nearly irresistible.

◖ WILLIAM DEAN
2790 W. Bay Drive, Belleair Bluffs, 727/593-0656,
williamdeanchocolates.com
HOURS: Mon.-Sat. 10 A.M.-7 P.M., Sun. noon-5 P.M.

Map 9

Opened in 2007, William Dean may be one of our most valuable local treasures (his chocolates were featured in the film *The Hunger Games*). Owner Bill Brown has won nearly every award there is to win in the chocolate world, recently receiving his third "grand master" award in a row in the 2012 Best Chocolatiers and Confectioners of America Awards. He traffics in gelatos, macarons, even sophisticated pastries like a "puff-puff" (part cream puff, part flaky puff pastry), but his growing staff of chocolatiers spends the lion's share of its time on crafting 35–40 varieties of small-batch chocolates.

Cigars

Can you remember as a kid checking out the shelf near the cash register in your hometown drugstore and seeing a slim, rectangular box, its opened lid displaying a smiling brunette in a colorful toga, her arms outstretched? If you can remember that, squint your eyes hard and see if you can read the type around the figure: "Hav-A-Tampa," it said across the bottom, "2

CIGAR BASICS

Want to try a cigar but don't know the first thing? Even before you light up, a cigar's visual specifications can give clues to its character. The outer wrapper's color indicates a great deal about a cigar's flavor. A *maduro* wrapper is a rich, deep brown, imparting a cigar with deep, unctuous flavors. A *claro* wrapper, on the other hand, is a light tan and lends little additional flavor to a cigar. There are essentially six color grades. Roughly from lightest to darkest, these are: *candela* (pale green), *claro, natural* (light brown), *colorado* (reddish brown), *maduro,* and *oscuro* (almost black).

Shape is another central factor in cigar selection. Among *parejos* or straight-sided cigars, there are three basic categories. A *corona* is classically six inches long, with an open foot (the end that is lighted) and a closed head (the end that is smoked). Within this category, **Churchills** are a bit longer and thicker, *robustos* are shorter and much thicker, and a double *corona* is significantly longer. **Panetelas,** the second category, are longer and much thinner than *coronas,* and the third category, Lonsdales, are thicker than panetelas and thinner and longer than *coronas.*

Figurados comprise the other class of cigar, which spans all of the irregularly shaped types. This includes torpedo shapes, braided *culebras,* and pyramid shapes that have a closed, pointed head and an open foot.

A cigar band is generally wrapped around the closed head of a cigar. Its original function was to minimize finger staining, not to identify brands. Nonetheless, on the band you will find the name a manufacturer has designated for a particular line of cigars—names like Partagas, Macanudo, Punch, and Montecristo. Keep in mind that after 1959, many cigar manufacturers fled Cuba to open shop elsewhere, taking their brand names with them. Thus, a brand name does not always betray a cigar's country of origin.

For neophytes lighting up for the first time, a milder cigar may ease you in. The Macanudo Hyde Park is a mild smoke, as is the Don Diego Playboy Robusto or Lonsdale. For a fuller-bodied cigar, the Punch Diademas and the Partagas Number 10 are both popular. If you're looking for a robust, ultra full-bodied taste, you might try the Hoyo de Monterrey Double Corona. The best way to discover your own personal tastes is to stop into a fine tobacconist or cigar-friendly restaurant and have a chat.

for 15 cents." Those were the days. When Hav-A-Tampa began operations in the city in 1902, Tampa was the nation's No. 1 cigar-producing city, even calling itself the Cigar City. (Not quite The Big Apple, but it had a ring to it.)

Less than a century ago, an estimated 12,000 residents, many of them recently arrived from Cuba, Spain, Italy, and Germany, worked in about 200 multistory brick factories around Ybor City. They rolled the stogies by hand: Making more cigars more cheaply was hardly a priority, so mechanization came relatively late to the industry. Northern states had usually been in the forefront of inventing, improving, and installing machinery, and they took the lead again when it came to cigar-rolling.

While several of the old factories still loom

above the retail and residential streets of Ybor, none is utilized for cigar production. A European conglomerate that had bought the Hav-a-Tampa brand and employed about 500 workers east of Tampa closed the building in 1997; now the brand is made in Puerto Rico.

Rolling by hand, formerly a serious mètier, is now practiced by only a few.

EL SOL HAND-MADE CIGARS
4951 E. Adamo Dr., Ste. 230, Tampa, 813/248-5905, www.elsolcigars.com
HOURS: Mon.-Sat. 11 A.M.-5:30 P.M.
`Map 5`

Hand-rolled cigars are available at El Sol Hand-Made Cigars, which sells its own and other cigars but does not roll the stogies for public viewing. El Sol features a wood-paneled showroom crammed with glass cases of cigars, a full complement of cutters, lighters, and pouches, as well as specialty ashtrays to support the ancillary needs of cigar aficionados.

TAMPA SWEETHEARTS CIGAR CO.

1603 E. 6th Ave., 813/247-3880,

www.tampasweetheart.com

HOURS: Mon. 10 A.M.–4 P.M., Tues.–Fri. 9 A.M.–6 P.M., Sat.

9 A.M.–2:30 P.M.

Map 3

For a wide selection of cigars, head to Tampa Sweethearts Cigar Co., headquarters for what used to be the Arturo Fuente cigar brand. It is now operated by the fourth generation of Fuentes, and while that brand is now made in the Dominican Republic, this location retails several dozen products from eight labels.

Specialty Stores

(DOWNTOWN DOGS

1604 W. Snow Circle, 813/250-3647,

www.shopdowntowndogs.com

HOURS: Mon.–Wed. 10 A.M.–7 P.M., Thurs.–Sat. 10 A.M.–8 P.M., Sun. noon–5 P.M.

Map 2

Located in the posh Hyde Park Village area, Downtown Dogs is devoted to carrying only the most coveted, hard-to-find pooch accessories (items so dear that they verge on ridiculous) on the planet. You can find an imaginative selection of lavish collars, leashes, apparel, bedding, and whimsical toys for the canine in your life.

MILAGROS

1104 Central Ave., 727/821-7555, www.sisteragnes.com

HOURS: Mon.–Fri. 10 A.M.–6 P.M., Sat. 10 A.M.–5 P.M.

Map 6

At Milagros, glycerin soaps—half-pound bars!—are handmade daily by Sister Agnes in whimsical and fragrant designs. In addition to candles, soaps, and bath salts, the funky shop imports Latin American religious art, *milagros,* and statuary. There is also a second location in Tampa's Hyde Park Village (1603 W. Snow Circle, Tampa, 813/251-1255).

HOW SWEDE IT IS

If you didn't have the good fortune to grow up within 100 miles of the big blue and yellow furniture superstore from Sweden, you may not know that **IKEA** (1103 N. 22nd St., Tampa, 813/623-5454, Mon.-Sat. 10 A.M.-9 P.M., Sun. 11 A.M.-7 P.M.) has a restaurant that serves Swedish food. You spend hours slogging through a maze of room tableaux, filling out order forms for oddly named goods (the Ektorp or the Skarpt), and then, before you pick up your merchandise in the airplane hangar-sized warehouse, you rest your weary feet and eat Swedish meatballs washed down with fizzy Swedish pear soda.

The Tampa Bay area got its first IKEA in 2009 at the edge of Ybor City in an area that was heretofore a no man's land. Now on weekends you'll regularly see college kids, young families, office managers, and retail tourists making the trek, with hatchbacks and truck beds ready to receive the huge cardboard boxes that will soon be unpacked and assembled.

Vintage Clothing and Accessories

Everything old is...well, if not new again, at least much of it is hip again. And through an odd circumstance, the Tampa Bay area is prime shopping territory if you want to decorate yourself or your home with vintage or retro gear.

While the area is chockfull of young families (more than 300,000 youngsters enrolled just in the public schools in Hillsborough and Pinellas counties), much of the area's explosive growth in the second half of the 20th century was due to families and retirees moving from northern climes. A lot of WWII vets had been trained in the area due to its year-round good climate, and those fellas liked the idea of no snow to shovel in January.

But as happens to newcomers and natives alike, they die. If the deceased was living alone, it's common to invite estate sales entrepreneurs to walk through the home, and they in turn may offer a flat amount for all the contents, rather than preside over a bits-and-pieces sale. These estate buyers then re-purpose the contents where they can. Hence, much inventory in some retro stores is the original version, mixed with 21st century knock-offs.

For everything from bustiers to bridal gowns, aprons to fedoras, costumes to couture, accessories to advertising signs, check these stores.

BUFFALO GAL VINTAGE CLOTHING ACCESSORIES AND GIFTS
911 Central Ave., 727/290-8468,
http://buffalogalvintage.com
HOURS: Tues.-Sat. 11 A.M.-6 P.M., Sun. noon-4 P.M.
Map 6
Offering a large sampling of what they were wearing from 1900 into the 1970s, Buffalo Gal can put you in a revealing bikini, 1940s women's business suit, or cocktail dress with full skirt in which Lucy Ricardo or Marsha Brady might have flounced about. They have menswear, too.

DESIGNERS' CONSIGNER
1033 Central Ave., 727/894-3326,
www.designersconsigner.com
HOURS: Mon.-Sat. 10 A.M.-5 P.M.
Map 6
This store, in downtown St. Petersburg, emphasizes designer-label clothing and accessories, and carries consignment items as well as inventory purchased outright. If you can't stop yourself from buying shoes, do NOT enter this store: Ferragamo, Prada, Manolo Blahnik, and Jimmy Choo may be found here.

LA FRANCE
1612 E. 7th Ave., 813/248-1381
HOURS: Mon.-Thurs. 11 A.M.-8 P.M., Fri.-Sat. 11 A.M.-10 P.M., Sun. noon-7 P.M.
Map 3
Voted by *Creative Loafing's* readers as 2012's Best Vintage Clothing Store in the Bay Area, La France understands its customers drop in to have fun—and then have fun again, when wearing kicky labels such as Trashy Diva and Hell Bunny. The store also holds Fill-a-Bag sales for $10 or $20.

PAPER STREET MARKET
915 Central Ave., 727/894-7777,
www.paperstreetantiques.com
HOURS: Tues.-Sat. 10 A.M.-5 P.M., Sun. noon-4 P.M.
Map 6
What do you need more to perfectly finish your place: a wooden, rolling work table with shelves, or a French-style buffet? Or must you have an 1800 map of the federal capital of Washington (oops, too late: that one's been bought). Paper Street Market owners Sean and

Celesta admit this vintage store grew out of their own over-purchases for their home.

REVOLVE CLOTHING EXCHANGE

2000 4th St. N., St. Petersburg, 727/399-7788,
http://revolve.cx

HOURS: Mon. 10 A.M.–6 P.M., Tues.–Fri. 10 A.M.–7 P.M., Sat. 10 A.M.–6 P.M., Sun. 11 A.M.–5 P.M.

Map 9

Revolve's St. Petersburg location is the most exciting of the three, with a vibrantly painted exterior and broad window showcasing their merchandies in hipster tableaux. A change of pace from the typical vintage operation, Revolve allows customers to swap their own "experienced" clothing and accessories for major discounts on items on the racks or the shelves. They favor upscale brands and carry women's clothing and accessories at reasonable

prices. They carry menswear, but less than their stock of womens clothing. There are also locations in southern Tampa (4023 W. Kennedy Blvd., 813/406-7788) and Ybor City (1620 E. 7th Ave., 813/242-5970).

SHERRY'S YESTERDAZE VINTAGE CLOTHING AND ANTIQUES

5208 N. Florida Ave., Tampa, 813/231-2020,
http://yesterdazevintage.com

HOURS: Tues.–Sat. 11 A.M.–6 P.M., Thurs. until 8 P.M., Sun. 11 A.M.–4 P.M.

Map 5

Sherry's seems to cover all mid-20th-century needs from tiki drinking glasses to costume and fine jewelry, with lots of clothing for men and women, too. So, if you want to bring out your inner Don Draper or Flower Child, start your shopping here.

HOTELS

Tampa's hotel scene is stymied by one thing: Tampa has no beaches. Although it's on the water—with the active Port of Tampa and waterside residential communities such as Davis and Harbour Islands—there is no possibility for a luxury resort hotel or charming bed-and-breakfast just steps from the waters of Hillsborough Bay. For that kind of experience you must head across any of three bridges over Tampa Bay to St. Pete or Clearwater.

Still, Tampa has a preponderance of pleasant, fairly priced accommodations, a mix of business travel and vacation lodgings spread around this side of Tampa Bay, from the Latin Quarter of Ybor City to the Westshore business district or the Tampa Convention Center,

to near Busch Gardens and the University of South Florida.

St. Petersburg and Pinellas County, on the other hand, are on a peninsula formed by Tampa Bay and the Gulf of Mexico and provide more accommodations options: The county does about five million room nights a year, fueled by visitors' desire to soak up the sun along well over 20 miles of Gulf beaches. The city of St. Petersburg stretches between Tampa Bay, on the eastern side of the peninsula, west to the Gulf. St. Petersburg has more history, more of a sense of place and sophistication than the roughly 20, pocket-sized, beach towns along the Gulf. There are romantic bed-and-breakfasts, fine restaurants, and cultural attractions.

COURTESY OF SANDPEARL RESORT

HIGHLIGHTS

COURTESY OF PONCE DE LEON BOUTIQUE HOTEL

Ponce De Leon Boutique Hotel

(Conventioneer's Dream Hotel: The 27-story **Tampa Marriott Waterside** is a dramatic presence in the downtown district, aiming largely for corporate groups and conferences. A full-service marina makes it ideal for visiting boaters (page 155).

(Best Place for Sumptuous Retail Therapy: Attached to Tampa's swankiest mall, the grand **Renaissance Tampa International Plaza** is in the middle of the Westshore business district (page 158).

(Best Place to Roll the Dice Before Bed: Tampa's **Seminole Hard Rock Hotel and Casino** is a rock 'n' roll gaming complex and four-diamond hotel just east of downtown. It is a 24-hour venue, with a nightclub that is open until 6 A.M. (page 158).

(Easiest Access to St. Petersburg's Museums and Culture: The historic **Ponce de Leon Boutique Hotel** is dead-center in St. Petersburg's cosmopolitan downtown, with 80 recently renovated rooms (page 160).

(Loveliest Piece of Local History: Listed on the National Register of Historic Places, the **Renaissance Vinoy Resort & Golf Club** was built by wealthy oilman Aymer Vinoy Laughner in 1925 (page 160).

(Most Luxurious Beachside Stay: The recently opened **Sandpearl Resort** features 700 feet of white-sand beach, just a quarter-mile from shopping and dining at Pier 60 (page 163).

Clearwater Beach and St. Pete Beach, both on the Gulf, have the densest concentrations of beachside accommodations—in Clearwater this often means tall resort hotels and condos right on the beach; in St. Pete Beach they are mostly low-rise motels that date back a few decades. The 10 communities between these two—Belleair, Belleair Shore and Belleair Beach; Indian Rocks Beach and Indian Shores; Redington Shores, North Redington Beach, and Redington Beach; Madeira Beach; and Treasure Island—are more residential, but with pockets of beachside hotels, motels, and rentals.

CHOOSING A HOTEL

Where you stay depends on your priorities. Beach lovers will obviously opt for either the low-rise (and affordable) lodgings around and north of St. Pete Beach, or the more high-rise (and, generally, pricier) options to the north, in the Clearwater Beach area. Culture hounds may choose accommodations downtown in St. Petersburg, or downtown in Tampa, in one of

PRICE KEY

💲 Under $100
💲💲 $100-250
💲💲💲 Over $250

the large chain properties near the David A. Straz Jr. Center for the Performing Arts (formerly the Tampa Bay Performing Arts Center) and the convention center.

At this point, nearly every property has a website with photos. Find the best rate available online, then call the property in question to see if you can negotiate a better one. Military affiliation, AAA or AARP membership, and professional affiliations may sweeten the deal. As with all metro areas in Florida, rates vary wildly by season. If affordability is of paramount importance, consider traveling in the off season (especially July and August, and post-Labor Day until just before Thanksgiving).

Downtown Tampa and Channelside   Map 1

EMBASSY SUITES TAMPA, DOWNTOWN CONVENTION CENTER 💲💲
513 S. Florida Ave., 813/769-8300,
http://embassysuites3.hilton.com
Linked by a skybridge to the convention center and seven miles from Tampa International Airport, this large hotel boasts an outdoor swim spa and sun deck located on the 3rd floor of the hotel, a Starbucks in the atrium, a free fitness center, and a full business center. All accommodations are spacious two-room suites, and room rates include cooked-to-order breakfast and a nightly manager's reception. There's a relaxing conversation area in the lobby, featuring live palms and a partial moat fed by a fountain.

HYATT REGENCY TAMPA 💲💲
211 N. Tampa St., 813/225-1234,
http://tamparegency.hyatt.com
Despite the fact that this is one of the most business-friendly hotels downtown (generous work space, wireless Internet, 30,000 square feet of meeting space), it's still a luxurious getaway possibility. Its 521 rooms were recently overhauled (granite and marble baths, those cool iPod docking stations); there are jogging paths, a rooftop deck with outdoor whirlpool, 24-hour fitness (with a fitness concierge and in-room yoga workouts) and business centers, and a huge outdoor heated pool. The Hyatt also boasts a very competent Italian restaurant.

SHERATON TAMPA RIVERWALK HOTEL $$$

200 N. Ashley Dr., 813/223-2222,
www.sheratontampariverwalk.com

Right on the Hillsborough River as part of a former mayor's thoughtful and elaborate Riverwalk vision for downtown (a few portions still remain to be done), the Sheraton has 277 guest rooms and 16 suites, renovated in 2008. Out back there's a 500-foot riverfront pool deck with a lovely swimming pool. For business meetings, the hotel has eight meeting rooms, with over 12,000 square feet of space (heavy on the weddings). There is free Wi-Fi throughout the property. From this Sheraton it's an easy Rollerblade along Bayshore Boulevard or over to the convention center.

◖ TAMPA MARRIOTT WATERSIDE $$

700 S. Florida Ave., 813/221-4900, www.marriott.com

Part of the walkable/bikeable Channel Riverwalk, with two cafés front and center for Port of Tampa viewing action, the hotel has 683 nicely appointed guest rooms and 36 suites, most with balconies or views that look over Hillsborough Bay. It's a huge meetings hotel, with 50,000 well-thought-out feet of space, in up to 30 rooms. Added allures include a fitness center plus full-service spa (scrubs,

COURTESY OF VISIT FLORIDA

HOTELS

Tampa Marriott Waterside

wraps, waxing, massages) and an array of solid on-site restaurants (where the chefs source produce and herbs from their own rooftop garden and greenhouse). It's adjacent to the Tampa Convention Center, thus an obvious choice for business travelers, but a 32-slip full-service marina makes it suitable for leisure boat travel.

Davis Islands   Map 2

WESTIN TAMPA HARBOUR ISLAND $$

725 S. Harbour Island Blvd., 813/229-5000,
www.starwoodhotels.com

Harbour Island is connected to downtown via a causeway. It still has a neat island-away-from-it-all appeal while being adjacent to the Tampa Convention Center and just two blocks from the Tampa Bay Times Forum, a venue both for the NHL Lightning and headliner musical acts. Thus, this 299-room property seems fairly split

between business and leisure travelers. It's got the signature Heavenly Beds with pillow-top mattresses, an outdoor pool, and full-service business center. In addition to the fitness center, you can work out privately by booking a guest room equipped with a treadmill, stationary bike, resistance bands, and so on. There are 13 flexible meeting rooms, many with nice harbor views. Dogs up to 15 pounds are allowed with a $50 nonrefundable cleaning fee.

Ybor City
Map 3

DON VICENTE DE YBOR HISTORIC INN ❸❸

1915 Avenida Republica de Cuba, 813/241-4545, www.donvicenteinn.com

For an experience steeped in history, head to the Don Vicente, constructed in 1895 by Cuban patriot Vicente Martinez Ybor. The boutique hotel's 16 guest rooms contain genteel flourishes such as four-poster beds, Persian rugs, and cast-iron balconies, but the Inn also offers broadband, voicemail, and in-room desks. Even if you don't stay here, the opulent grand salon is worth peeking at.

HAMPTON INN & SUITES TAMPA/YBOR CITY ❸❸

1301 E. 7th Ave., 813/247-6700, www.hilton.com

Located one mile from the Tampa Convention Center and the Port of Tampa Cruise Terminal, this pleasant mid-price hotel is right on the trolley line (also, there's a free shuttle to anywhere within three miles) and smack-dab in the middle of Ybor City's rollicking nightlife scene and Cuban restaurants. The hotel has 138 smoking and non-smoking guest rooms and suites, with accessible rooms available and meeting space for up to 50. Accommodations include free hot breakfast, free high-speed Internet access in every room, and pool and fitness center use.

Busch Gardens and North Tampa
Map 4

EMBASSY SUITES TAMPA USF ❸❸

3705 Spectrum Blvd., 813/977-7066, www.embassysuites.com

The USF hotel of choice is this tall, suites-only hotel with a soaring atrium. Rooms are pretty, with spacious living rooms and private bedrooms with either a king or two double beds. There are two TVs in every room, nice if the kids want to watch something execrable in the next room. Although the room costs are a little more, included in the price is a nice cooked-to-order breakfast buffet and nightly manager's reception, where you get a free cocktail and some chips. There is a free shuttle to Busch Gardens.

LA QUINTA INN TAMPA NEAR BUSCH GARDENS ❸

9202 N. 30th St., 813/930-6900, www.lq.com

This familiar chain is a mile from the Busch Gardens entrance, with 144 nicely appointed rooms with roomy bathrooms, good lighting, large desks, and computer-friendly dataport telephones. There's also a good-size pool and complimentary hot or cold breakfast.

Greater Tampa
Map 5

DOUBLETREE BY HILTON HOTEL TAMPA AIRPORT–WESTSHORE ❸❸
4500 W. Cypress St., Tampa, 813/879-4800,
http://doubletree1.hilton.com

A contemporary-looking paint job and a new restaurant (the tongue-twister ItaliAsia, offering both Italian and Asian cuisines) finishes nearly $17 million of improvements at DoubleTree by Hilton Hotel Tampa Airport—Westshore. The 489-room lodging offers 16,000 square feet of flexible space and 15 meeting rooms, all located on the first floor. Complimentary 24-hour airport shuttle service, in-room Wi-Fi, fitness center, and (alright, it may negate the fitness center efforts) those gooey chocolate-chip cookies complete the scene.

GRAM'S PLACE HOSTEL ❸
3109 N. Ola Ave., Tampa, 813/221-0596,
www.grams-inn-tampa.com

For when you're looking for a wild experience at a tame price, Gram's Place will surely fit the bill. It's eccentric, with a different music theme (jazz, blues, rock) in each of the private suites and youth hostel–style bunks. All rooms come with a "music menu" of 400-plus CDs. The hostel part looks like a railroad car fashioned around a 100-year-old train depot. The rooms are set in two circa 1945 cottages and share an oversized in-ground whirlpool tub, a BYOB bar in the courtyard, and a 16 multi-track recording studio. Lest you are imagining some cool old Grandma jamming in the recording studio with a bunch of longhairs, the "Gram" in question is Gram Parsons, once member of the Byrds and the Flying Burrito Brothers, the deceased musician responsible for the heartbreakingly beautiful song, "Grievous Angel," which Emmylou Harris made famous.

GRAND HYATT TAMPA BAY ❸❸❸
2900 Bayport Dr., Tampa, 813/874-1234,
www.grandtampabay.hyatt.com

One of the big kahuna hotels in these parts, the Grand Hyatt is a large hotel near the airport that caters mainly to road warriors. This four-diamond property recently refurbished all

COURTESY OF DOUBLETREE BY HILTON

HOTELS

DoubleTree by Hilton Hotel Tampa Airport—Westshore

of its accommodations—the 377 guest rooms, including hypo-allergenic rooms, 38 Spanish-style casita rooms and 7 casita suites—utilizing a palette of tropical colors, especially blues, and large patterned wall coverings. The rooms include safes large enough to store (and charge) your laptop, a desk large enough to actually work on, and plush bedding. Hyatt has tennis courts, a lap pool, and a free-form pool. The hotel is in a secluded area at the south end of a 35-acre wildlife preserve along Tampa Bay. The Hyatt contains two of the best restaurants in town, Armani's and Oystercatchers.

INTERCONTINENTAL TAMPA $$$

4860 W. Kennedy Blvd., Tampa, 813/286-4400, www.intercontampa.com

This relative newcomer is a business traveler's dream. The 323 rooms, 17 junior suites (a handful of which are business suites), and 2 presidential suites feature fresh decor, feather-top mattresses with luxurious linens, functional working areas, flat-screen TVs, and iPod docking stations. The hotel offers 17,000 square feet of flexible meeting space, a 40-seat "amphitheatre," Wi-Fi throughout the hotel, a fitness center, a full-service concierge program, as well as a rooftop pool with views of the bay and city. Three miles from the airport and five miles from the convention center, the hotel contains a Shula's Steak House and Shula's No Name Lounge.

(RENAISSANCE TAMPA INTERNATIONAL PLAZA $$$

4200 Jim Walter Blvd., Tampa, 813/877-9200, www.marriott.com

One of Tampa's nicest luxury hotels, the Renaissance Tampa International Plaza is near the Westshore business district and adjacent to the area's finest shopping center, International Plaza. The lush decor is reminiscent of a Mediterranean villa, an illusion bolstered by things such as the jewel-toned, high-style Pelagia Trattoria, with its open kitchen, at its

center. The hotel has 293 guest rooms, including six suites on a club level with its own lounge. Service is personal and attentive, and it seems especially geared to the repeat-business, high-end business traveler.

SAILPORT WATERFRONT SUITES $$

2506 N. Rocky Point Dr., Tampa, 813/281-9599, www.providentresorts.com/sailport-waterfront-suites

For a more independent approach amongst the many chain names in the Rocky Point area, try Sailport, a four-story, all-suites hotel (all rooms have a queen sleeper sofa in the living room, convenient for families) with full-sized kitchens, barbecue grills, outdoor heated pool, sunning deck, and fishing pier.

(SEMINOLE HARD ROCK HOTEL AND CASINO $$$

5223 Orient Rd., Tampa, 866/502-7529, www.hardrockhotelcasinotampa.com

The What Is This Doing Here (?!) Award goes to the Hard Rock. This huge luminous purple tower rises up in the middle of nowhere off of I-75 (well, it's not totally in the middle of nowhere, as the Live Nation Amphitheatre is just across the highway from it). With an illuminated 12-story tower that shifts colors, the signature huge guitar at the entrance, a 220,000-square-foot casino that debuted a massive expansion in summer 2012, and see-and-be-seen restaurants such as Council Oak and Rock 'n Raw Sushi, it's like a little piece of Vegas right here in Tampa. The complex opened in 2004 and has been swamped with casino and overnight guests ever since; it has undergone about $195 million in expansion, enlarging the casino and adding parking spaces. The 250 guest rooms and suites have a hipster art deco design, with unique extras such as Tivoli stereo and CD systems and ultra-luxury beds. The most luxurious part is the pool area, with cascading fountains and cool private cabanas with televisions and refrigerators. More expansion is planned, including possibly enlarging the hotel to 22 stories; the Seminole Tribe has not disclosed details.

TAHITIAN INN $

601 S. Dale Mabry Hwy., Tampa, 813/877-6721, www.tahitianinn.com

If you find yourself on the western side of Tampa near the residential area named Palma Ceia and you prefer independently owned hotels, the Tahitian Inn is a lovely two-story, family-run motel that had a huge remodel in 2003, yielding 60 Tahitian-theme (dark wood, tropical accessories) moderately priced rooms and 20 executive suites, a lovely pool with tiki huts and hammocks, and the Serenity Spa with massage and Tahitian hot stone treatments. There's also a lovely little on-site café with patio seating near a koi pond. The location is about six blocks south of busy Kennedy Boulevard, a little farther from I-275, and near lots of commerce.

TAMPA MARRIOTT WESTSHORE $$$

1001 N. Westshore Blvd., Tampa, 813/287-2555, www.marriott.com/hotels/travel/tpawe-tampa-marriott-westshore

Fourteen stories tall, this Marriott offers 308 rooms and two suites, and two concierge levels. It's well situated, minutes from Tampa International Airport, two of the city's top malls, and, if you need that NFL fix, quite close to Raymond James Stadium, home of the Tampa Bay Bucs. Awarded the Green Hotel distinction in the Florida Green Lodging Program, the facility has 13,000 square feet of meeting space and is fully accessible. The public areas offer Wi-Fi, all rooms have 32-inch flat screen HD TVs, and parking is complimentary.

WYNDHAM TAMPA WESTSHORE $$$

700 N. Westshore Blvd., Tampa, 813/289-8200, www.wyndhamhoteltampa.com

Located in the heart of the Westshore business district, this Wyndham was formerly the Quorum Hotel Tampa. On the western side of the city, it is just two miles from Tampa International Airport and Raymond James Stadium and sits squarely between Westshore Plaza and International Plaza shopping centers. The largely business-oriented property offers 272 spacious guest rooms, including six 600- and 900-square-foot suites. The executive club level, 26 rooms on the 11th floor, features a comfortable private lounge with complimentary continental breakfast, evening cocktails, and hors d'oeuvres. Wi-Fi is free in the lobby, but a slight charge in the guest rooms.

Downtown St. Petersburg   Map 6

HOTEL INDIGO $$

234 3rd Ave. N., 727/822-4814, www.downtownstpetersburghotel.com

Just 2.5 blocks from upscale Beach Drive, nestled in a residential neighborhood, Hotel Indigo is aglow with vibrant pastels, and many guest rooms have giant wall murals of tropical leaves or shells. There's free Wi-Fi and flat-screens in the rooms of this newish, smallish lodging. There is a full bar and limited-seating restaurant for breakfast and dinner, but it's just a few minutes to walk to several of the city's finer dining venues.

LA VERANDA BED AND BREAKFAST $$

111 5th Ave. N., 727/824-9997, www.laverandabb.com

Especially for romance seekers, La Veranda Bed and Breakfast is wonderful for couples as it's near the heart of downtown St. Petersburg but still quiet and romantic. It's set in a 1910 mansion girdled by wide wraparound porches

HOTELS

and sweet tropical gardens, its five suites furnished the way your rich granny might have, with canopy beds, antiques, and Oriental rugs. Each suite opens directly onto the large veranda, ergo the name.

🏰 PONCE DE LEON BOUTIQUE HOTEL $$

95 Central Ave., 727/550-9300,
www.poncedeleonhotel.com

Right in the thick of things downtown, this was one of St. Petersburg's first hotels. Opened in 1922 and hosting many of the city's most famous visitors, it has charm and a real sense of place (without having a superabundance of amenities). There are 79 rooms, decorated in a variety of styles. Its restaurant, Ceviche, is one of the biggest draws downtown, with great tapas and live music (ask for a top floor if music and street noise will bother you), and the tiny Pincho y Pincho café serves up fabulous coffees and Spanish-style snacks and breakfast. Weekly rates are available.

🏰 RENAISSANCE VINOY RESORT & GOLF CLUB $$$

501 5th Ave. NE, 727/894-1000,
www.renaissancehotels.com

Some of this area's greatest landmarks are grand old hotels. In order to feel comfortable with the splurge, tell yourself it's like the price of the hotel plus the admission to a local historical attraction. It's a historical attraction with room service. Simply referred to as The Vinoy (vin-OY), the hotel was built by Pennsylvania oilman Aymer Vinoy Laughner in 1925. At $3.5 million, the Mediterranean revival–style hotel was the largest construction project in Florida's history. Exquisitely restored in 1992 at a cost

Renaissance Vinoy Resort & Golf Club

COURTESY OF VISITSTPETECLEARWATER.COM

of $93 million (that included redesigning the golf course, which is a free shuttle ride three miles away), this grand dame exudes the rarefied glamour that helps put life's quotidian woes behind you. There are 345 guest rooms and 15 suites, many with views of its marina on Tampa Bay. The hotel also has a spa, a lovely pool with a waterfall, five restaurants, and tennis courts. Is lovely lobby was revamped in 2011–2012 to increase the seating area for the small bar, but those in the know are content to relax on the spacious verandah and enjoy the cross-street views of a park and the bay. And that might have been just what such guests as Calvin Coolidge, Babe Ruth, and Herbert Hoover used to do. The Vinoy is listed on the National Register of Historic Places.

St. Pete Beach

Map 7

ALDEN BEACH RESORT 🟡🟡

5900 Gulf Blvd., 727/360-7081,
www.aldenbeachresort.com

Most visitors to the Gulf side of the peninsula want to stay *on* the beach, and the Alden is an attentively staffed, family-owned resort. It has 140 suites, especially beloved by kids. It also has tennis, volleyball, two pools (a little far from the beach, so the walk back and forth takes time for little ones), and a video game room. Rooms on the pool side are significantly cheaper than on the Gulf side, which is typical for lodgings on Florida's barrier islands.

LOEWS DON CESAR HOTEL 🟡🟡🟡

3400 Gulf Blvd., 727/360-1881, www.doncesar.com

The huge, Pepto Bismol–pink Don CeSar is a landmark on Florida's Gulf Coast and a long-time point of reference on maritime navigation charts. Named after a character in the opera *Maritana,* the Don CeSar hosted F. Scott Fitzgerald and wife Zelda, Clarence Darrow, Al Capone, Lou Gehrig, and countless other celebrities, plus it was featured in a Robert Altman movie filmed in the 1970s, *Health.* Originally opened in 1928, the property was commandeered by the military during World War II and eventually abandoned. These days, it's a Loews hotel, with 340 lovely if somewhat small rooms, fishing, golfing, tennis, and the soothing Beach Club & Spa. If it's too rich for your blood, take the tour and stop in for ice cream at its old-fashioned ice cream parlor (get the coffee flavor).

POSTCARD INN 🟡🟡

6300 Gulf Blvd., 727/367-2711, www.postcardinn.com

It takes some imagination to see this beach-chic

Loews Don CeSar Hotel

facility as having started life as a Travelodge. Now, the decor is a riot of vivid colors and geometric designs. Each of the 196 rooms is differently painted and furnished—though actual surfboards are a frequent accessory, and photo galleries or wall-size photo murals of surfing themes are ubiquitous. Each room has Wi-Fi and a flat screen TV, and all are a few steps from the powdery sand. The guest-room choice includes poolside cabanas. If the PCI Beach Bar was any closer to the Gulf, happy hour would be tuned to high tide.

SIRATA BEACH RESORT ⑤⑤

5300 Gulf Blvd., 727/363-5100, www.sirata.com

Sirata Beach Resort used to be connected to the TradeWinds but is now an independent, family-run midsize hotel, with a range of children's programs and activities. It's the kind of place that locals in Tampa take their brood for a weekend of R&R, with 13 unspoiled acres of beachfront. Its three pools are open daily 9 A.M.–10 P.M., the two on-site beach bars (Harry's and Rumrunner's) are hopping, and there's a Durango's Steak House attached. A beach services kiosk will set you up with rental cabanas (complete with fridge and TV), parasailing, Wave Runners, Jet Skis, or a dinner sunset cruise.

TRADEWINDS ISLAND RESORTS ⑤⑤

5500 Gulf Blvd., 727/367-6461,
www.tradewindsresort.com

For families, blow with the TradeWinds. It's just completed a $20 million spruce-up of guest rooms and public areas, and it offers families a bunch of accommodation choices with nary a clinker among them. The resort, supposedly the largest on the Gulf Coast with 584 rooms, comprises the TradeWinds Island Grand ($168–457) and the adjacent Sandpiper Hotel and Suites ($149–226), and whichever one you choose includes playtime privileges at the other. The Island Grand is the fancier, a four-diamond property with soaring palms, a grand lobby, and lovely rooms. Sandpiper would be our choice with little ones. The whole complex offers seven pools, 14 places to eat and drink, fitness centers, tennis courts everywhere, a paddleboat canal meandering through the grounds, and a wide, private expanse of beach. Behind the properties you can enjoy a 20,000-square-foot water park anchored just offshore, you can rent equipment for snorkeling or fishing, and try your hand at the latest gadgets: a water-propelled, vertical jet pack device—you're tethered, so 30 feet is the maximum height—and battery-powered surf boards, to give you some motion in the usually placid Gulf. The children's program (KONK, Kids Only No Kidding!) is tremendous, with

THE BELLEVIEW BILTMORE RESORT & SPA

Built in 1897 by railroad magnate and west-central Florida pioneer Henry Plant, the 292-room Belleview Biltmore (25 Belleview Blvd., www.belleviewbiltmore.com) is said to be the largest continuously occupied wooden structure in the world (its roof covers 2.5 acres). Situated high on a coastal bluff, and surrounded by its golf course, the hotel has hosted Thomas Edison, Henry Ford, the Duke of Windsor, and Bob Dylan. Sadly, that was then .... The Biltmore has changed hands several times in recent years and while the current owners are trying to devise a plan to retain—and overhaul—the main structure, the landmark is currently closed, though its golf course is still open and functioning.

On March 3, 2012, Belleview Biltmore Partners, LLC, signed a sales option agreement with the current owner, Raphael and Daniel Ades. The group is trying to raise capital to buy the hotel and restore it, with hopes that it will open to the public again in the coming years.

seasonal offerings like the Swashbucklin' By the Sea pirate package, sand-sculpture lessons, and even discussions on ecology. And with the staff having undergone training, the entire facility has been certified autism-friendly by the Center for Autism and Related Diseases.

Clearwater and Clearwater Beach　Map 8

HYATT REGENCY CLEARWATER BEACH RESORT & SPA ❸❸❸
301 S. Gulfview Blvd., 727/373-1234, www.clearwaterbeach.hyatt.com

At 17 stories, this AAA four-diamond hotel is tall for the Gulf beaches, but its space is spread among 250 guest rooms, some measuring a startling 2,000 square feet. All units, some of them two-bedroom, have a living room and kitchen, plus a balcony overlooking either the Gulf of Mexico (absolutely glorious sunsets) or the Intracoastal Waterway (sunrises). The decor might be called island elegant/romantic. For the road warriors, there is 32,500 square feet of meeting space plus a business center and Wi-Fi throughout. Guests can utilize the 24-hour fitness area—it has a concierge—and can dial up the poolside experience to "decadent" by renting one of 20 cabanas that have air-conditioning, Wi-Fi, a flat screen HDTV, wet bar, and a bathroom.

PIER HOUSE 60 MARINA HOTEL ❸❸
101 Coronado Dr., 727/683-0002, www.pierhouse60.com

Located across the street from the Gulf of Mexico beach, the Pier House 60 overlooks the municipal marina— giving guests something nautical to dream about. There is Wi-Fi throughout the hotel, and each of the rooms and suites has a flat screen HDTV, microwave, and mini fridge. The hotel does not have its own restaurant, though several casual places are a short walk away, but the Pier House does offer a complimentary breakfast. To swoon at must-see over-the-Gulf sunsets, head to the 10th floor lounge, Jimmy's Crow's Nest, and view another panorama fit for dreams.

❰ SANDPEARL RESORT ❸❸❸
500 Mandalay Ave., 727/441-2425, www.sandpearl.com

This four-diamond property was the first all new resort to be built on Clearwater Beach in about 30 years, and it is absolutely spectacular. The combined resort and condominium project features a 253-room hotel, a full-service spa, upscale dining, state-of-the-art meeting and event space, 117 condominium units, and 700 feet of gorgeous Gulf of Mexico beachfront. Rooms have an open, airy feel with balconies and high ceilings and each includes elegant yet comfortable furnishings, fixtures, and rich textured fabrics. Fifty suites, located on the top two floors of the resort, offer one- and two-bedroom floor plans. Since opening, the Sandpearl has emerged as the destination for countless feet-in-the-sand weddings.

Greater Pinellas County　Map 9

INNISBROOK ❸❸❸
36750 U.S. 19 N., Palm Harbor, 727/942-2000 or 800/492-6899, www.innisbrookgolfresort.com

Rolling across 900 wooded acres, this golf and tennis (and swimming and spa) kingdom defies a basic fact: About 35 minutes from both downtown St. Petersburg and Tampa, this resort is tucked into the northern corner of Florida's most-densely populated county. Yet guests in its 560 villas and suites (from 225 to 1,400 square feet) come here to relax, and once they are off congested U.S. 19, the only decisions are where to unwind and where to eat. Innisbrook opened in 1970, as a pioneer condominium golf resort. It now boasts four courses (one, the Copperhead, has hosted a PGA Tournament for decades); six pools, including a waterpark; and 11 Har-Tru tennis courts. Added during a recently completed $30-million renovation was an 18,000-square-foot Indaba brand spa and fitness center. There are four restaurants, including a steakhouse, a decidedly upscale convenience store that will prepare picnic baskets, and room service if you just want to stay away from it all. Innisbrook also has about 100,00 square feet devoted to meeting space, both indoors and out.

SAFETY HARBOR RESORT AND SPA 🪙🪙

105 N. Bayshore Dr., Safety Harbor, 727/726-1161, www.safetyharborspa.com

Plenty of places along the Gulf Coasts claim

ties to the early Spanish explorers, including the Safety Harbor Resort and Spa. Disputed is whether Hernando de Soto came ashore to this site in 1539 and proclaimed its five mineral springs as the Fountain of Youth. But not debated is that for nearly a century, health-seekers have come to this quaint town to "take the waters." The original springs now sit beneath the 50,000-square-foot spa and tennis academy. The waters, which used to be shipped around America in big jugs, are now piped to fill three pools and are used in the spa treatments. The resort is also home to a fairly sophisticated restaurant called 105 North, and a fancy-pants salon. The 189 guest rooms and four suites are spacious and offer nice views of Old Tampa Bay.

ST. PETERSBURG MARRIOTT CLEARWATER 🪙🪙

12600 Roosevelt Blvd., St. Petersburg, 727/572-7800, www.marriott.com

Boasting an "Outstanding Business of the Year

Safety Harbor Resort and Spa

Award" from the local Chamber of Commerce, this lodging in turn aims toward business travelers. It is about 15 minutes from Tampa International Airport and just 3 minutes from the St. Petersburg-Clearwater International Airport (its tags read PIE). Similarly, the lodging is less than 20 minutes from St. Petersburg and Clearwater, and on a good-traffic day, that close to Tampa's downtown. For the meetings crowd, there is 30,000 square feet of event space. All 197 rooms come with either one king or two queen beds, a 37-inch flat screen HDTV, specially designed working desk with all the necessary plugs, and a safe large enough for your laptop. There are also suites and a concierge level. There is a smallish fitness center and outdoor pool.

EXCURSIONS FROM TAMPA AND ST. PETERSBURG

An hour due north from Tampa and St. Petersburg and you run smack into what's called the Nature Coast, complete with manatee viewing, fishing, and tramping around in the palmetto-festooned flatwoods. An hour due south and you encounter all the sophisticated cultural allures in the city of Sarasota and its barrier islands. An hour northeast? That's where you throw your hands in the air and scream during the triple inversion. It's Walt Disney World Resort, Universal, and all the theme park madness that is Orlando.

PLANNING YOUR TIME

Your whim decides which way you head for an excursion from the home base of Tampa and St. Petersburg. Well, your whim, your wallet, and your wardrobe. The Nature Coast's allures are inexpensive and casual, with enough to entertain you for two or three days (the hardcore angler, however, will be endlessly amused). Everything in Orlando requires deep pockets and comfortable shoes; jacket not required but those mouse ears help. Orlando, like the universe, seems to be ever expanding, with more and greater attractions added all the time. You might easily add a day or a week to your trip, depending on your stamina for theme parks. (To be fair, downtown Orlando and Winter Park are destinations in their own right, free of theme parks and rich with culture.)

Sarasota, on the other hand, would make

© HOWARD BURCH/123RF

HIGHLIGHTS

LOOK FOR ◖ TO FIND RECOMMENDED SIGHTS, RESTAURANTS, ACTIVITIES, AND HOTELS.

© 123RF.COM

Downtown Orlando is home to a thriving arts community.

◖ **Most Thrilling Ride:** At **Walt Disney World Resort,** Expedition Everest should be high on your list of rides. Disney Imagineers built a scaled-down Mount Everest (now the tallest mountain in Florida) upon which you'll find a state-of-the-art thrill ride (page 169).

◖ **Best Art Within Driving Distance of Orlando's Theme Parks:** **Downtown Orlando** is a cultural hotspot, where you'll find the stunning Orlando Museum of Art (page 172).

◖ **Best Place to See Large Animals:** See manatees up close in the underwater "fishbowl" at **Homosassa Springs State Wildlife Park** (page 181).

◖ **Best Place to Wet Your Line:** There

seem to be more fish than ever on the Nature Coast, enlivening a day of **offshore fishing** in Steinhatchee (page 182).

◖ **Weirdest Plants:** Enjoy a day at **Marie Selby Botanical Gardens,** the open-air and under-glass museum that has more than 6,000 orchids and more than 20,000 other plants. Most impressive is the vast array of otherworldly air plants (page 186).

◖ **Best Rainy-Day Activity:** The **John and Mable Ringling Museum of Art** is a must-see for fans of Flemish and Italian baroque art, with rooms of breathtaking canvasses, including a series by Peter Paul Rubens known collectively as *The Triumph of the Eucharist* (page 188).

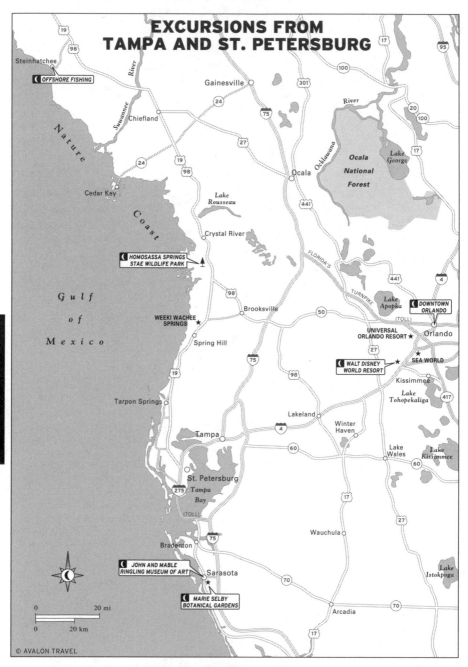

EXCURSIONS FROM TAMPA AND ST. PETERSBURG

EXCURSIONS

Steinhatchee

OFFSHORE FISHING

Nature

Gainesville

Chiefland

Cedar Key

Coast

Gulf

of

Mexico

Crystal River

HOMOSASSA SPRINGS
STAE WILDLIFE PARK

WEEKI WACHEE
SPRINGS

Spring Hill

Tarpon Springs

Tampa

St. Petersburg

*Tampa
Bay*

(TOLL)

Bradenton

JOHN AND MABLE
RINGLING MUSEUM OF ART

Sarasota

MARIE SELBY
BOTANICAL GARDENS

Arcadia

Ocala

Ocklawana

*Lake
Rousseau*

Brooksville

Lakeland

River

*Lake
George*

Ocala

National

Forest

FLORIDA'S

TURNPIKE

*Lake
Apopka*

DOWNTOWN
ORLANDO

(TOLL)

UNIVERSAL
ORLANDO RESORT

Orlando

SEA WORLD

WALT DISNEY
WORLD RESORT

Kissimmee

*Lake
Tohopekaliga*

Winter
Haven

Lake
Wales

*Lake
Kissimmee*

Wauchula

*Lake
Istokpoga*

0   20 mi

0   20 km

© AVALON TRAVEL

a pleasant outing for dinner and a show (its theater, opera, and other arts efforts beat those in Tampa and St. Petersburg handily). Hotels and restaurants in Sarasota proper are expensive, but more affordable digs are to be found on the barrier islands of Siesta Key and Anna Maria (many accommodations offered only by the week in high season). Another barrier island, Longboat Key, is designed to thrill the high-end golfer.

Orlando

A little like Las Vegas, Orlando draws people with the lure of fantasy, magic, and fun, with fewer vices or ladies in feathered headdresses. But unlike Vegas—where what happens there, stays there, subdued in a fog of excess—what happens in Orlando is the content of scrapbooks, subject of the lion's share of those family holiday photo cards, fodder for countless "what I did on my summer vacation" essays, and, maybe most important of all, the stuff of oft-recounted family memories.

Walt Disney World Resort sets the tone for all the other ancillary and tertiary theme parks and visitor attractions in Orlando. The sprawling Central Florida tourism hub features a brand of magic and fun that is by and large wholesome, but changing all the time as theme parks add, revise, and try to outdo the competition. The thing that holds it all together, that gives it a sense of continuity, is the destination's ongoing flair at appealing to many different kinds of people.

At each attraction, fun has been calibrated to appeal to many different interests and abilities. What started with a shrill-voiced mouse introduced at the Colony Theater in New York on November 18, 1928 has become a whole industry devoted to sussing out the unfulfilled dreams of generations of visitors. Like the sage Cinderella once said, "A dream is a wish your heart makes," which makes all of Orlando something like a psychic cardiologist.

SIGHTS
◖ Walt Disney World Resort
Walt Disney World (WDW, 407/939-1289,

http://disneyworld.disney.go.com) is spread across 30,080 acres, about twice the size of Manhattan, half in Orlando and half in Lake Buena Vista. It encompasses four distinct theme parks, two water parks, shopping and entertainment complexes, 24 resort hotels (plus another 8 that aren't Disney owned, but are on the property), five golf courses, a sports complex, and other attractions. For the uninitiated who have a vague notion that WDW is that park with the castle in the middle, thorough investigation cannot be undertaken on a single day. Magic Kingdom, the first of the parks, is divided into six themed lands, with lots to do for little ones. Epcot, what used to be EPCOT, an acronym for Experimental Prototype Community of Tomorrow, has two "worlds": Future World, which is mostly about science and technology, and World Showcase, pavilions representing countries around the world. Epcot appeals most to adults, whereas the third park, Disney's Hollywood Studios (formerly MGM) lures teens and tweens with its movie-themed rides and attractions. The fourth and newest park, Animal Kingdom, is not a zoo, but rather an animal-themed assemblage of exhibits and thrill rides. All four parks tend to host a festive afternoon parade, an evening celebration (many with fireworks), and special events throughout the year. Costumed Disney characters mill around at all four parks for photo ops and autograph signing.

Typhoon Lagoon and Blizzard Beach are the two themed water parks, each requiring separate entry. Downtown Disney is a shopping

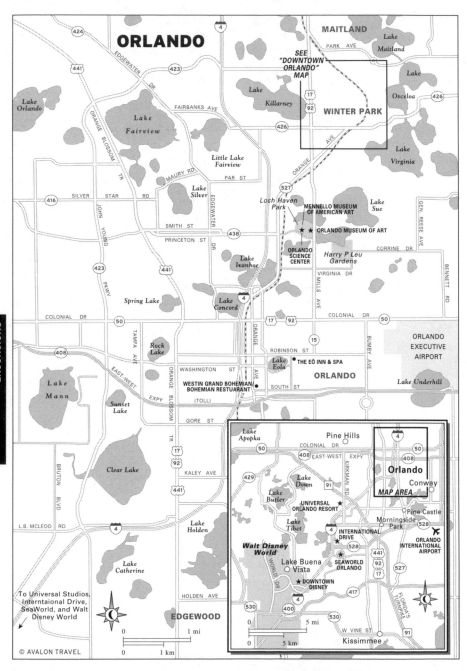

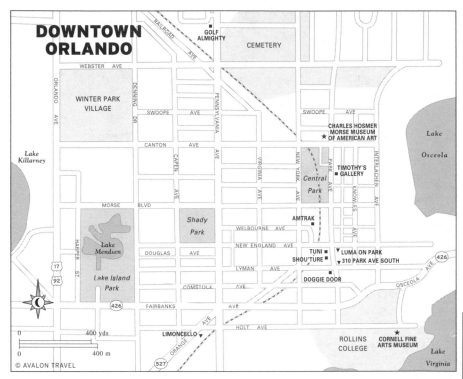

and dining complex with an adult nightclub area called Pleasure Island, a huge virtual-reality and video arcade called DisneyQuest, and a theater in which Cirque du Soleil performs La Nouba. The Wide World of Sports complex hosts sporting events like the Atlanta Braves spring training; the Richard Petty Driving Experience enables you to drive a real race car; and, 15 miles south, the Nature Conservancy oversees Disney Wilderness Preserve.

Universal Orlando Resort

Universal Orlando Resort (407/363-8000, www.universalorlando.com) began as a direct competitor to Disney's Hollywood Studios (formerly Disney-MGM). The idea was the same: build a working film and TV studio that is also a theme park in which guests are immersed in the world of the movies, its

dynamic rides, attractions, 3-D movies, and exhibits celebrating the cinema. A massive growth spurt in 1999 yielded a second park, Islands of Adventure, as well as three resort hotels, and a dining and nightlife complex called CityWalk. The tagline for Universal Studios Florida is Ride the Movies, whereas the phrase for Islands of Adventure is Live the Adventure. The distinction is a little blurry, but what you need to know is that Islands of Adventure has some of the most hair-raising, sweaty-palmed thrill rides in all of Orlando, cases in point being Incredible Hulk Coaster and The Amazing Adventures of Spider-Man, but also cool stuff like the Wizarding World of Harry Potter, which opened in 2010. And whereas Disney's Hollywood Studios focuses a little more on nostalgic old films, Universal Studios's efforts are more inspired by popular

COURTESY OF VISIT FLORIDA

SeaWorld Orlando

films, divided into seven themed areas within the park. Islands of Adventure draws from classic comics and comic book heroes.

SeaWorld Orlando

It's not an amusement park, but it's certainly no aquarium or zoo. SeaWorld Orlando (800/327-2420, www.seaworld.com) is a celebration of sea life, with a special emphasis on those amazingly smart marine mammals. Shamu and friends are put through their paces in a variety of shows that are constantly being updated and added to. The current killer whale show, *One Ocean* and the dolphin show, *Blue Horizons,* are offered several times daily along with other live shows that make up the core of the park's attractions. There are a couple thrill-ish rides, but the park's real strengths are the animal shows and educational walk-throughs of animal environments.

Just across the road from SeaWorld Orlando is its more upscale sibling, Discovery Cove. Limited to 1,000 guests per day by reservation,

the lush Caribbean resort allows visitors to swim with a dolphin, snorkel along a saltwater coral reef, frolic amongst stingrays, or just loll in a chaise on a sandy beach. Aquatica opened in 2008, a water park with slides, lazy rivers, wave pools, and far too much flesh exposed to the Florida sun.

C Downtown Orlando

Downtown? Yes, Orlando has one, located about 20 minutes northeast of the tourist sprawl. The downtown area and the nearby historic town of Winter Park are home to many of the area's top museums: See Tiffany stained glass at the **Charles Hosmer Morse Museum of American Art;** the work of folk artist Earl Cunningham and others at the **Mennello Museum of American Art;** a great permanent collection of American art, including works by Georgia O'Keefe and Ansel Adams at the **Orlando Museum of Art;** or a thoughtfully curated show at the **Cornell Fine Arts Museum,** considered one of the country's top college art museums. Kids are entertained at the hands-on **Orlando Science Center** or the 50-acres of botanical gardens at the nearby **Harry P. Leu Gardens,** while sports fans might want to catch an NBA's Orlando Magic game at **Amway Center.**

International Drive

Often shortened to I-Drive, this is the most intensive tourist strip of the greater Orlando area, running southwest of downtown roughly parallel to I-4 and linking SeaWorld Orlando and Universal Orlando Resort with the Orange County Convention Center and the two monster outlet malls. For visitors splitting their time between the various theme parks, I-Drive is an ideal and centralized place to stay, offering mid-priced and luxury high-rise hotels along its length. Some of the area's nicer restaurants crowd along I-Drive with many of the half-day tourist attractions (WonderWorks, Ripley's Believe It or Not, iFly Orlando). The downside is grueling, bumper-to-bumper traffic during rush hour. It is less crowded in its southern end near the convention center, unless there's a huge convention going on (check the website, www. occc.net, to find out).

Kissimmee

Some say the name was that of a 17th century mission created here to convert the Jororo tribe to Christianity, but everyone agrees that Kissimmee wins Central Florida's Hardest City to Pronounce award. Kissimmee, the Osceola County seat, is 18 miles due south of Orlando and just east of Walt Disney World Resort. Its roots are firmly planted in cattle ranching, with a lingering rough-and-tumble cowboy image. It's where folks go to see the rodeo, do a little bass fishing, ride an airboat through gator-studded waters, or tramp around on the beautiful Florida Trail. Through Kissimmee, the long strip of multi-laned highway called U.S. 192 or Irlo Bronson Memorial Highway is the jackpot for budget-minded Disney visitors. Moderately priced motels, family restaurants and fast food, and a staggering number of mini-golf emporiums dot its length.

Between Kissimmee and Walt Disney World Resort lies the town of Celebration. Clusters of eerily perfect Victorian homes align on neat streets of the Disney Corporation's prototypical community of the future. It's not exactly what Mr. Disney had in mind with EPCOT, but it's close.

RESTAURANTS
Walt Disney World Resort

Dining options are so plentiful as to be dizzying—each Disney park has on-site dining ranging from walk-up casual to white-tablecloth fine, and each of the 32 Disney resort properties offer their own eats. A handful of the better options are listed here.

The **Hoop-Dee-Doo Musical Revue** (Fort Wilderness Resort & Campground, 407/939-3463, three shows daily: 4 P.M., 6:15 P.M., and 8:30 P.M., $54–64 adult, $28–33 child) is the big dining kahuna here, and advance reservations are a must (up to 180 days). It's an all-American hoedown with family-style barbecued ribs, corn, baked beans, draft beer, wine, and soft drinks, all enjoyed with a musical comedy review that always gets highest marks from longtime Disney fans. It's one of the longest-running shows at WDW.

Making lists of Orlando's top restaurants nearly every year, **California Grill** (Contemporary Resort, 407/824-1576, https:// disneyworld.disney.go.com, daily 5:30–10 P.M., $36–60) draws locals as well as tourists. It was one of Disney's earliest efforts at luxurious destination dining, with panoramic windows showing off Magic Kingdom (and its fireworks) and a dynamic open kitchen. The food is a very apt facsimile of what made San Francisco such a culinary mecca in the late 1980s—flatbreads, Sonoma goat cheese ravioli, grilled pork tenderloin with polenta and balsamic-sparked cremini mushrooms: simple, bright flavors, with a heavy reliance on seasonal produce. The wine list is a treasure trove for the California Cabophile, even by the glass. But be aware, California Grill will be under refurbishment from January 6, 2013 through late summer 2013.

Jiko–The Cooking Place (Animal Kingdom Lodge, 407/938-4733, https://disneyworld.disney.go.com, daily 5:30–10 P.M., $36–60) is the top offering, with a broad palette of cuisines that range across the Mediterranean, Europe, and the 52 countries on the African continent. It's a lovely dining space, vaguely evocative of *The Lion King,* enlivened by two huge wood-burning ovens. Appetizers tend to be more imaginative than entrées, and the array of wines from South Africa is laudable.

Universal Orlando Resort

Set off to one side of Universal's CityWalk is the biggest **Hard Rock Café** (407/351-7625, daily

EXCURSIONS

11 A.M.–midnight, $11–30) in the world—a veritable "Roman Coliseum of rock," replete with memorabilia from KISS, Elvis, The Beatles, and Bob Dylan, along with an all-American menu of burgers, ribs, and salads. Or kick it up a notch and head to **Emeril's Restaurant Orlando** (407/224-2424, daily 11:30 A.M.–3 P.M. and 5–10 P.M., Fri. and Sat. until 10:30 P.M., $25–50) for Emeril Lagasse's upscale spins on Louisiana-style oyster stew, duck, and rib eye. The cocktails are good, but the 12,000-bottle wine list merits some robust consideration. There's also a notable cigar bar and all prime beef—an expense-account paradise.

SeaWorld Orlando

Makahiki Luau Dinner and Show used to be the big daily dinner event, but it closed at the end of 2012. Instead, **Sharks Underwater Grill** (800/327-2424, www.seaworldparks. com, daily 11 A.M. until one hour before park closing, $18–35) is SeaWorld Orlando going fancy-pants. It's first come, first served, but you can put your name in for priority seating and come back at a designated time. There's a very commendable à la carte menu of Floribbean dishes—sushi-grade tuna with tropical slaw, lobster bisque, jumbo lump crab cakes with Key lime mustard mayonnaise—served in an elegant, "underwater" dining room. Not really, but the enormous walls of shark tanks are truly compelling if dinner conversation lapses.

Downtown Orlando

Some of the best dining in this area is to be had in the charming town of **Winter Park,** just northeast of downtown. It's a serious food city, where restaurants engage in fierce competition for the approbation of the sophisticated, worldly locals. **Luma on Park** (290 S. Park Ave., 407/599-4111, www.lumaonpark. com, daily 5:30–11 P.M., $23–37) may currently get top honors for its incredible array of wines by the glass as well as its contemporary

dishes such as Idaho rainbow trout with Israeli couscous and Myakka Farms fennel coulis, or pizzas like the roasted apple, gorgonzola crema, and speck. At the corner of Park and New England Avenues, it's in a perfect corner spot in the recently remodeled Bank of America building, with a striking two-story illuminated wine vault.

The No. 2 spot is nipping at its heels, **The Ravenous Pig** (1234 Orange Ave., 407/628-2333, www.theravenouspig.com, Tues.–Sat. 11:30 A.M.–2 P.M. and 5 P.M.–10 P.M., $14–29) being a nationally regarded gastropub, a wizard of pork belly and all things charcuterie. **Prato** (124 Park Ave., 407/262-0050, www.prato-wp. com, Wed.–Sun. 11:30 A.M.–3 P.M., nightly 5:30–11 P.M., $7–18) gets more mixed reviews for service, but this relative newcomer has set the standard for indoor/outdoor patio dining, with a regional Italian small plate menu that seems super contemporary.

SHOPS

Each of the theme parks boasts its own shopping, mostly of the themed gewgaw variety. For more extensive retail therapy, head to **Prime Outlets Orlando** at the northern tip of International Drive, **Orlando Premium Outlets** at the southern tip of International Drive, or the 120-acre **Downtown Disney** (1780 E. Buena Vista Dr., Lake Buena Vista). This last is a shopping and dining complex comprised of the **Marketplace** (common areas open 8 A.M.–1 P.M.) and the 66-acre **West Side** (common areas open 8 A.M.–2 A.M.). The shopping consists of souvenirs, luxury goods, and zany impulse buys, like chili-cheese dog refrigerator magnets (very lifelike) and cans of Flarp!, described euphemistically as "noise-making goop." If one were so inclined, one could also buy just-dipped candy apples, a spinning sphere that appears to hover in space, a battery-operated hamster that runs incessantly inside a clear plastic ball, or a premium cigar.

Universal CityWalk is a 30-acre adult playground of restaurants, nightclubs, and music venues. It sits right at the entrance to both Universal Studios and Islands of Adventure, with a gorgeous 20-screen AMC movie theater. Shopping is nothing particularly upscale or notable, mostly impulse-buy souvenir shops, from the super cool skateboard-obilia at **Element** to the incendiary delights of **Cigarz at CityWalk** to the bright cotton clothing for the whole family at **Fresh Produce.**

In Orlando, the biggest draw is the relatively new **Mall at Millenia** (4200 Conroy Rd., Orlando, www.mallatmillenia.com). In Winter Park there are 10 blocks of shops and galleries interspersed with restaurants along Park Avenue, from Swoope Avenue south to Fairbanks Avenue. You'll see ubiquitous national names (Gap, Talbot's), but independent shops abound, from clothing boutiques like the trendy **Tuni** (301 S. Park Ave., Winter Park, 407/628-1609) or **Blue Door Denim** (316 N. Park Ave., Winter Park, 407/647-2583). There are galleries like **Timothy's Gallery** (236 N. Park Ave., Winter Park, 407/629-0707) with ceramics, jewelry, and home accessories; **Peterbrooke Chocolatier** (300 S. Park Ave., Winter Park, 407/644-3200) when you need a sweet; and **Doggie Door** (356 S. Park Ave., Winter Park, 407/644-2969) when you need a treat for the canine back home.

Winter Park Village (500 N. Orlando Ave., 407/571-2502, www.shopwinterparkvillage. net) is a nearby small shopping center with retail shops, about a dozen restaurants, a great chocolate shop, and a 20-screen movie theater.

HOTELS
Walt Disney World Resort
Walt Disney World (WDW, 407/934-7639, http://waltdisneyworld.disney.go.com) has 33 different resorts, with more than 31,000 guest rooms and 784 campsites—this includes seven Disney Vacation Club resort properties, and 10

resorts that are not Disney owned and operated. If the bulk of your time in Orlando will be spent at Walt Disney World Resort theme parks, it makes a lot of sense to stay in one of the Disney Resorts. They are offered at nearly every price point, many of them just adjacent to one of the parks, and there are a host of benefits afforded Disney Resort guests. There are also perks like getting to use your Disney Resort ID like a credit card, or having a package delivery right to your room. Resort identification (your plastic Disney Resort ID) and theme park admission tickets are required to take advantage of these perks.

Universal Orlando Resort
There are three hotels on the property, each with its own flavor and price point, included here from least expensive to most. Each is within walking distance of Universal Studios, Islands of Adventure, and CityWalk, and guests get Universal Express preferred access to theme park rides and attractions, along with priority seating at most on-site restaurants and shows. There's also courtesy water taxi and bus transportation between the resort and park, complimentary package delivery of in-park purchases to guest rooms, and you can use your resort ID to charge things throughout Universal Orlando.

The Loews's **Royal Pacific Resort** (6300 Hollywood Way, 407/503-3000, www.loewshotels.com/Royal-Pacific-Resort, from $240) has a South Pacific vibe, complete with luscious tropical landscaping and lagoons on a 53-acre property. It's big, with 1,000 rooms and 85,000 square feet of meeting space, so you'll see a preponderance of business and convention travelers here, swirling around the central fountain of the lobby's Orchid Court or the active lobby bar. If you want to spend a little time up close with one of Elvis's rhinestone jumpsuits or a little footwear from Elton John's closet, head straight for the **Hard Rock Hotel** (5800

Universal Blvd., 407/503-7625, www.hardrock-hotelorlando.com, from $319), designed in a hip California mission style with 650 rooms. As with other Hard Rocks, the public spaces are chockablock with rock memorabilia, and huge video screens run concert footage. The **Portofino Bay Hotel** (5601 Universal Blvd., 407/503-1000, www.universalorlando.com, from $350) aims at Mediterranean luxury. Opened in 1999, the hotel features 750 rooms in a kind of Italian seaside village environment. It has won awards like the AAA Four Diamond Award and a place in *Travel + Leisure* magazine's Top 500 Hotels in the World, mostly for its lovely rooms with garden or bay views, and its wide array of amenities.

SeaWorld Orlando

The **Residence Inn Orlando SeaWorld/ International Center** (11000 Westwood Blvd., 800/889-9728, www.marriott.com, from $139) is six stories in a Floribbean motif, with 350 rooms and one- and two-bedroom suites with fully equipped kitchens. There's a very nice hot breakfast buffet that is thrown in, with waffles, pancakes, and all the fixings, which you can eat out by the pool. It's a great family hotel, entertaining the kids with a big heated pool, playground, game arcade, and sports courts. **Renaissance Orlando Resort at SeaWorld** (6677 Sea Harbor Dr., 407/351-5555, www.renaissanceseaworldorlando.com, from $299) is located directly across from SeaWorld Orlando, Discovery Cove, Aquatica, and one mile from Orlando's Orange County Convention Center. The hotel boasts 185,000 square feet of meeting and event space with a 10-story atrium (full of waterfalls, exotic birds, and goldfish ponds), 18-hole championship golf course, three lighted tennis courts, and an Olympic-size swimming pool with a 120-foot water slide. The 778 rooms have recently been renovated, along with 64 suites. All rooms feature 32-inch flat-panel televisions and king beds with a sleeper sofa or double queen-size beds.

Downtown Orlando

Hotelier Richard Kessler opened the AAA four-diamond **Westin Grand Bohemian** (325 S. Orange Ave., 407/313-9000, www.grandbohemianhotel.com, from $249) in 2001 and people thought he was a little touched. The laughs on them because the hotel has been a hit amongst business travelers, with its 247 guest rooms gorgeously kitted out with velvet drapes, plush leather headboards, and crisp white bed linens on pillow-top beds. The hotel's Boheme Restaurant consistently wins kudos from food magazines, its luxurious menu featuring dishes like seared foie gras with fig bread pudding and a warm huckleberry sauce, and surprising Asian fillips as in the sushi bento box for two or the Thai spiced duck breast with black bean sauce. A Sunday jazz brunch draws a huge following, and the Bösendorfer Lounge (with one of only two Imperial Grand Bösendorfer pianos in the world) features nightly jazz.

On a much more intimate scale, **The Eō Inn & Spa** (227 N. Eola Dr., 407/481-8485, www.eoinn.com, from $139) boasts 17 suites tucked into a 1923-era building overlooking Lake Eola Park and the downtown skyline. A rooftop terrace with whirlpool, a day spa, and an in-house Panera restaurant make it an extremely pleasant stay.

GETTING THERE AND AROUND

From the Tampa Bay area, Orlando is about an hour northeast along I-4. This route is notoriously under construction and often just clogged with tourists, so leave yourself plenty of time in either direction.

Once in the Orlando area, you will find excellent signage that makes it easy to navigate throughout the area and around the various theme parks. **I-4** is the main route to the theme parks and in the greater Orlando area, but it's tricky: It's an east–west highway, but takes a north–south jog from Kissimmee up through Downtown Orlando to the north. Traffic can

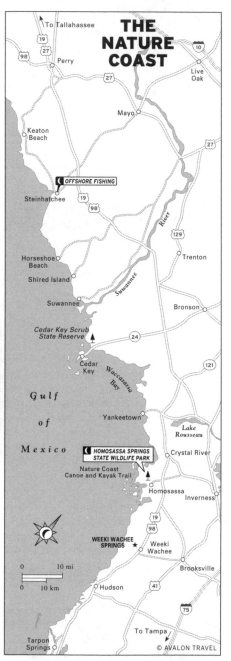

THE
NATURE
COAST

To Tallahassee
19
98
27
Perry
10
Live
Oak
27
Mayo
Keaton
Beach
27
OFFSHORE FISHING
Steinhatchee
19
98
River
129
Horseshoe
Beach
Trenton
Shired Island
Suwannee
Suwannee
Bronson
Cedar Key Scrub
State Reserve
24
Cedar
Key
Waccasassa
Bay
121
Gulf
of
Yankeetown
Lake
Rousseau
Mexico
**HOMOSASSA SPRINGS
STATE WILDLIFE PARK**
Crystal River
Nature Coast
Canoe and Kayak Trail
Homosassa
Inverness
19
98
**WEEKI WACHEE
SPRINGS**
Weeki
Wachee
0   10 mi
Brooksville
0   10 km
Hudson
41
Tarpon
Springs
To Tampa
75
© AVALON TRAVEL

apparatus to north of Tampa around 1900 and persuaded friends and family, sponge divers all, to relocate from Hydra and Aegena, Greece, to this little Florida backwater. Greeks begot more Greeks and a booming town of Greek restaurants, Greek Orthodox churches, and Greek festivals grew up around the sponge industry. Tarpon Springs was the largest U.S. sponge-diving port in the 1930s, but a sponge blight and new synthetic sponge technology caused business to dry up.

The town is still more than one-third Greek, with a sweet, kitschy, Old Florida tourist attraction charm and several fine restaurants. Sponges are everywhere, most of them imported from more sponge-rich far-flung lands.

It's well worth an afternoon of your time—see the museum and the sponge docks, shop a little, and have dinner.

First stop, **Spongeorama** (510 Dodecanese Blvd., 727/943-2164, www.spongeorama. com, Mon.–Sat. 10:30 A.M.–5 P.M., Sun. 11:30 A.M.–5 P.M., free). The building itself is also called the Sponge Factory, but let's stick with Spongeorama. A little down at the heels, the shop/attraction has mannequins dressed as sponge divers and shows an old crackly movie called *Men and the Sea,* which you view before wandering around the little sponge museum with dioramas of sponge-diving history (one gory diorama depicts a diver dying of the bends—kids hang out for a long time in front of this one). Afterwards, you buy a couple of specimens (the "wool" ones are highly prized) at the gift shop. There are rumors that Spongeorama is haunted; maybe it's that diver with the bends.

If you're still angling for more sponge action, **St. Nicholas Boat Line** (693 Dodecanese Blvd., 727/942-6425, $8 adult, $4 child age 6–12, free for child under 6) offers a fun, 35-minute narrated boat cruise through the sponge docks, with its own sponge-diving demonstration.

natural sea sponges drying in the sun

Out on the main drag, Dodecanese Boulevard, there are seven blocks of shops and restaurants. Before you settle on a place to eat, stop into nearby **St. Nicholas Greek Orthodox Cathedral** (18 Hibiscus St., 727/937-3540, www.epiphanycity.org, office hours Mon.–Fri. 10 A.M.–4 P.M., hours for services vary), made of 60 tons of Greek marble once on display at the Greek exhibit at the first New York World's Fair. The church is a copy of the Byzantine Revival St. Sophia in Constantinople, with beautiful Czech chandeliers and stained glass. If you happen to be here in January, time a visit for Epiphany on the 6th—this church is the center of the biggest Epiphany celebration in the country. Festivities move from the church to nearby Spring Bayou, where young Greek men dive for a cross that has been blessed and thrown into the water.

Weeki Wachee Springs

The job requirements are tough: a winning smile, powerful athleticism, and a great body. Now add to that the ability to hold one's breath for 2.5 minutes. Florida is home to a variety of rare aquatic creatures, but perhaps none are so singular as the 21 mermaids and mermen who swim through their daily choreographed show at Weeki Wachee Springs (6131 Commercial Way, Spring Hill, 352/596-2062, http://weeki-wachee.com, daily 9 A.M.–5:30 P.M., $13 adult, $8 child age 3–10).

In 1947, former U.S. Navy frogman Newton Perry thought of a way to bring added draw to one of the United States's most prolific fresh-water springs. More than 170 million gallons of 72°F water pour dramatically into the Weeki Wachee River daily. Perry's notion was to gussy up the headwater with a bevy of beautiful mermaids. To this end, he taught a group of powerful swimmers to breathe through submerged air hoses supplied by an air compressor, the upshot being a remarkable 30- to 45-minute, entirely underwater extravaganza.

Conceived in the heyday of MGM's trademark aquatic musical spectaculars starring Esther Williams, the show at Weeki Wachee Springs is nonetheless a family affair. There are plenty of ogling opportunities, but these bathing beauties are put through their paces in a show that usually draws from past Disney movies (recent shows have included, unsurprisingly, *The Little Mermaid* and *Pocahontas*).

The audience sits in a small underground amphitheatre in front of a four-inch-thick plate-glass window, behind which the blue waters of the springs teem with fish, turtles, eels, and women in oversized, shimmering tails who twirl, undulate, and lip-synch on cue. Many of the mermaids have been with the show for decades, a fact that can be ascertained with a quick look through photos and memorabilia in the small **Mermaid Museum** (a wall of fame includes early sea nymphs cavorting with Elvis and Don Knotts), opened to commemorate the show's 50th anniversary in 1997.

After getting your picture taken with a mermaid, check out the rest of the 200-acre family entertainment park, Florida's only natural spring water park. This includes a flume ride at Buccaneer Bay, a low-key Birds of Prey show, a petting zoo, and jungle river cruise.

The admission price includes Buccaneer Bay. Weeki Wachee is open year-round but Buccaneer Bay is closed during the winter months and reopens each mid-March.

RESTAURANTS
Tarpon Springs

Everyone has a different favorite Greek restaurant here. Ours is **Hellas** (785 Dodecanese Blvd., 727/943-2400, www.hellas-restaurant.com, daily 11 A.M.–10 P.M., $10–26), a lively spot with a full bar and a wonderful Greek bakery attached to it. The best entrée is slowly braised tomatoey lamb shanks, served somewhat mysteriously atop spaghetti. There are addictive garlic shrimp, nice gyros in warm Greek pita, and a delicious Greek salad that comes with a scoop of potato salad hidden in its midst. Others swear by **Mykonos** (628 Dodecanese Blvd., 727/934-4306, daily 11 A.M.–10 P.M., $10–24) for the lamb chops, Greek meatloaf, and slightly more refined atmosphere. Still, **Mama's** (735 Dodecanese Blvd., 727/944-2888, www.mamasgreekcuisine.net, daily 11 A.M.–10 P.M., $7–14) often gets the nod for casual, family-friendly booths and delicious but messy chicken souvlaki sandwiches. If you're visiting on a Saturday night, head over after dinner to the bouzouki club called **Zorba** (508 W. Athens, 727/934-8803, Thurs. noon–2 A.M., Fri.–Sat. 8 P.M.–2 A.M., Sun. 8 P.M.–midnight), for some zesty belly dancing and an ouzo.

Weeki Wachee Springs Area

For something a little splurgy, **Brian's Place** (3430 Shoal Line Blvd., 352/597-5101, Tues.–Sun. 4–9 P.M., www.briansonthebeach.com, $13–25) is presided over by Brian Alvarez, with a slightly quirky Italian-Spanish fusion menu, from artichoke basil crab cakes to chipotle sesame seared tuna.

Cedar Key

Built in 1859, the **Island Hotel and Restaurant** (2nd St. and B St., 352/543-5111, www.island-hotel-cedarkey.com, Tues.–Sun. 6–9 P.M., $15–24) is purportedly haunted by 13 ghosts, particularly during grisly weather. Even if you don't believe the story of the restless spirit of a murdered former owner, you'll enjoy the hearts of palm salad (supposedly invented here by the hotel's original owners), the crab bisque, or just a drink in the chummy bar.

For elegant waterside dining, head to the **Island Room Restaurant at Cedar Cove** (10 E. 2nd. St., 352/543-6520, www.islandroom.com, Mon.–Sat. 5–10 P.M., Sun. 10 A.M.–9 P.M., $14–28) for Chef Peter Stefani's house-grown veggies and greens or his oh-so-local Cedar

Key seafood boil. After dinner, if you're not quite ready to turn in, head over to Dock Street for a game of pool, darts, or some game viewing at **Coconuts of Cedar Key** (590 Dock St., 352/543-6390, www.coconutsofcedarkey.com, daily 11 A.M.–2 A.M.) or a drink with the locals at **Black Dog Bar and Tables** (360 Dock St., 352/325-0050, www.cedarkeybar.com, Wed.–Thurs. and Sun. 3–10 P.M., Fri. and Sat. 3 P.M.–midnight) or **Seabreeze** (310 Dock St., 352/543-5738, Mon.–Wed. 11 A.M.–9 P.M., Thurs. 4:30–9 P.M., Fri. and Sat. 11 A.M.–10 P.M., Sun. noon–9 P.M.). And when you're feeling fortified and emboldened, order the single weirdest dish the island has to offer: Seabreeze's signature salad is a mélange of lettuce, hearts of palm, peach, pineapple, and dates, "dressed" with a slowly melting scoop of peanut butter ice cream.

Steinhatchee

The dining scene here is dominated by **Fiddler's Restaurant** (1306 Riverside Dr., 352/498-7427, http://fiddlersrestaurant.com, Mon.–Thurs. 4–10 P.M., Fri.–Sun. 11 A.M.–10 P.M., $10–20), a sprawling, lively spot populated by anglers swapping big fish stories and tucking into fried grouper (you can bring your own cleaned catch and have them cook it up). **Roy's** (100 1st Ave. SW, 352/498-5000, www.roys-restaurant.com, daily 11 A.M.–9 P.M., $13–16), a local favorite since 1969, doesn't serve any booze but has an exhaustive salad bar, fried seafood, and fat burgers that keep people happy.

RECREATION
Swimming with Manatees

The West Indian manatee is still listed as an endangered species, but the population has rebounded tremendously in the past few years in this area. Manatee "season" is October 15–March 31, but you'll spot them all year long. Kings Bay in Crystal River has the densest concentration, but the Blue Waters area of the

Homosassa River is a little less trafficked by boats, thus a bit quieter. Either way, you can commune with these lumbering mammals from the distance that suits you (up close their size is unsettling—just remember they are herbivores, with blunt teeth so far back in their heads that you could, were it legal, hand feed them with no worries). **Manatee Tour & Dive** (267 NW 3rd St., Crystal River, 888/732-2692, www.manateetouranddive.com, $39 adult, $24 child) offers two-hour manatee swim and snorkeling trips suitable for the whole family in the waters of Crystal River, and scuba trips in Crystal Springs and Kings Spring, an underwater cavern praised for its excellent visibility, size, and potential for underwater photography (thousands of saltwater fish congregate at the cavern's two exits).

Sunshine River Tours (1 SW 1st Pl., Crystal River, 352/628-3450, www.sunshinerivertours.com, $40) has a similar range of guided ecotourism escapades in Homosassa. If a manatee swim and snorkel tour doesn't sound like a good way to take the waters, you can try your hand at scalloping (July 1–Sept. 10) or just a boat ride to follow the river out to the Gulf of Mexico.

◖ Homosassa Springs State Wildlife Park

How could even the most myopic and woman-starved ancient mariner have mistaken these slow and lugubrious sea cows for mermaids? Manatees, so famous in these parts, can weigh up to 2,000 pounds and look like submerged, limbless elephants, often festooned with algae and barnacles. You'll catch sight of them most often during cooler months, December–March, in the Suwannee River or at Manatee or Fanning Springs State Parks. From boat or shore, look for swirly "footprints" on the water's surface or torpedo-like shapes ambling across the shallow bottom. If you want a guaranteed viewing, stop into Homosassa Springs

The warm water of Homosassa Springs is a natural attraction to manatees during winter.

State Wildlife Park (4150 S. Suncoast Blvd., Homosassa, 352/628-5343, daily 9 A.M.– 5:30 P.M., $13 adult, $5 child), where you can see these marine mammals several ways. Visitors are loaded onto pontoon boats and shuttled through the canopied headwaters of the Homosassa River to a refuge for injured manatees and other animals. Alternately, at 11:30 A.M., 1:30 P.M., and 3:30 P.M., a manatee program allows you to watch docents wade out to feed stubby carrots to a slow-moving swarm of these creatures, many etched with outboard motor scars from run-ins with boats, after which you can walk down to the glass-fronted Fishbowl Underwater Observatory and see eye-to-eye with the gentle giants and the park's other indigenous aquatic creatures. (Mysteriously, the park hosts a hippo named Lucifer—a washed-up animal actor—that former governor Lawton Chiles declared an honorary Florida native.)

⟨ Offshore Fishing

Folks visiting this area most often spend their time, and considerable money, on half-day or full-day charters out into the Gulf in search of amberjack, kingfish (the most terrible-tasting of the fiercely beautiful sportfish), redfish, cobia, and grouper. Black grouper limits are five per person, per day, and they must be at least 22 inches long. **Big Bend Charters** (352/498-3703, www.bigbendcharters.com) takes groups of up to six far out on offshore trips ($750), nearshore trips ($400), and on a "thrill" fishing trip that targets a range of species ($1,200). Keep the grouper you catch, and pawn the rest of it off on someone else. Fresh-caught local grouper is a revelation.

Farther in, spotted sea trout, catfish, and redfish can be coaxed out of the grass flats of Deadman's Bay or the slow-moving Steinhatchee River. Kingfish travel through Steinhatchee spring and fall to stay in the perfect water temperature (72°F or so), and the

THE SILVER KING

Any fly-fisher will tell you Homosassa, a little Old Florida town, is where the big tarpon congregate, for no reason anyone can fathom. Many of the world record catches, approaching 300 pounds on different tackle, were caught right here. It's a respectful, almost reverent endeavor, with patience often yielding nothing but sunburn. On any given day, you'll see the river dotted with 25 or 30 flats boats navigated with push poles in a hushed silence of profound concentration, everyone waiting to see one roll along the surface in water depths of 5–25 feet. People come from all over the world to the Nature Coast to sight fish, spin casting or fly-fishing for these behemoths before releasing them gently into the warm, clear waters. Tarpon begin to run the last weeks of April and fade out in July. What many consider the "Super Bowl of fishing," tarpon fishing requires a special tag to keep one, and some serious know-how. If you catch one (using live crabs, baitfish, or hand-tied flies), the initial jumps and runs of that angry hooked fish will take your breath away.

If you want to try your hand at chasing giant tarpon on the Gulf or, even better, fly-fishing with light tackle in the backwaters from Homosassa to Cedar Key, try **Capt. Rick LeFiles** (Osprey Guide Services, 6115 Riverside Dr., Yankeetown, 352/447-0829, ospreyguides.com, $350 for a day of reds and trout, $450 for tarpon or spin tackle) or fourth-generation Homosassa **Capt. William Toney** (352/621-9284, www.homosassainshorefishing.com, $350 for a half day, $400 for full day for 1–2 people, $50 each additional person).

town is a legendary trout and redfish fishery in the wintertime when the fish move up into the river. Freshwater fishing can be accomplished dockside or from a rented canoe, but it's more fun in a shallow-draft boat with a motor: A 24-foot deck boat with a 200-horsepower Yamaha motor with a bimini will run you $150 per half day, plus fuel at the **River Haven Marina** (1110 Riverside Dr. SE, Steinhatchee, 352/498-0709). First-timers should hire a guide (it's an eminent place to learn saltwater fly-fishing techniques), but if you're striking out on your own, head to one of the local marinas (Sea Hag, River Haven, or Gulf Stream) and listen carefully to suss out the latest hot spots and irresistible baits. (Tip: Wear sunglasses with polarized lenses so you can see into the water more effectively.)

SHOPS

Inveterate shoppers will be a little flummoxed by the Nature Coast's meager retail options. There is a serviceable **mall in Crystal River** (1801 NW U.S. 19, 352/795-2585) with ubiquitous stores such as Sears, Kmart, and Payless, and Cedar Key's **Dock Street** is host to the kinds of shell-themed giftware and handicrafts stores found in many little seaside towns. For a real local frisson of excitement, sift through the 300 or so booths at **Howard's Flea Market** (6373 S. Suncoast Blvd., Homosassa Springs, 352/628-3532, Fri. 7 A.M.–2 P.M., Sat.–Sun. 6:30 A.M.–3 P.M.). To safeguard against rain and muggy weather, the market is enclosed, with vendors hawking Nascar merchandise, leather goods, tools, and even puppies. A bird aviary and food vendors (good barbecue, excellent old-fashioned root beer) make it fun for the whole family.

HOTELS

People are drawn to the Nature Coast for a raw, unmediated view into the natural world. They come with rods and reels, without hair dryers or sometimes even a decent change of shirt. Thus, this swath of Florida is replete with RV parks, campgrounds, and fish camps that run from rough wooden cabins to no-frills motels.

EXCURSIONS

In nearly all the small towns that dot U.S. 19 or the little roads west to the Gulf, you can bet on finding a clean room in a mom-and-pop venture where the decor is uninspired and the amenities limited.

But in addition to these or the more upscale lodgings listed here, the area provides opportunities to indulge a lot of people's moony-eyed fantasy of endless, tranquil mobility: a houseboat stay. You can go "way down upon the Suwannee River" with a 44-foot houseboat rented from **Miller's Marine & Suwannee Houseboats** (County Road 349, Suwannee, 800/458-2628, $640 Fri. afternoon–Sun. afternoon, $599–800 for two days). The crafts rent by the day, weekend, or week, sleep up to eight, and are equipped with showers, bathroom facilities, linens, full kitchens, and cookware. The owners take renters on a warm-up cruise to teach them the basics, then you're on your own with 70 miles of river, countless springs, and an up-close view of the area's wildlife.

We got the anchor stuck, saw a bald eagle, fished from the comfort of our beds, scratched chigger bites, and generally pretended we were Huckleberry Finn.

Crystal River

The Nature Coast doesn't offer the glut of golfing opportunities as elsewhere in Florida. If you're jonesing to tee off, the **Plantation Inn and Golf Resort** (9301 W. Fort Island Trail, Crystal River, 352/795-4211, www.plantationinn.com, rooms $124–350, includes greens fees) boasts a par-72, 18-hole championship course and a 9-hole executive course for training and practice, in addition to manatee snorkeling tours, guided scuba diving, and 145 guest rooms (with 12 golf villas and 6 condos). Given all the amenities and glitz, room rates are fairly reasonable.

Cedar Key

A fairly recent addition, **The Faraway Inn** (3rd and G Sts., 888/543-5330, www.farawayinn.com, $75–160) is set within a quiet, attractive residential area away from traffic and nightlife, but within a short five-minute walk past Victorian and traditional Cracker homes to restaurants, convenience stores, shops, boat launches, the public beach, and the city dock. Faraway Inn was built in the early 1950s on the original site of the 19th-century Eagle Pencil Company Cedar Mill. The inn has little freestanding efficiencies and cottages as well as more motel-like accommodations. It's pet friendly.

Steinhatchee

Steinhatchee Landing Resort (228 NE Hwy. 51, 800/584-1709, www.steinhatcheelanding.com, $146–612) is as swanky as it gets along the Nature Coast. The brainchild of patrician Georgian gentleman Dean Fowler, its 35 acres are dotted with dozens of individual one-, two-, and three-bedroom Victorian and Florida Cracker cottages, most equipped with French country furniture, oversize spa tubs, and wildly luxurious appointments for such a down-home fishing village. There's a new swimming pool and patio area, and it accepts pets up to 28 pounds.

If that's too rich for your blood, the same folks own the nearby 17-room budget-friendly **Steinhatchee River Inn** (1111 Riverside Dr., 352/498-4049, www.steinhatcheeriverinn.net, $79–129), where the rates fluctuate depending on the season.

GETTING THERE AND AROUND

Florida's Nature Coast is west of I-75 and is accessible by the north–south corridor of U.S. 19. Most of the Nature Coast is accessible by car or boat only. There is no public transportation to speak of (okay, there are two southbound and two northbound Greyhound buses that stop daily in Crystal River and Chiefland—but

PASCO COUNTY

Pasco County, the sleepy, landlocked area to Tampa's north, has at least a day's worth of kooky fun. It's definitely worth a side trip, a couple of meals, and maybe even an overnight at one of the area's luscious spa/golf/tennis resorts.

Lake Como Family Nudist Resort in the town of Lutz is the area's original nudist community, started in 1947. Since then, Pasco County has become a hotbed of naturist activity, with six all-ages nudist communities and recreational activities (until recently there was naked bowling at the local lanes). These days the biggest player is the 120-acre **Caliente Resort and Spa** (21240 Gran Via Blvd., Land O' Lakes, 800/326-7731, calienteresorts.com/tampa).

Another Pasco original requiring a little bit of chutzpah is **Skydive City** (4241 Skydive Ln., off Chancey Rd., 813/783-9399, skydivecity.com, $199, $294 with video) in Zephyrhills. The town has been a world-famous drop zone since the 1960s, with a world meet in 1972. Tandem jumping (where a rookie jumps harnessed to an instructor) has opened skydiving up to a wider audience.

It takes about an hour to prepare, with a 20-minute briefing. The whole experience is a 3-4-hour adventure, with freefall at 120 mph for about a minute from 13,500 feet, followed by up to six minutes of steering with the parachute open.

After that, take it down a notch and enjoy a walking tour of downtown **Dade City.** In the rolling hills of eastern Pasco County, the town has more than 50 antiques stores, gift shops, and boutiques. Stop into the historic 1909 Pasco County Courthouse and look at the sweet collection of artifacts from the turn of the 20th century. And then have a slice of history with a slice of pie at **Lunch on Limoges** (14139 7th St., 352/567-5685, $12-18). It's a darling throwback to a former era of refined and leisurely lunching, with a daily-changing menu served on Limoges china by nice waitresses in nurses' uniforms with sensible orthopedic shoes. The chocolate cake is excellent, but they have a fairly steep minimum order to dine here.

Not far from downtown and worth maybe an hour, **The Pioneer Florida Museum** (15602 Pioneer Museum Rd., 352/567-0262, www.pioneerfloridamuseum.org, Tues.-Sat. 10 A.M.-5 P.M., $6 adult, $5 senior, $2 child under 18) consists of nine period buildings dating back to 1878. There's the John Overstreet House, the Lacoochee School, and the Enterprise Methodist Church, all displaying period furniture, clothing, toys, and tools. There's also a spooky collection of miniature big-eyed dolls of Florida's first ladies. The museum has good raw material, but it should spend a chunk of volunteer hours redoing some of their signage, which looks a little tired. There often isn't quite enough explanation of what we're looking at—in a historical museum, signs so often tell the story.

If there's time, take a tour around **New Port Richey's Main Street** (www.newportrichey-mainstreet.com) and then board a boat and ride the **Pithlachascotee River** to see historic homes once owned by Gloria Swanson, Thomas Meighan, and Babe Ruth. Then walk around **Centennial Cultural Park,** which contains the Pasco Fine Arts Council, the Centennial Library, and the 1882 Baker House, one of the oldest structures in Pasco County. If you're hungry, stop in at waterside **Catches** (7811 Bayview St., 727/849-2121, www.catcheswaterfrontgrille.com).

Saddlebrook Resort & Spa (5700 Saddlebrook Way, 800/729-8383, www.saddlebrook.com, $300-600) is a four-star resort hotel in the sleepy town of Wesley Chapel. It has 800 gorgeous guest rooms and suites, pools, tennis courts, the Palmer and the Saddlebrook golf courses (and the Arnold Palmer Golf Academy), and a variety of dining options (eat on the Tropics Terrace to see nesting wood storks).

For more information about Pasco County, visit www.visitpasco.net.

EXCURSIONS

then once you've arrived, you still need a car to see anything). From south to north, Spring Hill (the town in which Weeki Wachee Springs lies), Homosassa, and Crystal River are lined up adjacent to each other right along U.S. 19. To get to Cedar Key, head north on U.S. 19 and then 23 miles southwest on Highway 24, the only road in and out of town (much of which is a quite rural two-lane highway until you cross the causeway into town). Steinhatchee is 33 miles north of Cedar Key on U.S. 19 and then 12 miles west on Highway 51.

Driving in Florida during the summer months can be especially challenging, with periods of heat and humidity punctuated by tremendous thunderstorms. It pays to have your car equipped with the following: first-aid kit, jumper cables, flashlight with new batteries, a jack, and cellular phone (although cell phone service can be sketchy in the more rural communities).

Sarasota

Want a stiff shot of culture? Sarasota's the place to go. Arts vie with more than 35 miles of dazzling Gulf Coast beaches for top draw. An influx of wealthy socialites settled the area starting around 1910, establishing Sarasota as a winter resort for affluent northerners. It was during this time that Sarasota's performing and visual arts institutions were established, to entertain those first hoity-toity tourists. Among the early tourists to be smitten by the town was circus magnate John Ringling. He scooped up property all around Sarasota, moving the circus's winter home here, building himself a winter residence, art museum, circus museum, and college.

All these years later, the city of Sarasota is the undisputed cultural center of the area, with theater, opera, symphony, ballet, art museums, and restaurants to rival those in much bigger cities. Each of the keys maintains its own identity, with glorious beach access being the central unifying theme. Lido and St. Armands are really just extensions of downtown Sarasota, connected by a causeway and fairly urban. Started as a quiet fishing village, Longboat Key is now strictly the purview of the posh, with tall resort hotels and condominiums and a glut of golf courses. Siesta Key is much more low-rise, with a personality to match. It's relaxed, laid-back, with a high funk-factor. It's the most youthful spot on this part of the Gulf Coast. Casey Key is less of a tourist draw, mostly dotted with single-family homes.

SIGHTS
🄲 Marie Selby Botanical Gardens
The word epiphyte comes from the Greek words "epi," meaning "upon," and "phyton," meaning "plant." Beginning their life in the canopy of trees, their seeds carried by birds or wind, epiphytes are air plants, growing stubbornly without the benefit of soil on the branches or trunks of trees. Orchids, cacti, bromeliads, aroids, lichens, mosses, and ferns can even grow on the same tree, a big interspecies jamboree. And if you want to see some heartbreakingly beautiful and alien epiphytes, spend a long afternoon at Marie Selby Botanical Gardens (811 S. Palm Ave., 941/366-5731, www.selby.org, daily 10 A.M.–5 P.M., $17 adult, $6 child age 6–11, free for child under 6). The 14-acre gardens on the shores of Sarasota Bay are one of Sarasota's absolute jewels. Marie Selby donated her home and grounds "to provide enjoyment for all who visit the gardens." Meandering along the walking paths through the hibiscus garden, cycad garden, a banyan grove, a tropical fruit garden, and thousands of orchids—there's a lot of enjoyment to be had. The botanical gardens also host lectures and gardening classes, and

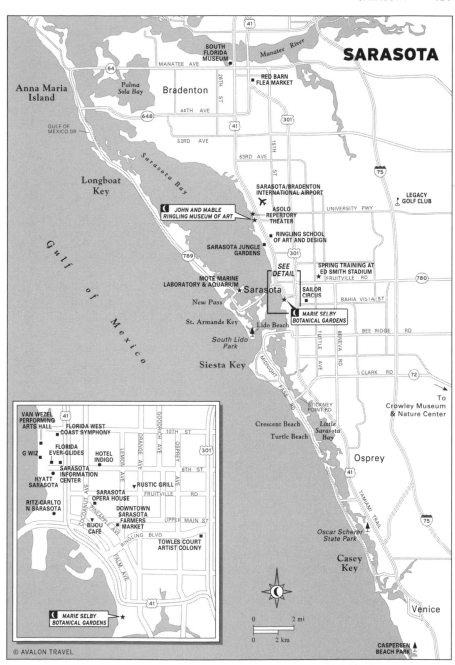

EXCURSIONS

cactus orchid flower at the Marie Selby Botanical Gardens

have a lovely shop (beginners should opt for a training-wheels phalaenopsis—very hard to kill—or an easy-care bromeliad) with an exhaustive collection of gardening books (80 on orchids alone).

John and Mable Ringling Museum of Art

John Ringling's lasting influence on Sarasota is remarkable, but the John and Mable Ringling Museum of Art (5401 Bay Shore Rd., 941/351-1660, www.ringling.org, daily 10 A.M.–5 P.M., $25 adult, $20 senior, $5 student and child age 6–17, $6 Florida teacher and student with ID) makes it simply incontrovertible.

The museum recently underwent a six-year, $140 million makeover, one of the most extraordinary transformations of any museum in North America. It's now one of the 20 largest art museums in North America. Since 2006, the Ringling Museum has opened four new buildings, the Tibbals Learning Center,

the John M. McKay Visitors Pavilion, the Ulla R. and Arthur F. Searing Wing, and the Education/Conservation Building, as well as opening the restored Historic Asolo Theater.

The whole museum complex is spectacular, but the art museum is definitely worth its fairly hefty admission price, having been built in 1927 to house Ringling's nearly pathological accretion of 600 paintings, sculptures, and decorative arts, including more than 25 tapestries. The Mediterranean-style palazzo contains a collection that includes a set of five gargantuan paintings by Peter Paul Rubens, lots of wonderful Spanish work (soulful El Grecos, Velázquez's portrait of King Philip IV of Spain, etc.), and the music room and dining room of Mrs. William B. Astor (Ringling bought all this in 1926 when the Astor mansion in New York was scheduled to be demolished).

The complex also houses the **Museum of the Circus,** a peek into circus history. It achieves a certain level of hyperbole in the interpretive signs when it parallels the ascendance of the circus with the growth of the country more generally. The single most impressive thing about the museum, the thing that caused rampant loitering and inspired commentary like, "Whoa, cooool," is the Howard Bros. Circus model. It takes up vast space—the world's largest miniature circus, after all—and is a 0.75-inch-to-the-foot scale replica of Ringling Bros. and Barnum & Bailey Circus when the tented circus was at its largest. The model itself takes up 3,800 square feet, with eight main tents, 152 wagons, 1,300 circus performers and workers, more than 800 animals, a 57-car train, and a zillion wonderful details.

Fully restored, John Ringling's home on the bay, **Cà d'Zan** (House of John) is also open to the public, an ornate structure evocative of Ringling's two favorite Venetian hotels, the Danieli and the Bauer Grunwald. Completed in 1926, the house is 200 feet long with 32 rooms and 15 baths (a comfort to those with small bladders). All kidding aside, there's something about the quality of light much of the year in Sarasota that seems utterly appropriate as host to such a magnificent Venetian Renaissance–style mansion.

RESTAURANTS
Downtown

A standout in Sarasota's sophisticated culinary landscape, **Derek's Culinary Casual** (514 Central Ave., 941/366-6565, http://dereks-sarasota.com, Tues.–Sat. 5–10 P.M., $19–39) is the brainchild of chef/owner Derek Barnes, former chef at 5-One-6 Burns. In a much larger, high-ceilinged space, he has brought exciting, contemporary American cuisine (complete with a glossary on the back of the menu) to Sarasota's Rosemary District. Tuna gnocchi, pork confit with monkfish medallions, and duck "two ways" (a seared breast paired with crispy pecan-crusted leg confit, German spaetzle, and bitter greens) all aim to bring a new level of sophistication to classic French/Italian/Californian dishes. The wine list is similarly ambitious and fairly priced, but small.

Darwin Santa Maria first introduced his stylish Peruvian vision to locals at Selva Grill, which he sold some time back. He now has inherited a fabulous Rosemary District restaurant space (formerly occupied briefly by Mad Crow Brewery, and Rustic Grill before that) for his **Darwins on 4th** (1525 4th St., 941/343-2165, http://darwinson4th.com, Sun.–Thurs. 5–10 P.M., Fri. and Sat. until 1 A.M., $14–32). He has lightened up the space but kept the beer equipment, brewing house beers that are nearly as enticing as the house pisco sour, all of which go well with the house ceviches accessorized with salted corn nuts and a jaunty skewer of fat cuzco corn kernels impaling a wedge of roasted sweet potato. Seating tip: Want to be in the thick of things? Sit downstairs. Upstairs at Darwin's is quieter, less of a scene.

John and Mable Ringling Museum of Art

Sarasota's **Bijou Cafe** (1287 1st St., 941/366-8111, www.bijoucafe.net, Mon.–Fri. 11:30 A.M.–2 P.M., Mon.–Thurs. 5–9 P.M., Fri. and Sat. until 10 P.M., Sun. until 9 P.M., $19–39) has been a local sparkling jewel since 1986, making everyone's top 10 list and garnering lots of drippy adjectives from *Zagat*, *Bon Appetit* and *Gourmet*. It's what you'd call continental-American fare, presided over by chef Jean-Pierre Knaggs and his wife, Shay. Located a couple blocks from Ritz-Carlton Sarasota in a 1920s gas station turned restaurant, the vibe is special-occasion or big-time-business dining. A fairly recent renovation (after a fire) has yielded a new bar, lounge, private room, and outdoor dining courtyards. The wine list is unusual, with a fair number of South African wines (Knaggs is South African), and the menu contains dishes like velvety shrimp and crab bisque, crispy roast duck napped with orange-cognac sauce, or luscious crab cakes with Louisiana rémoulade. All hail the crème brûlée.

It's not exactly downtown, but just slightly south. Still, any list of important downtown restaurants has to include **Michaels On East** (1212 East Ave. S., 941/366-0007, www.michaelsoneast.com, Mon.–Fri. 11:30 A.M.–2 P.M., daily 5:30–10 P.M., $18–31). It's won best-of-Florida accolades from nearly everyone since its opening at the beginning of the 1990s—and it has kept up with all the newcomers, consistently pushing the envelope and wowing diners with its New American take and opulent decor. During the day it's a power-lunching crowd enjoying Wendy's warm chicken salad with dried cranberries, goat cheese, and candied pecans in honey-lemon-basil vinaigrette and a big bottle of bubbly water; at night, romantic dinners à deux include a grilled duck breast paired with Bermuda onion and shiitake fondue, and fig and pecan risotto, all flavors elegantly showcased with a gorgeous big-ticket burgundy or California pinot noir.

St. Armands Circle and Lido Key

Two of the oldest on the stretch are **Café L'Europe** (431 St. Armands Cir., 941/388-4415, www.cafeleurope.net, daily 11:30 A.M.–3 P.M. and 5–10 P.M., Sun. brunch 11:30 A.M.–3 P.M., $23–40) and the **Columbia Restaurant** (411 St. Armands Cir., 941/388-3987, www.columbiarestaurant.com, Mon.–Sat. 11 A.M.–11 P.M., Sun. noon–10 P.M., $8–28). Close together, both feature beautiful dining rooms and wonderful sidewalk dining, but the food is better at Café L'Europe. The Columbia opened in 1959, making it the oldest restaurant in Sarasota. (Its sister restaurant in Tampa goes one better, being the oldest restaurant in the state of Florida.) The Cuban food is pretty dated, and even its "world-famous" dishes—the 1905 Salad with chopped cheese, olives, and a ho-hum vinaigrette; the sangria; the red snapper Alicante—don't thrill the way they used to. The black bean soup and pompano in parchment seldom disappoint, though. As for Café L'Europe, it's a sophisticated stew of culinary influences that's hard to pin down: The kitchen does an equally adept job with shrimp pad Thai, veal cordon bleu with luxe chanterelle mushroom risotto, and a Mediterranean chicken Kavalla that pairs chicken breast with feta, spinach, and crab.

Southside Village

In the space once occupied by Fred's in the charming Southside Village, **Libby's Café and Bar** (1917 South Osprey Ave., 941/487-7300, http://libbyscafebar.com, daily 11:30 A.M.–10 P.M., $14–36), is among the most stylish restaurants in the city. Owned by the Seidensticker family, who cut their chops at the fabled Gasparilla Inn on Boca Grande, this is a paean to the good old U.S. of A. At lunch, think stunning spins on BLTs and burgers, served with fries and homemade ketchup that can cause compulsive behavior. With its generous French doors thrown open to the street, it has the bustle of an urban hotspot, crowded with families, businessfolk, and Hillview neighborhood scenesters. The lively bar and spacious dining rooms get a little moodier at night, though the sidewalk tables are still the hottest commodity after the dusk cools. The dinner menu is vast unto stupor-inducing, with simple grilled meats and fishes and a whole lot of more sophisticated options.

Pacific Rim (1859 Hillview St., 941/330-8071, Mon.–Fri. 11:30 A.M.–2 P.M., Mon.–Thurs. 5–9:30 P.M., Fri. and Sat. 5–10:30 P.M., $7–15) takes you on a very pleasant pan-Asian romp, from Thai curries redolent of basil and galangal to expertly rolled tekka maki sushi and beyond. You can play chef here and select your combinations of meats and veggies to be grilled or cooked in the wok.

ARTS AND LEISURE
Asolo Repertory Theatre
Celebrating 48 years of professional theater in Sarasota, the Asolo (5555 N. Tamiami Trail, 941/351-8000, www.asolorep.org, curtain times generally 2 P.M. and 8 P.M. Nov.–June, prices vary) is a professional company that performs primarily in the 500-seat Harold E. and Esther M. Mertz Theatre at the Florida State University Center for the Performing Arts, a theater originally built as an opera house in 1903 in Dunfermline, Scotland. There's a second, smaller 161-seat black-box Jane B. Cook Theatre on-site for performances of the conservatory season and smaller productions of the Asolo. Students also present a series of original works known as the LateNite series, and the FSU School of Theatre presents a variety of other special events and performances. Recently, the Asolo Rep and the Conservatory perform one show each in the Historic Asolo Theater, located in the Ringling Museum's Visitors Pavilion. All of this means more shows and more variety for Sarasota's theatergoers.

This means that in a single season you might see David Mamet's riveting *Glengarry Glen Ross,* followed by the one-woman *My Brilliant Divorce,* and good ole Bill Shakespeare's *Twelfth Night.*

Festivals
Sarasota supports not one, but two film festivals. By far the more famous of the two is the **Sarasota Film Festival** (332 Cocoanut Ave., 941/364-9514, www.sarasotafilmfestival.com) every April, and every November there's the Sarasota Film Society's 10-day **Cine-World Film Festival** (various locations, 941/364-8662, www.filmsociety.org).

February's not a bad month to visit because you can catch the month-long annual run of the European-style **Circus Sarasota** (various locations, 941/355-9335, www.circussarasota.org). Sarasota is the self-described "circus capital of the world," after all. Music lovers may want to come in February or March for the repertory season of the **Sarasota Opera** (61 N. Pineapple Ave., 941/366-8450, www.sarasotaopera.org), although in April there's **La Musica International Chamber Music Festival** (Sarasota Opera House, 61 N. Pineapple Ave., 941/366-8450, www.lamusicafestival.com). Also in April you'll encounter the **Florida Wine & Balloon Festival** (various locations, 941/952-1109, www.floridawinefest.org), where you can sample wine from local vineyards and wineries, as well as take a hot air balloon ride.

Recreation
SIESTA KEY BEACH
We have a winner of the international whose-beach-is-better competition. In 1987, scientists from the Woods Hole Oceanographic Institution in Woods Hole, Massachusetts, convened to judge the Great International White Sand Beach Challenge, with more than 30 entries from beaches around the world. To this day, Siesta Key Beach (948 Beach Rd.,

EXCURSIONS

Siesta Key Beach

Siesta Key, www.scgov.net) remains the reigning world champ. Its preeminence has long been known—supposedly in the 1950s a visitor from New York, Mr. Edward G. Curtis, sent a pickle jar of Siesta's sand to the Geology Department of Harvard University for analysis. The report came back:

> The sand from Siesta Key is 99 percent pure quartz grains, the grains being somewhat angular in shape. The soft floury texture of the sand is due to its very fine grain size. It contains no fragments of coral and no shell. The fineness of the sand, which gives it its powdery softness, is emphasized by the fact that the quartz is a very hard substance, graded at 7 in the hardness scale of 10.

The real test can't be done with sand in a pickle jar. You need to lie on the sloping strand, run the warmed granules through your fingers, sniff the salt air, and listen to a plaintive gull overhead. That way, too, Siesta Key Beach wins—it's been named America's Best Sand Beach and ranked in Florida's Top Ten Beaches multiple years on the Travel Channel.

Dr. Beach named it the No. 1 beach in America again in 2011 (it's made it into the top 10 numerous times); *National Geographic Traveler* has also named Siesta One of America's Best Beaches. The list goes on.

Siesta Key Beach is on the north side of Siesta Key (it is contiguous with another favorite beach called Crescent Beach—good snorkeling off this one), with white sand so reflective it feels cool on a hot day. Scientists estimate that the sand on this beach is millions of years old, starting in the Appalachians and eventually deposited on these shores. The water is shallow, the beach incline gradual, making it a perfect beach for young swimmers. There are 800 parking spots, which tend to fill up, and the lifeguard stands are painted different colors (as points of reference, so you don't lose your way).

POLO

There are scads of spectator sporting opportunities in Sarasota, but polo trumps a fair number of them. Games are enormous fun, the horses racing around tearing up the lush sod of the polo grounds while their riders focus fiercely on that pesky little ball. For a sport with such an effete pedigree, it's amazingly physical and exciting to watch, whether you're in your fancy polo togs (what's with all the hats?) or your weekend jeans. **Sarasota Polo Club** (Lakewood Ranch, 8201 Polo Club Ln., 941/907-0000, www.sarasotapolo.com, Sun. 1 P.M. mid-Dec.–early Apr., $12 adult, free child 12 and under) began in 1991, with professional-level players coming from around the world to play on the nine pristine fields. Bring a picnic or buy sandwiches and drinks once you're here. Gates open at 11:30 A.M. and dogs on leashes are welcome. You can also take polo lessons at Lakewood Ranch. Sarasota also boasts high-caliber cricket, lawn bowling, and pétanque.

SHOPS

The shops of **St. Armands Circle** on Lido Key have been a primary retail draw in Sarasota for a long time, historically known for high-end boutiques. These days the shops cover familiar ground—chains like **Tommy Bahama** (300 John Ringling Blvd., 941/388-2446), **Fresh Produce** (1 N. Blvd. of the Presidents, 941/388-1883), and **White House Black Market** (317 St. Armands Circle, 941/388-5033)—and a handful of upscale, independently owned boutiques. You'll have better luck noodling in the circle's novelty and giftware shops: **Fantasea Seashells** (378 St. Armands Circle, 941/388-3031), **Florida Olive Oil Company** (382A St. Armands Circle, 941/388-2640), or **Kilwin's** (312 John Ringling Blvd., 941/388-3200) for ice cream and fudge.

In downtown Sarasota, **Towles Court Artist Colony** (1938 Adams Ln., Sarasota, www.towlescourt.com) is a collection of 16 quirky pastel-colored bungalows and cottages that contain artists working furiously and the art they've been working furiously on. You can buy their work and watch them in action most Tuesdays through Saturdays noon–4 P.M., or

visit Towles Court on the third Friday evening of each month for the Art Walk.

Palm Avenue and **Main Street** in downtown Sarasota are lined with galleries and cute shops, and historic **Herald Square** in the SoMa (south of Main St.) part of downtown on Pineapple Avenue has a fairly dense concentration of antiques shops and upscale housewares stores. Also on Pineapple you'll find the **Artisan's World Marketplace** (128 S. Pineapple Ave., 941/365-5994, www.artisansworldmarketplace.com), which promotes self-employment for low-income artisans in developing countries worldwide by selling their baskets, clothing, and handicrafts.

HOTELS

There are scads of condos and beachfront rentals in the greater Sarasota area, but most of these rent only by the week. If that's your time frame, the weeklong rentals often are a more financially prudent choice. Try giving **Argus Property Management** (941/927-6464) a call, or visit **Vacation Rentals by Owner** (www.vrbo.com). There are also golf resort condo communities such as **Heritage Oaks Golf and Country Club** (4800 Chase Oaks Dr., 941/926-7602, www.heritageoaksgcc.com) and **Timberwoods Vacation Villas & Resort** (7964 Timberwood Cir., 941/923-4966, www.timberwoods.com) that rent by the week.

However, if you're only in for a few days, hotels and motels run the gamut from moderately priced and no-frills to truly luxurious. The 12-story **Hyatt Sarasota** (1000 Boulevard of the Arts, 941/953-1234, http://sarasota.hyatt.com, $119–439) finished a $22 million transformation a few years back. The results are a spectacular, and massive, convention hotel right downtown with easy access to Van Wezel Performing Arts Hall, the Municipal Auditorium, and other attractions. It's right in the downtown business district, but waterside, with its own private marina, a floating dock, and a beautiful lagoon-style pool. The 294 guest rooms all have a view of the bay or marina, most with little balconies.

It was controversial when it opened, but the **Ritz-Carlton Sarasota** (1111 Ritz-Carlton Dr., 941/309-2000, reservations 800/241-3333, www.ritzcarlton.com, $229–719), a 266-room, 18-story luxury hotel right downtown, has managed to blend in beautifully, as if it has always been here. Ritz-Carlton's signature service (warm, efficient, but seldom verging on obsequious), spacious rooms with balconies and marble baths, and great amenities make it the top choice among business and high-fallutin' travelers. The downtown location is convenient to restaurants (although there are two laudable ones on-site) and attractions; there's a lovely pool, and the wood-paneled Cà d'Zan Bar & Cigar Lounge is always hopping. The Ritz has a spa open to guests and members only, and the Members Golf Club located 13 miles from the hotel offers a Tom Fazio–designed 18-hole championship course. It is a par 72, located on 315 acres of tropical landscape with no real estate development.

One of the most attractive hotels to open in recent years is the **Hotel Indigo** (1223 Boulevard of the Arts, 941/487-3800, www.hotelindigo.com, $125–233), a sweet boutique job with a canny use of vibrant colors and whimsical design elements. Guest rooms have wall-sized murals and wonderful fabrics in rich blues and greens—altogether it's a fun, contemporary alternative, right in the thick of things. The onsite café is called the H2O Bistro, there's a little wine bar, and you can ride one of the hotel's bikes (complete with a handle bar basket to hold souvenirs or local fresh fruit) to the Downtown Farmers Market. Of course, you can always spend some time in one of the cushioned Adirondack chairs or out on the lovely patio.

GETTING THERE AND AROUND

Sarasota is along I-75, the major transportation corridor for the southeastern United States. Sarasota County is approximately one hour south of Tampa. U.S. 301 and U.S. 41 (Tamiami Trail) are the major north–south arteries on the mainland; the Gulf Drive (County Rd. 789) is the main island road. The largest east–west thoroughfares in Sarasota are Highway 72 (Stickney Point Rd.); County Road 780 (University Pkwy.); and (to the islands) Ringling Causeway, which takes you right to Lido Beach.

Downtown streets and roads run east–west; avenues and boulevards run north–south. The main street downtown is called, um, Main Street. From downtown, go east across the John Ringling Causeway to access St. Armands Circle and Lido Key. Continue north to Longboat Key, where there's not a lot of draw beyond swanky hotels, golf courses, a few restaurants, and slightly inconvenient beach access and parking. To reach Siesta Key, head south on U.S. 41 (also called the Tamiami Trail), then take a right onto either Siesta Drive or Stickney Point Road—the former takes you to the northern, residential section of the key; Stickney takes you closer to the funky Siesta Village. The public beaches on Siesta Key are among the finest in the state.

By Air
Sarasota-Bradenton International Airport (SRQ) (6000 Airport Cir., at the intersection of U.S. 41 and University Pkwy., 941/359-2770) is certainly the closest airport, served by commuter flights and a half dozen major airlines or their partners, including Continental, Delta, Northwest, AirTran, and US Airways. Still, many people fly into **Tampa International Airport** (4100 George J. Bean Pkwy., 813/870-8700, www.tampaairport.com), which offers more arrival and departure choices, and often better fares on flights and even rental cars.

BACKGROUND

The Land

Florida is bounded on the north by Alabama and Georgia, to the east by the Atlantic, to the south by the Straits of Florida, and to the west by the Gulf of Mexico. The east coast of the state is comparatively straight, extending in a rough line 470 miles long. The Gulf side, on the other hand, has a more sinuous and convoluted coastline, measuring roughly 675 miles. In all, Florida's 2,276-mile coastline is longer than that of any other state in the continental United States. It's nearly pancake flat, without notable change in elevation, and young by geological standards, having risen out of the ocean a scant 300–400 million years ago.

TAMPA

Busch Gardens, Ybor City, the Florida Aquarium, Tampa Bay Buccaneers, and Tampa Bay Lightning. Tampa fronts Tampa and Hillsborough Bays, not the Gulf of Mexico. A huge port city, Tampa doesn't have any beaches to speak of. It's an excellent vacation destination, especially for families. There's a magical confluence of warm weather, affordable accommodations, professional sports, children's

© 123RF.COM

WALKING TREES

This area's waterfront is in many places fringed with mangrove trees. They are often called walking trees because they hover above the water, their arching prop roots resembling so many spindly legs. The mangrove is one of only a handful of tree species on planet Earth that can withstand having its roots sitting in saltwater, immersed daily by rising tides, and that thrives in little soil and high levels of sulfides. The mangrove's hardiness is just one among many of its idiosyncrasies, however.

Mangroves are natural land builders. Seed tubules about the heft and length of an excellent Cuban cigar sprout on the parent tree, drop off, and bob in the brackish water until they lodge on an oyster bar or a snag in the shallows. There, the seed begins to grow into a tree, its leaves dropping and getting trapped along with seaweed and other plant debris. This organic slurry is the bottom of the food chain, supplying food, breeding area, and sanctuary to countless tiny marine creatures. In addition, it is the foundation upon which a little island or "key" begins to take shape, this buildup of sediment and debris creating a thick layer of organic peat upon which other plant species begin to grow. This first tree drops more seed tubules, which get stuck in the soft mud around the base of the parent tree and begin to grow. Soon, it's an impenetrable tangle of trees and roots extravagant enough to support birdlife and other animals.

Red mangrove forms a wide band of trees on the outermost part of each island, facing the open sea. The red mangrove encircles the black mangrove, which in turn encircles the white mangrove at the highest, driest part of each mangrove island (they are the least tolerant of having their roots sitting in saltwater). The mangroves' leathery evergreen leaves fall and stain the water a tobacco-colored tannic brown, but in fact the mangroves and all of the species dependent upon them do much to keep the waters clean and pure.

For all these reasons, mangrove trees are protected by federal, state, and local laws. Do not injure, spindle, or mutilate a mangrove or you will face steep penalties.

attractions, and strangely posh shopping that seems to suit every taste.

As the location of one of America's most user-friendly airports, Tampa is a natural embarkation point for a Gulf Coast vacation. It's located adjacent to Pinellas County and, when combined with St. Petersburg, is the second-largest metropolitan area in the state, behind only the Miami-Fort Lauderdale megalopolis. There is huge suburban sprawl in the north of the Tampa Bay area, where Busch Gardens, the University of South Florida, and plenty of middle-class homes are situated. But farther to the south it's cheek by jowl: There's the elegant historic residential and commercial neighborhood of Hyde Park, the Cuban center of town in Ybor City (once famous for cigars, now more famous for bars), and MacDill Air Force Base, which takes up the entire southern third of the Tampa peninsula and is home to the U.S. Central Command. The Hillsborough River runs through the city, providing a peaceful natural counterpoint to all the more frantic, citified pleasures.

ST. PETERSBURG AND PINELLAS COUNTY

St. Petersburg used to be a stolid retirement community. It's different now—an influx of high-tech firms, mostly employing youngish people, has prompted a shift in the demographics. Pinellas County as a whole has seen enormous growth and counts more than 100,000 kids just in the public school system; there are a multitude of religious and charter schools, too. A notable destination for family vacations, St. Petersburg itself faces Tampa to the east, with miles of inviting waterfront parkland touching placid Tampa Bay. The northwest side of the Pinellas peninsula is protected by barrier islands, starting with Honeymoon Island and Caladesi Island State Park. Clearwater Beach is a wide, welcoming swath of Gulf lapping at white sand, backed by restaurants, souvenir shops, and boogie-board-and-bikini boutiques. It's popular with both families and the spring-break set.

The city of St. Petersburg exerts its pull with a vibrant downtown of pastel art deco buildings and cultural attractions like the recently opened Salvador Dalí Museum and the Dale Chihuly Collection, the somber Florida Holocaust Museum, orchestral music at the Mahaffey Theater, or theater at American Stage. St. Petersburg is also home to some of the most sophisticated restaurants in the greater Tampa Bay area.

Along the Gulf side of Pinellas County, Clearwater is both the county seat and second-largest city after St. Pete among Pinellas's nearly two-dozen incorporated communities. St. Pete Beach to the south, which is a distinct community from the larger, more urban, St. Petersburg to its east, draws beach goers from around the world. It's a classic Florida beach town, with late-night waterside clubs, deepwater fishing charters, and low-slung motels with views of the luscious sand. And there's a lot of beach, many local strands ranking high in international beach polls. Caladesi Island, Honeymoon Island, and Fort De Soto, a sprawling county park so large you can camp overnight, have all been named to the famous Dr. Beach's list of top 10 beaches in America.

CLIMATE
Heat and Humidity
Located on the southeastern tip of North America, Florida is closer to the equator than any other continental U.S. state. Thus, Florida has a humid, subtropical climate and significant, almost daily, rainfall April–November.

St. Pete Beach

Its humidity is attributed to the fact that no point in the state is more than 60 miles from salt water and no more than 345 feet above sea level. If this thick steamy breath on the back of your neck is new to you, humidity is a measure of the amount of water vapor in the air. Most often you'll hear the percentage described in relative humidity, which is the amount of water vapor actually in the air divided by the amount of water vapor the air can hold. The warmer the air becomes, the more moisture it can hold.

When heat and humidity combine to slow evaporation of sweat from the body, outdoor activity becomes dangerous even for those in good physical shape. Drink plenty of water to avoid dehydration and slow down if you feel fatigued or notice a headache, a high pulse rate, or shallow breathing. Overheating can cause serious and even life-threatening conditions such as heatstroke. The elderly, small children, the overweight, and those on some medications are particularly vulnerable to heat stress.

During the summer months, expect temperatures to hover around 90°F and humidity to be that high, too—except when it reaches near 100 percent, including the rain that is falling by then. The most pleasant times of the year along the length of the Florida peninsula fall between December and April—coinciding, not surprisingly, with the busiest time for tourism. The best approach for packing in preparation for a visit to Florida is layering, with a sweater for over-air-conditioned interiors or the occasional chilly evening breezes, and lots of loose, wicking material for the heat.

Rain

It rains nearly every day in the summer in the Tampa Bay area. And it's not just a sprinkle. Due to the abundance of warm, moist air from the Gulf of Mexico and the hot tropical sun, conditions are perfect for the formation of thunderstorms. There are 80–90 thunderstorms each summer, generally less than 15 miles in diameter—but vertically they can grow up to 10 miles high in the atmosphere. These are huge, localized thunderstorms that can drop four or more inches of rain in an hour, while just a few miles away it stays dry. The bulk of these tropical afternoon thunderstorms each summer are electrical storms.

Lightning

With sudden thunderstorms comes lightning, a serious threat here. About 50 people are struck by lightning each year in Florida. Most of them are hospitalized and recover, but there are about 10 fatalities annually. Tampa is the Lightning Capital of the United States, with around 25 cloud-to-ground lightning bolt blasts on each square mile annually. The temperature of a single bolt can reach 50,000 degrees Fahrenheit, about three times as hot as the sun's surface. There's not much you can do to ward off lightning except to avoid being in the wrong place at the wrong time. The summer months of June, July, August, and September have the highest number of lightning-related injuries and deaths. Usually lightning occurs during daylight hours, with the highest concentration between 3 and 4 P.M., when the afternoon storms peak. Lightning strikes usually occur either at the beginning or end of a storm, and can strike up to 10 miles away from the center of the storm. Keep your eye on approaching storms and seek shelter when you see lightning.

Locals use the 30-30 rule: Count the seconds after a lightning flash until you hear thunder. If that number is under 30, the storm is within six miles of you. Seek shelter. Then, at storm's end, wait 30 minutes after the last thunderclap before resuming outdoor activity.

Hurricanes

At the time of this writing, Tampa Bay has repeatedly dodged bullets. The last time the area took a direct hurricane hit was 2004, when Hurricane Charley came ashore with winds of about 105 mph, about 100 miles south of Tampa Bay. But the law of averages says that the Bay Area's luck won't last.

Hurricanes are violent tropical storms with sustained winds of at least 74 mph. Massive low-pressure systems, they blow counterclockwise around a relatively calm central area called the eye. They form over warm ocean waters, often starting as storms in the Caribbean or off the west coast of Africa. As they move westward, they are fueled by the warm waters of the tropics. Warm, moist air moves toward the center of the storm and spirals upward, releasing driving rains. Updrafts suck up more water vapor, which further strengthens the storm until it can be stopped only when contact is made with land or cooler water. In the average hurricane, just 1 percent of the energy released could meet the energy needs of the United States for a full year.

In Florida, the hurricane season is June–November. These storms have been named since 1953. It used to be just female names ("Hell hath no fury like a woman scorned," or some such nonsense), but now there's gender parity in the naming. Really powerful hurricanes' names are retired, kind of like sports greats' jerseys.

The 2004 hurricane season was the last really destructive year in Florida, with Charley, Frances, Ivan, and Jeanne wreaking quite a bit of havoc on the Gulf Coast in a period of just 46 days. Despite dire predictions, recent years have been meteorologically uneventful on Florida's Gulf Coast.

Hurricane Safety

Monitor radio and TV broadcasts closely for directions. Gas up the car, and make sure you have batteries, water supply, candles, and food that can be eaten without the use of electricity. Get cash, have your prescriptions filled, and put all essential documents in a large resealable bag. In the event of an evacuation, find the closest shelter by listening to the radio or TV broadcasts. Pets are not allowed in most shelters. There are designated pet shelters, but all animals must be up to date on shots. Alternatively, an increasing number of hotels and motels accept animals for a nominal daily fee.

History

The southernmost state in the United States, Florida was named by **Ponce de León** upon his visit in 1513, when he was clearly taken with the lush tropical wilderness. This expedition, the first documented presence of Europeans on the mainland of the United States, was ostensibly "to discover and people the island of Bimini." On the return voyage he rounded the Dry Tortugas, 190 miles south of Tampa Bay, to explore the Gulf of Mexico, entering Charlotte Harbor (about an hour south of Tampa and St. Petersburg). He soon realized that Florida was more than a large island. Near Mound Key he encountered the fierce Calusa people, and while on Estero Island repairing his ship, he narrowly escaped Calusa capture. Eight years later he returned and headed to the Calusa territory with 500 of his men, aiming to establish a permanent colony in Florida. In an ensuing battle with the Calusa, Ponce de León was pierced in the thigh by an arrow and carried back to his ship. He never returned again.

Many of the subsequent explorers' missions were less high profile. In 1516 **Diego Miruelo** mapped Pensacola Bay, in northwest Florida. In 1517, **Alonso Alvarez de Pineda** went the length of the Florida shore to the Mississippi River, confirming Ponce de León's assertion that Florida was not an island. In 1520, **Vasquez de Ayollon** mapped the Carolina coast (which at the time Spain claimed in the vast region they called "Florida").

Panfilo de Narvaez was a veteran Caribbean soldier, hired by Spanish authorities in 1520 to overthrow Hernán Cortés's tyrannical rule. After a lengthy imprisonment by Cortés, Narvaez went back to Spain and obtained a grant to colonize the Gulf Coast from northern Mexico to Florida. Together with **Cabeza de Vaca,** an armada of five ships, and 400 soldiers, Narvaez landed on the western coast of what would become St. Petersburg, in April 1528. Spanish–Native American relations deteriorated quickly during this period; the Spaniards' ruthless hunt for gold and riches met with violence on the part of the Indians.

Then came **Hernando de Soto.** In the spring of 1539 he sailed for Tampa Bay with seven vessels, at least 500 soldiers, three Jesuit friars, and several dozen civilians with the intent of starting a settlement. Where he went exactly is a topic of much debate: Some say he landed first in Manatee County, on the southern edge of the mouth of Tampa Bay, before sailing up the bay to its closed end, setting off on his journey from what is now Safety Harbor in the northeast corner of Pinellas. Like many of the conquistadores before him, de Soto was attracted to the stories of Indian riches to the north, so he sent his fleet back to Cuba and set off inland from the coast. He and his men never found what they sought, moving ever northward into Georgia, South Carolina, Tennessee, Alabama, Mississippi, and Arkansas, where he died of fever.

There were religious missions to the state during the same time. Dominican priest **Father Luis Cancer,** three additional missionaries, and a Christianized Indian maiden named Magdalene arrived on the beaches outside Tampa Bay in 1549. Given the Native Americans' experience with white men, it's probably no wonder that Father Cancer was quickly surrounded and clubbed to death.

The survivors in his party hightailed it back to Mexico to put the skids on future missionary proposals for Florida.

Long after Hernando de Soto sailed into the bay, the area went largely untouched by whites for another couple of hundred years. Dutch cartographer Bernard Romans named the Hillsborough River and the upper arm of Tampa Bay in 1772, in honor of Lord Hillsborough, British secretary of state for the colonies. The United States purchased Florida from Spain in 1821, with traders setting up shop along what is now downtown Tampa in 1855.

In 1842, on the other side of Tampa Bay, intrepid Frenchman Odet Philippe established a large orange grove near what is now Safety Harbor. In what was to become Pinellas County, Scottish merchants settled Dunedin, and a Russian immigrant who owned the Orange Belt Railroad laid tracks into a sandy village and named it St. Petersburg, after his Russian hometown.

It wasn't until Henry B. Plant extended his railroad into Tampa in 1884 and started a steamship line from Tampa to Key West to Havana, Cuba, that the area really began to grow. In 1891, Plant built the Tampa Bay Hotel, which launched the city as a winter resort for the northern elite. Around the same time, O. H. Platt purchased 20 acres of land across the Hillsborough River, creating Tampa's first residential suburb, Hyde Park (named after Platt's hometown in Illinois). Hyde Park was, and still is, the residential area of choice for many prominent citizens. Many of the late 19th-century bungalows and Princess Anne–style cottages are still occupied today, and the Old Hyde Park Village collection of boutiques and restaurants is one of the city's biggest draws.

In 1885, Don Vicente Martinez Ybor (pronounced EE-bor), an influential cigar manufacturer and Cuban exile, moved his cigar business from Key West to a scruffy stretch of land east of Tampa. His first cigar factory drew others, and the Spanish, Italian, German, and Cuban workers who settled here to work in the area's more than 200 cigar factories created a vivacious Latin community still known as Ybor City. When the United States declared war on Spain in 1898, Tampa was the port of embarkation for troops headed to Cuba. A vital colonel named Theodore Roosevelt organized his Rough Riders at the Tampa encampment. More than a century of development has erased any trace of T.R.'s boys, though some locals like to dress up as the Rough Riders for various public galas. Not long after that, another Tampa neighborhood, Davis Islands, developed during the Florida land boom. Two little islands off downtown Tampa, where the Hillsborough River empties into Hillsborough Bay, became booming real estate developments.

In some ways, Henry Ford's affordable $400 Model T abetted the real estate boom in the early 1920s. It was the beginning of road-tripping, folks hopping in the car in search of sun, sand, and a little fun. They found what is now Pinellas County, the peninsula that hangs down Florida's west side like a thumb, with its beaches and Intracoastal Waterway, and they found the growing city of Tampa to the east. People liked what they saw. They bought up land, building big resort hotels, affordable motels, and homes.

Growth continued apace through the Roaring Twenties, slowing, as it did everywhere, during the Great Depression. But with tens of thousands of military trainees based in the area during World War II, the delight of warm, sunny winters was spread by word of mouth. Innumerable vets decided to move here, especially when they retired. With economic diversification in the last decades of the 20th century, the Tampa Bay area has depended less on just the tourist dollar to the degree other Gulf Coast cities have. Thus the Bay Area has been less susceptible to the ups and downs of

downtown Tampa

vacationing in Florida (first 9/11, then the walloping hurricane season of 2004, counterbalanced by Europeans' enthusiasm about the weakness of the dollar). But the worldwide recession has even reduced the number of Europeans flying over, though the market for South American visitors has helped offset that.

Government and Economy

STATE GOVERNMENT

In 1968, Florida adopted a new state constitution. The governor is elected for a term of four years, and the Legislature has a Senate of 40 members and a House of Representatives of 120 members. The state also elects 25 representatives and two senators to the U.S. Congress and has 29 electoral votes.

It's easy enough to say that the state is fairly solidly Republican. But it's more complicated than that. In a state that was historically Democrat, recent explosive population growth has brought with it many Republicans, leaving the state approximately evenly split between the two parties. It's because of that, combined with its large number of electoral votes, that Florida is considered by political analysts to be a key swing state in presidential elections. Tampa, once a hotbed of Democratic union support, is now much more heavily influenced by pro-business Republicans. As a whole, Florida went for Nixon in 1968 and 1972, but Carter in 1976, Reagan in 1980 and 1984, Bush in 1988, Bush, just barely, in 1992, Clinton in 1996, then depending on your take on the 2000 election, either Bush by a hair or Gore by a bigger hair, and Bush again by a little in 2004. With about 51 percent of the popular vote, Barack Obama edged John McCain in 2008, taking both Pinellas (think St. Petersburg) and Hillsborough (Tampa) counties.

The 2012 election cycle proved, once again, that Florida is the most electorally dysfunctional state. With 49 out of 50 states officially weighing in (including states like New Jersey, which had just been walloped by superstorm Sandy), Florida took its sweet time to announce election results. The final tally in the state was 50 percent for Obama to 49.1 percent for Romney, a difference of about 74,000 votes (which was outside the half-percent margin that would have triggered an automatic recount).

As for state government, Democrat Lawton Chiles, elected governor in 1990 and re-elected in 1994, was succeeded by Republican John Ellis "Jeb" Bush, elected in 1998 and re-elected in 2002. Republican Charlie Crist (a St. Pete native and attorney general under Bush) was elected in 2006. Newcomer and Republican Rick Scott edged Democrat and former state CFO Alex Sink, 49 percent to 48 percent, in the 2010 election.

INDUSTRY

Florida has historically been a poor state. It spent its early years luring any kind of industry here with big tax breaks and incentives, sometimes even free land. And there have been many waves of takers. The deepwater ports along the Gulf prompted ship-building booms as far back as the 1830s, with industries such as cotton and lumber shipping utilizing the gentle open water and connecting rivers and the Intracoastal Waterway.

Cheap labor, lax laws, rich natural resources, a general anti-union sentiment, and no state income tax—it's a recipe for get-rich-quick, environmentally-damaging industries. And Florida has had them, from timber and turpentining to paper mills and chemical plants. It wasn't until the Clean Water Act in 1972—which regulates the discharge of pollutants into U.S. waters and makes it illegal for industry to discharge pollutants without a permit—that people in Florida started scratching their heads about all the dead fish washing up on the shores. It has gotten better, but the Gulf states (Florida, Texas, and Louisiana in particular) are still among the top offenders for allowing permit violations for high-hazard chemicals. The industries in question are varied, linked mainly by their propensity for toxic discharge and their political clout. State and federal agencies charged with monitoring are perennially hamstrung by Florida politicians, who tend to favor industry over the environment. Pollution of the spectacular Everglades due to agribusiness run-offs has been a decades-long battle with, arguably, a notable lack of restoration.

But agriculture does play a mighty role in the commercial well-being of the state. In 2009, Florida ranked first in the value of citrus (it produced 65 percent of the nation's total in the 2009–2010 harvest seasons) and first in producing sugar cane, snap beans, sweet corn, and watermelon, among other crops. As of January 1, 2011, there were about 1.63 million head of cattle on Florida ranches. Horticultural products (meaning plants and floriculture) are big business, too, with Florida ranking second in the production of greenhouse and nursery products, with cash receipts in 2010 of $1.67 billion.

Cattle ranches and dairy farms are most dense in the middle of the state, though before the real estate crash of the 2000s, they often were being converted to subdivisions. From Gulf waters, commercial fishers haul millions of pounds of fish and shellfish, and sport fishers haul millions more. The lumber industry is still going strong in some parts of the state, while high-tech companies have flocked to the St. Petersburg/Tampa area the past couple of decades, making it the western terminus of a highly regarded I-4 corridor that stretches more than 100 miles from the Gulf to Orlando. The

Florida oranges

lures for many companies moving south remain the same as they have for the past century: good weather and low housing costs.

All this is still beside the point in some ways. Tourism is the state's number one industry, plain and simple. From January 1 through December 31, 2011, more than 86.5 million people visited Florida, according to data released by Visit Florida, the state's marketing arm. It's an approximately $67.2 billion business, with about 900,000 people employed in the estimated 50,000 restaurants, 4,000 hotels and accommodations, and some of the world's top tourist attractions (Walt Disney World, Universal Studios, Busch Gardens).

FLORIDA'S MILITARY

There are 13 Air Force, Navy, and Marine bases, plus 14 Coast Guard stations, in Florida. Though shrinking, the military has in recent years been the state's third top economic sector behind tourism and agriculture, with about 43,000 members of the military and another 28,000 civilians employed at Florida installations.

Many of the bases and two of the unified commands are along the Gulf Coast. **U.S. Special Operations Command and the U.S. Central Command** (CENTCOM) are both at MacDill Air Force Base in south Tampa. Special Ops (USSOCOM) is the controller for America's special warfare all over the world, while CENTCOM is responsible for U.S. security interests in 20 nations that stretch from the Horn of Africa, through the Gulf region, into Central Asia. CENTCOM was activated in January 1983 as the successor to the Rapid Deployment Joint Task Force. A few years after that, in 1987, USSOCOM was established as a unified combatant command also at MacDill; it's composed of Army, Navy, and Air Force special operations forces. Its mission is to support the geographic commanders-in-chief, ambassadors, and their country teams and other

government agencies by preparing special operations forces.

EDUCATION

For the 2010–11 school year, the Legislature appropriated about $2,000 less per child than the national average, placing Florida in the bottom fifth of per-pupil contributions for all states. The Legislature allows corporations to substitute paying their taxes to the state treasury by instead contributing the same amount to funds to operate private schools. The state similarly has boosted the creation and operation of charter schools, though imposing less oversight on the quality of their faculty and educational programs than there is for public schools. Politicians cannot seem to keep from tampering with even the public universities, at various times trying to pack the various boards of overseers for each college with political appointees who share the incumbent party's view of things. In 2012, one powerful state senator was able to get the Legislature to agree to split a satellite campus from the burgeoning University of South Florida (full campuses in both Tampa and St. Petersburg) and to thus create a "polytechnic institute" in his hometown.

Further, though it is years into the process, Florida still cannot get a handle on its mandatory standardized testing system, known by the acronym FCAT. There have been problems with the grading of the K-12 tests by commercial firms, regular complaints that teachers feel they must abandon their preferred topics and methods in order to "teach to the test" to try to boost their pupils' FCAT scores. Further, the Legislature and some governors have sought to use those scores as a means of teacher accountability, withholding funds from schools whose students fail to meet certain standards. This ranks schools with a letter grade, the highest-ranked schools getting the greatest funding, and then handing state vouchers to pay for private school tuition to students in the "failing" public schools. And the incumbent governor, Rick Scott, has sought to end teacher tenure.

The bottom line: Florida's public education is not competitive on a national level. In areas such as scores on the ACT and SAT college-entrance exams, student-teacher ratios, high-school graduation rates, and reading and math scores on the National Assessment of Educational Progress exams administered to students across the country, a national report conducted in the late 2000s deemed Florida public education to be subpar.

Money is part of the problem. In addition to the relatively low per-pupil state expenditure, the state also lags in average teacher salary and funding of colleges (adjusted for cost of living, though, beginning teachers' salaries are slightly above average). Crowding is another problem.

Class-size maximums, mandated by the state Constitution, have not kept up with those of other states, and the schools have seen a significant demographic bubble in elementary-age kids in the past few years.

But the problems are clearly just as much about ideology. The state has failed to prioritize the education of its students, as much at the elementary school levels as at the college level. With some of the lowest tuitions and teacher salaries in the country, Florida universities prove one thing: Cheap tuition means inferior education, with poor services, crowded classrooms, delayed graduation (because classes aren't available), and disgruntled faculty. Repeated surveys of industry personnel find dissatisfaction with Florida education as a reason to not move a business facility to the state, i.e., those executives don't believe the current employee pool is sufficiently educated, and the executives do not want to put their own children into state schools.

ENVIRONMENTAL ISSUES

In 1827, Ralph Waldo Emerson visited the Florida territory's new capital city and wrote in his diary that the place had been "rapidly settled by public officers, land speculators, and desperadoes." That seems to still be the case.

In reading the *New Yorker*'s review of the biopic *Monster*, the story of multiple-murderer Aileen Wuornos, David Denby's assessment of the state in which the real-life Wuornos was executed in 2002 is striking:

The roseate spoonbill pictured here is a resident of the St. Petersburg and Clearwater area.

The scuzzy central-Florida setting gives [Charlize] Theron some acting ground to stand on. In such recent American movies as the Matt Dillon thriller *Wild Things*, Larry Clark's *Bully*, John Sayles's *Sunshine State*, the Charlie Kaufman-Spike Jonze fantasia *Adaptation*, and Frederick Wiseman's documentary *Domestic Violence*, as well as Carl Hiaasen's novels, Florida has appeared as a kind of bedraggled kingdom of chaos. The swamps, the threadbare woods, the sagging, loose-hinged bungalows, the roadhouses with their grizzled and beer-bellied bikers, the long, droning freeways, cars tooling along to somewhere or other.... Florida is the place where life doesn't shape up...[where] there's no structure, nothing hard or dense enough to mold people into coherent human beings."

Sounds pretty grim, huh? But still, he has a point. There's a Wild West, frontier spirit in this state, a state in which environmentalism has been slow to catch on. For nearly two centuries, land speculators have ridden roughshod over the wilderness, buying and selling it in ever-smaller parcels. Mismanaged growth has been the norm, with government officials routinely called to the carpet for cozying up to land developers.

Millions of acres have been bulldozed to make way for strip malls and condo developments—nothing new, really, it happens all over. It's the same story of insufficient infrastructure, deficient water supply, and oversubscribed highways that is told of most recently plundered natural settings. And with something like 1,000 new residents moving to Florida every day, something's gotta give.

Still, the state's commitment to the environment is not hopeless. There's been an enormous grassroots effort in the past decade in Florida, regular people who have balked at the shady characters and get-rich-quick schemes that have so wantonly reduced the state's resources and diminished natural habitats. If their efforts gain purchase, the state's natural treasures—which are truly so vast and so breathtaking—might be preserved and, in some cases, restored.

People and Culture

DEMOGRAPHICS

Florida ranks fourth in the United States in population, behind California, Texas, and New York. In 2010, the U.S. Census put the population at 18,801,310 (up from 9,746,961 in 1980). The 2011 estimate by the Census Bureau was 19,057,542. If you count Tampa/St. Petersburg/Clearwater as a single metropolitan area, the estimate for 2011 was 2.79 million. For the sake of comparison, the Miami-Dade area estimate was 2.52 million, but adding in the neighboring Fort Lauderdale metro area, that southeastern metropolis had an estimated 4.27 million. On the Gulf Coast, the other most populous areas are Sarasota/Bradenton/Venice (789,000), Fort Myers/Cape Coral (714,000), Pensacola (470,000), Tallahassee (348,000), and Naples/Marco Island (405,000). Nearly 1,000 new people move to Florida each day, making it one of the fastest-growing states in the nation.

Age

Florida's age distribution is in a state of flux: In 1990, Floridians aged 65 and older were 18.2 percent of the state's population, whereas in 2010 the census counted 17.7 percent of the Florida total. The slight decline can probably be attributed to increases in the birth rate and to in-migration of families with young children. But while the percentage of those over 65 has shrunk some, the number of people 85 and older has grown tremendously (maybe people just live longer in this climate). The area around Tampa has gotten younger in recent years. For instance, the youth population (ages 0–19) has shown increasing growth rates over the last 40 years, from 15.5 percent in 1970–1980 to 21.9 percent in 2010.

Race

The population of the Gulf Coast is still primarily white (20 percent nonwhite at the last

COURTESY OF VISITSTPETECLEARWATER.COM

fun on the beach

census, in 2010), with the greatest ethnic diversity in the Tampa Bay area. Of the state's 19 million residents, 18.7 percent of them are foreign-born, and 22.5 percent are Latino (making Florida home to the third-largest Latino population in the United States).

Religion

In modern times, the Gulf Coast is primarily Christian. Jewish retirees seldom, for whatever reason, settle along the Gulf Coast, with the exception of Sarasota (3–6 percent Jewish, as compared to the east coast of the state from Coral Gables up through Palm Beach, which is roughly 13–15 percent Jewish). The southernmost part of the state is dominantly Catholic, as is the area just north of Tampa up through what is known as the Nature Coast. By and large, though, Floridians are Protestant, especially as you get closer to the Georgia and Alabama borders.

Snowbirds

First, what's a snowbird? It's a temporary resident in Florida, someone who comes from a colder, less hospitable, winter climate to bask in the Sunshine State all winter. Snowbirds are usually of retirement age, or nearing it. But it gets more specific. New Yorkers account for 13.1 percent of Florida's temporary residents, followed by Michiganders at 7.4 percent, Ohioans at 6.7 percent, Pennsylvanians at 5.8 percent, and Canadians at 5.5 percent. The average length of stay is five months. If Florida has roughly seven million households, there are an estimated 920,000 temporary residents during the peak winter months and another 170,000 during the late summer.

ESSENTIALS

Getting There

BY PLANE

Tampa International Airport (TPA, 4100 George J. Bean Outbound Pkwy., Tampa, 813/870-8700, www.tampaairport.com) is the largest airport on the Gulf Coast, with 72 non-stop destinations. The 30th busiest airport, with more than 16 million passengers annually, it was recently ranked one of the 10 most beloved airports by CNN online, and with good reason. Forty percent of the airport's concessions were under construction in 2012, yielding a number of new amenities and restaurant tenants aimed to "bring Tampa into the airport."

Tampa fine-dining institution Mise en Place opened a café called First Flight, a Columbia Restaurant Café launched, as did Cigar City Brewing (the only spot in the country brewing right in an airport). Burger titan Green Iguana opened on Concourse A, and on Concourse C Don Shula's new Shula's Bar and Grill and Shula Burger were unveiled. Visitors hardly have a reason to leave the airport these days.

Southwest Florida International Airport (RSW, 11000 Terminal Access Rd., Fort Myers, 239/590-4800, http://flylcpa.com) in Fort Myers has also experienced enormous expansion

Tampa International Airport

in the past few years. Generally, the most direct routes and cheapest fares can be found through these airports, but it's worth pricing flights through Orlando, which is an hour east of Tampa (mostly from Orlando International Airport, but there is a second airport that is increasingly popular for international travelers called Sanford International Airport).

From Europe

The most international flights on the Gulf Coast arrive and depart out of Tampa, a smaller number out of Southwest Florida International in Fort Myers. Tampa services destinations in Canada, Mexico, Switzerland (Edelweiss Air started flying direct in 2012), the United Kingdom, and to destinations throughout the Caribbean.

Airfare

All of the online travel resources (Orbitz, Travelocity, Expedia, etc.) offer last-minute specials and weekend deals on travel. The way to get a good fare in advance on air travel or hotel rooms is by traveling off peak season. Peak season is from after Thanksgiving to just after Easter, but the most frenetic of all is during spring break in March and April. Fall and winter are still lovely times to visit (summer, not so much).

BY CAR

The main arteries into Florida include I-95, which crosses the Florida-Georgia border just north of Jacksonville and hugs the east coast of the state all the way down, and I-75, which runs south from Georgia through the state's middle, then works its way west to the coast just south of Tampa. I-4 extends southwest across the state from Daytona through Orlando and then connects to I-75 in Tampa. On the Panhandle, I-10 is the big east–west road, which can be accessed from the north by U.S. 29, U.S. 231, or U.S. 19.

BY BOAT

Most boaters are familiar with the 1,090-mile, toll-free, East Coast channel that is the Intracoastal Waterway (ICW), linking Norfolk, Virginia, to Miami, Florida, through gorgeous sheltered waters. Well, the Gulf has one too, the **Gulf Intracoastal Waterway,** extending about 1,300 miles from Carrabelle, Florida, to Brownsville, Texas. (And there's a noncontiguous section of the waterway connecting Tampa Bay with the Okeechobee Waterway.) The Gulf Intracoastal Waterway follows a course of sheltered bays, rivers, and canals along the Gulf of Mexico, perfect for recreational cruising. The sheltered Gulf waters aren't as punishing as the Atlantic Ocean, but still the Gulf Intracoastal Waterway makes for varied and scenic cruising.

Speaking of cruising, the **Port of Tampa** is a huge home port for a variety of cruise lines (Carnival Cruise Lines, Holland America, Royal Caribbean, and Norwegian Cruise Line, offering the variety of 4, 5, 7, and 14-day cruise itineraries). Nearly a million passengers pass through its cruise terminals each year on their way to days upon the open sea, shuffleboard, and cocktails on the Lido deck. So, another vacation itinerary might be taking a cruise, followed or preceded by an exploration of Tampa and St. Petersburg.

Getting Around

BY CAR

Florida's Gulf Coast is an ideal destination for those with a poor sense of direction. There are only a few major roads you have to master, and even the urban areas are mostly laid out in a grid (except Tampa, sadly, where driving visitors are known to browbeat the map-reading visitors in the passenger seat). U.S. 19 extends along the coast all the way down to St. Pete. I-75 is the huge north–south artery on the Gulf Coast side of the Florida peninsula, stretching from where it enters the state at Valdosta, Georgia, all the way south to Naples, where it jogs across the state to the east along what is called Alligator Alley. One of the more famous north–south routes in Florida is U.S. 41, also known as the Tamiami Trail, which extends from Tampa down to Naples, where it, too, shoots east across the state (significantly south of I-75). The Tamiami Trail and I-75 run parallel, fairly close together—which you choose depends on your preference: I-75 has the speed, Tamiami Trail has the charm.

Once in Tampa, from north to south, Bearrs, Fletcher, Fowler, and Busch Boulevards are the big east–west roads. Dale Mabry and Bruce B. Downs are the biggest north–south roads. This all sounds fairly simple, but once you get downtown in Tampa you really need GPS to find your way out. There are lots of one-way streets, and the highway on-ramps are a bit difficult to find. The Busch Gardens area and USF lie between I-75 and I-275 northeast of downtown. The airport is just southwest of downtown.

St. Petersburg and Tampa are connected by two major bridges (Gandy Bridge in the south and Howard Frankland Bridge to the north). Once in Pinellas, Clearwater is in the north along the Gulf, St. Petersburg is in the south along the bay. To reach St. Petersburg from Clearwater, head south on U.S. 19A, a slow, densely trafficked mess. Farther east, the regular U.S. 19 cuts down through the center of the peninsula to St. Petersburg.

In St. Petersburg, streets are set up in a grid pattern, with avenues running east–west and streets running north–south. Central Avenue divides north and south St. Petersburg, with the numbered avenues on either side—it's tricky, though, as to the left of Central there's

1st Avenue North, to the right it's 1st Avenue South. There are some sections of town that are all one-way streets, so you may make a lot of little squares while driving. From St. Pete Beach all the way up through Clearwater, all you need to know is that Gulf Boulevard (Hwy. 699) runs right up the coast and through each little town. The city of Clearwater is on the mainland, but Clearwater Beach is on a barrier island connected by Memorial Causeway.

BY BUS

Greyhound (800/231-2222, www.greyhound. com) service has gotten spottier in recent years, but there are still regular routes that run from Naples up through Fort Myers, then up to Tampa and St. Petersburg, and all the way around the Panhandle. If traveling by Greyhound is new to you, here is some general information: There are no assigned seats (do not, under any circumstances, take the seats adjacent to the bathroom, it's olfactory suicide), no smoking, no pets, no meal service (but there are regular meal stops so you can jump out and buy something). There are no reservations, so you buy a ticket and show up. Stopovers at any point along the route are permitted if you've paid a regular fare. The driver gives you a notation on your ticket, or a coupon, and you can get back on whenever.

BY TRAIN

Amtrak (800/872-7245, www.amtrak.com) offers some service to and from Tampa, with a full-service train station at 601 N. Nebraska Avenue.

BY BIKE

Tampa is a particularly biker-unfriendly town, with very few bike lanes and drivers unaccustomed to watching out for the two-wheeled. St. Petersburg is more progressive, with downtown bike lanes, bike racks, and a general bike-savvy tenor. All cautions aside, Tampa is pancake-flat, thus an easy place to ride, but heat and humidity can be daunting, as can regular afternoon thunderstorms in the summer months.

ACCESS FOR TRAVELERS WITH DISABILITIES

Tampa and St. Petersburg are tremendously accessible, but as one would expect, the more remote areas that reflect a more "Old Florida" sensibility may not have ramps, handicapped-accessible bathrooms, and other amenities. You may want to consider buying a copy of **Wheelchairs on the Go: Accessible Fun in Florida**. The 424-page paperback covers wheelchair-accessible and barrier-free accommodations, tourist attractions, and activities across the state.

Society for Accessible Travel & Hospitality (212/447-7284, www.sath.org) provides recommendations and resources to help travelers with disabilities plan their vacations, and **Able Trust** (888/838-2253, www. abletrust.org) offers helpful links to disability resources throughout Florida.

Most major car rental companies have hand-controlled cars in their fleets (give them 24- to 48-hours' notice to locate one). If you need to rent a scooter or wheelchair during your visit, **ScootAround** (888/441-7575, www.scootaround.com) is a mobility enhancement company with scooter and wheelchair rental service for seniors or travelers with disabilities in Tampa and a number of other Gulf Coast cities.

Diabetic travelers can call the **American Diabetes Association** (800/342-2383) to get a list of hospitals that provide services to diabetics, or log on to **Dialysis Finder** (www.dialysisfinder.com).

The **American Foundation for the Blind** (800/232-5463, www.afb.org) provides information on traveling with a seeing-eye dog.

Visas and Officialdom

FOREIGN VISITORS

Visas

Even coming from Canada and Mexico, you need a valid passport and a tourist visa (a Non-Immigrant Visitors Visa B1, for business, or B2, for recreation). Keep your passport in a safe place, and make a copy of the passport number and other critical information and keep it elsewhere.

Money

U.S. currency looks pretty fancy these days, with watermarks, lots of anti-counterfeit devices, and huge heads (in the case of Ben Franklin, not a pretty turn of events), but working with dollars is fairly simple—bills come in $1, $5, $10, $20, and, less common, $50. The $100 bill is very seldom used and very seldom accepted without a lot of scrutiny. (The old, small-head bills are still good, don't worry.) In coins, 1-cent pennies are practically only good for gumball machines and wishing wells, then there's the 5-cent nickel, the 10-cent dime, the 25-cent quarter, as well as the more rare 50-cent piece.

Money can be exchanged at Tampa International Airport. Exchange money before you arrive, or work in U.S. travelers' checks. For the most part, if you have a Visa or MasterCard, put all of your accommodations, restaurant meals, and attractions expenditures on that—an easy way to keep track of how you spent your money on vacation.

Conduct and Customs

TRAVELING WITH CHILDREN

The Tampa Bay area is suited to a rambling family car trip. But how to face the open road with a car full of antsy travelers? Consider carrying a master list of all that you've packed. Although it sounds monstrously fastidious, it helps to see where your gaps are, it allows you to easily keep track of things from car to motel to final destination, and if you generate this list on the computer, it can be used as the basis for future trip lists.

The list should be divided into categories: clothes and equipment (these are the things that go in the trunk, to be exhumed at your final destination) and the stuff that makes or breaks your travel time—food, entertainment, and car comfort. Older kids can each be put in charge of a category checklist as the car gets loaded.

When traveling in the car with small children, allow more time to reach your destination. Count on stopping every hour to stretch your legs and run around. Churches are good stopping spots if rest areas aren't available, as they often have open, grassy areas and playgrounds. Traveling at night or during nap times is a good way to make up time. Put blankets, pillows, and any necessary stuffed animals in the back seat at the ready.

Your local party goods and dollar stores are perfect places to find inexpensive new forms of amusement. Wrap each new toy as a gift, to make the excitement last. Maze books, magic-pen books, stickers, a magnetic puzzle of the United States, even car bingo can keep everyone entertained. For long car trips, the book *Miles of Smiles* is filled with car games. Picture-puzzle books (like *I Spy* and *Where's Waldo*) can be made into games as well: One person names an object for the rest to find in the picture.

Bring lap desks and art supplies for projects.

Kids love Florida beaches.

Dated spiral-bound drawing pads can be a nice way to chronicle a trip, with each child keeping the finished pad (parents can annotate as instructed). Encourage older kids to journal with a cool pad and a set of gel pens.

TRAVELING WITH PETS

More and more hotel chains are accepting people's canine companions (other pets, from potbellied pigs to naked mole rats, are a harder sell). Best Western, Motel 6, Holiday Inn, and even swishy chains such as Four Seasons often accept pet guests for an additional fee. To get good information, pick up a copy of *The Dog Lover's Companion to Florida,* by Sally Deneen and Robert McClure, or visit www.petswelcome.com.

Flying with your pet to and from the Tampa Bay area can be problematic, as most major airlines have an embargo against pets as checked baggage during the summer months (any day in which the outdoor temperature might reach 90 degrees), and even for small pets that fit under an airplane seat, the airlines only allow one pet per cabin. The ASPCA strongly discourages pets as checked baggage.

Dogs are prohibited on many walking trails in the Tampa Bay area, as well as most beaches. There are designated dog parks and dog beaches on Davis Islands, in Gulfport, on Honeymoon Island and Fort DeSoto Park, with amenities such as fenced play areas, dog water fountains, and poop bags. Be aware that in much of the Gulf Coast's wilderness areas, poisonous snakes and alligators pose more of a threat to your dog than to you.

TRAVELING ALONE

All the offerings in the area are blissfully suited to traveling alone, including beach walking, fishing, kayaking, and even the area's many cultural attractions. The only exception to that is backwoods camping in deep wilderness. Be extremely careful to give rangers your exact schedule and detailed whereabouts. The Tampa Bay and all of Florida's Gulf Coast make for a great spot for quiet, contemplative solo travel.

GAY AND LESBIAN TRAVELERS

The Tampa Bay area is not Miami or Key West, but it's gotten much better in recent years. St. Petersburg is hugely gay friendly, with an enormous annual Gay Pride Parade and lots of gay nightlife, and Ybor City is similarly festive. Even beyond those areas, very little seems in any way homophobic toward gay or lesbian travelers. As with most places, the more rural the area, the more likely any discernible difference is likely to prompt unwanted notice.

For further resources to the area, check out http://tampa.gaycities.com or www.gayflorida.com.

SENIOR TRAVELERS

Snowbirds account for a huge percentage of the winter population of Pinellas County's beachside towns, as well as nearby cities such as Sarasota. Because of this, the whole area is extremely welcoming to senior visitors in terms of accessibility, reduced ticket and admission prices, "early-bird specials," and other incentives to draw a senior crowd.

Health and Safety

Florida has good emergency services and medical care. Why, from Tampa to Sarasota you'll see more medical facilities, pharmacies, and billboards for MRI scanners than nearly anywhere else, a remnant of the area's recent past as a mostly retirement-age region (as the Bob Dylan song says, "it's younger than that now").

Still, you want to do what you can to stay healthy during a visit here. The sun is probably the biggest underestimated foe. **Sunburn** can be wicked, so be sure to slather with at least an SPF of 30, and because you'll be in and out of water, and sweating in the steamy humidity, opt for waterproof or water-resistant cream such as Banana Boat Sport Sunblock Lotion (waterproof/sweatproof, SPF 30). Even better, Avon now makes an SPF 30 Skin So Soft cream with a DEET-free pesticide in it to cope with the Gulf Coast's other big bully, the **mosquitoes.** DEET-based products are more effective in preventing mosquitoes from landing on you, but you may not want it sitting on your skin all day. Lather up with the Avon product, then apply a DEET-based spray only if the mosquitoes are bad. Mosquitoes in Florida don't carry any diseases such as malaria, but their itching can certainly be preoccupying.

Another itchy subject is **fire ants.** If you see loose, sandy mounds on the ground, do not stand in them. These little devils get incensed at the foot in their house and swarm up your shoe and beyond to leave raised white or red welts that really hurt and itch for days. There is no known treatment for their bites.

Many travel articles suggest getting medical travel insurance. If you have insurance, though, that's probably all the coverage you'll need. Contact the **Centers for Disease Control and Prevention** (800/311-3435, www.cdc.gov) for information on health hazards by region.

HOSPITALS AND EMERGENCIES

In any emergency, dial 911 for immediate assistance. If you need police assistance in a nonemergency, visit or call the **Tampa Police Department** (411 N. Franklin St., 813/276-3200). The police department operates three districts that serve the greater Tampa Bay area; they will assign your problem to the proper

ALLIGATORS

Alligators were first listed as an endangered species in 1967, their numbers threatened by hunting and habitat loss. Then the American alligator was removed from the endangered species list in 1987 after the U.S. Fish and Wildlife Service pronounced a complete recovery of the species. Conservative estimates put the population at around a million just in Florida. Because they can tolerate brackish water as well as freshwater, they can be found in rivers, swamps, bogs, lakes, ponds, creeks, canals, swimming pools, and lots of Florida golf courses.

The American alligator is the largest reptile in North America. They can live 35-50 years in the wild, 60-80 years in captivity. The average adult male is 13 feet in length, although they can grow up to 18 feet long. Bulls are generally larger than females, weighing 450-600 pounds.

They're everywhere in Florida, and they eat just about anything. Usually that means lizards, fish, snakes, turtles, even little gators.

Florida residents have learned to be blasé about gators. They're an everyday part of living in this subtropical climate. In the past decade, there have been dozens and dozens of reported gator attacks on humans, though only one fatality.

The problems are not just a function of large numbers. People feed the gators and thus the alligators have gotten chummy and less fearful of humans. So new policies were put in place. In many spots along the Gulf Coast, if gators get large (over eight feet) they are taken away and "processed" (not a good euphemism). Smaller ones get relocated.

STAY SAFE
Alligators are cold-blooded. They don't need to eat as much or as often as their warm-blooded counterparts. In fact, they can't eat unless their internal body temperature is 90 degrees. Thus, they don't eat all winter, and in the spring

they can be seen basking on the banks in a sunny spot. They're hungry in April and May, a good time to steer clear. In the summer, the females lay their eggs (up to 70) in a nest and cover them over, then the eggs incubate for 65 days. The mom stays close, carrying the freshly hatched babies to the water. Even after they're swimming around, mama is protective for up to the first two years.

Things to keep in mind, for your safety and the safety of others:

- Don't feed the gators. And if you see others doing so, give them a hard time.

- Don't bother the babies or come between a mother and her young.

- Don't bug them during their spring mating season.

- Closely supervise kids playing in or near fresh or brackish water. Never allow little ones to play by water unattended. The same goes for pets. In fact, just don't let your dog swim in fresh or brackish water in Florida.

- Alligators feed most actively at dusk and dawn, so schedule your lake or river swim for another time.

- They don't make good pets. They are not tamed in captivity, and it's illegal.

- If you are bitten, seek medical attention, even if it seems minor. Their mouths harbor very infectious bacteria.

- If you see a big one that seems interested in humans, call the local police nonemergency number.

- Don't throw your fish scraps back into the water when fishing. This encourages gators to hang around boats and docks.

district. Tampa has several hospitals equipped with emergency rooms: If you have a medical emergency in the Hyde Park area, go to **Memorial Hospital of Tampa** (2901 Swann Ave., 800/341-7729). In Carrollwood, visit the

University Community Hospital Carrollwood (7171 N. Dale Mabry Hwy., 813/558-8068). In the Westshore area, go to **University Community Hospital** (2223 N. Westshore Blvd., 813/615-7272). In the downtown area, make your way to **Tampa General Hospital** (2 Columbia Dr., 813/844-7000) near the causeway to Davis Islands.

In Pinellas County, try **St. Petersburg General Hospital** (6500 38th Ave. N, St. Petersburg, 727/341-4870) and **St. Anthony's Hospital** (1200 7th Ave. N., St. Petersburg, 727/825-1100) in the south of the county, and **Suncoast Hospital** (2025 Indian Rocks Rd., Largo, 727/581-9474) in northern Pinellas County. For a nonemergency police need, contact the **St. Petersburg Police Department** (1300 1st Ave. N., St. Petersburg, 727/893-7780).

PHARMACIES

This may be totally anecdotal, even false, but it sure seems like the Tampa Bay area is more densely dotted with pharmacies than anywhere else in the galaxy. Walgreen's, CVS, you name it, your smartphone will find you one pronto, many of them laid out along Dale Mabry Highway in Tampa, U.S. 19 in North Pinellas County, or 4th Street North in St. Petersburg.

THE STINGRAY SHUFFLE

It's not a dance, exactly.

Pinellas County beaches have their share of flat, seafloor-living stingrays. Visitors occasionally step on these creatures, their winglike fins hidden in the sandy shallows. When trod upon, a stingray flips up its tail in self-defense and delivers a nasty stinging puncture with its barb. To avoid this, drag your feet along the sandy bottom (as opposed to stepping up and down). The "shuffle" may not look too swift, but it alerts stingrays to your approach. They are just hanging around the shallows to catch shellfish and crustaceans and they'd rather not waste their time on stinging you.

If you are unlucky enough to be stung, it's important that you clean the wound with fresh water immediately (other bacteria in seawater can infect the area). As soon as you can, soak the wound in the hottest water you can stand for up to 90 minutes to neutralize the venom. The pain can be severe, often accompanied by weakness, vomiting, headache, fainting, shortness of breath, paralysis, and collapse in people who are allergic to the venom. You may want to see a doctor, who might add insult to injury with a tetanus shot.

Always report stingray injuries to the lifeguard on duty.

Information and Services

COMMUNICATIONS AND MEDIA

Mail

Mail service within the United States generally takes 2–3 days, except during the Christmas holiday season when all bets are off. Within Florida, post takes about two days to get anywhere (you speed things up if you use the full nine-digit zip code). A first-class stamp currently costs $0.45.

Telephone

If you are calling long distance, dial 1, then the three-digit area code, then the seven-digit phone number. If calling from abroad, the international code for the United States is 1. Within the United States, the 800, 888, 877, and 866 area codes are toll-free, meaning they cost you nothing to dial. Tampa and all of Hillsborough County are within the 813 area code; St. Petersburg and Pinellas County are within the 727 area code. You must dial the area code when dialing from one side of the bay to the other.

Fax

Most hotels and motels will send and receive a fax for a fee, and multipage documents can be sent at any Kinko's shop.

Internet Access

The cheapest hotels offer free Wi-Fi, then mid-priced hotels charge you for it, then at the luxury hotels it's free again. Go figure. More and more, public buildings, coffee shops, and quick-serve restaurants offer free Wi-Fi. Even if you're not packing a laptop or smartphone on your trip, you can check web-based email from almost any hotel or motel, often for no fee.

Newspapers

The *Tampa Bay Times* (490 1st Ave. S., St. Petersburg, 727/893-8111, www.tampabay. com), with a useful website for locals and visitors, is St. Petersburg's serious metro daily with hard-hitting investigative journalists, Pulitzer-winning columnists, and great arts coverage. You'll see kiosks everywhere. All right, we both have been on staff here, so maybe we're biased. The *Tampa Tribune* has been through a rough period, as have so many U.S. newspapers, but it still gives you the basic daily news.

Creative Loafing (813/739-4800, www. creativeloafing.com), the area's free alternative weekly, has great entertainment schedules, restaurant reviews, and a view into local politics. For quick and easy info on events, attractions, and restaurants, visit www.tampabay.citysearch.com. There are also numerous magazines: *Tampa Bay Magazine* is a little stodgy, and there are many glossy freebies in Hyde Park (many of them are here today, gone tomorrow).

Radio and Television

Of the local radio stations is **WMNF 88.5 FM,** which has a huge following for its independent and quirky programming: Tune in and you'll hear salsa, or maybe Hawaiian slack-key guitar, or maybe a little alt-country. It has a snuggly relationship with Skipper's Smokehouse, and together they sponsor many of the city's best concerts. You can also tune in to **WUSF 89.7 FM** for NPR and classical programming. For a mix of light rock, turn to **MIX 100.7 FM. WARM 94.9 FM** is "soft favorites with less talk," **107.3 FM The Eagle** is hits of the 1970s, and for sports talk turn to **WDAE 1250 AM.**

For local television programming, **Bay News 9** is Bright House Networks' 24-hour local news station, **WFLA Channel 8** is the local NBC affiliate, **WTSP Channel 10** is the CBS affiliate, **WTVT Channel 13** is the FOX affiliate, and **WFTS Channel 28** is the local ABC affiliate.

RESOURCES

Suggested Reading

CHILDREN'S LITERATURE

DiCamillo, Kate. *Because of Winn Dixie.* Cambridge: Candlewick Press, 2001. Also made into a major motion picture some years back, this book about 10-year-old India Opal Buloni and her ugly dog Winn-Dixie (named for where she found him) has captured the attention of lots of families. It's a great story, set in a fictional town of Naomi, Florida (likely modeled on someplace down toward Port Charlotte). Opal has had kind of a hard life, so it might be too much for a really sensitive kid.

Rawlings, Marjorie Kinnan. *The Yearling.* New York: Simon Pulse, 50th edition, 1988. Rawlings wrote 10 books while a resident in Cross Creek, Florida, the most popular of which was *The Yearling,* which won a Pulitzer Prize in fiction in 1939. It tells the story of scrappy young Jody Baxter and his pet fawn Flag, who together roam the Florida scrublands wrestling big swamp gators and cavorting with bear cubs. Rawlings's second-best book is called simply, *Cross Creek,* also with the same earthy Florida Cracker dialect.

Smith, Patrick D. *A Land Remembered.* Sarasota, FL: Pineapple Press, 1998. Beginning with Tobias MacIvey's arrival in Florida in 1858, this young-adult historical novel tells the story of three generations of Floridians carving out a hardscrabble life for themselves in the wilds of central Florida. This sweeping story is rich in Florida history.

DRAMA

Cruz, Nilo. *Anna in the Tropics.* New York: Theatre Communications Group, 2003. This play won Nilo Cruz the Pulitzer Prize for drama in 2003. It is a romantic drama, loosely a retelling of Tolstoy's *Anna Karenina,* that depicts a Cuban-American family of cigar makers in Ybor City (Tampa) in 1930. It tells the story of the factory's new "lector," a person hired to read aloud great works of literature and the day's news to the cigar workers. A beautiful stage play—keep your eyes open for any performances of it during your visit.

FICTION

Atkins, Ace. *White Shadow.* New York: Berkley Trade, 2009. A former *Tampa Tribune* reporter wrote this tremendous page-turner, which is loosely based on the real-life 1955 murder of gangster Charlie Wall. It's a great look at the historic turf wars in Ybor City, a crime drama as rich and atmospheric as that neighborhood's café con leche.

Hiaasen, Carl. *Star Island.* New York: Alfred A. Knopf, 2010. Carl Hiaasen is everywhere in Florida: bigger than a novelist, bigger than a *Miami Herald* columnist. He's like a rock star around here, with so many titles it's hard to really put forth a favorite with any kind of stalwart conviction. The most recent is *Star Island*, before that was *Nature Girl, Skinny Dip, Basket Case, Sick Puppy, Lucky You, Stormy Weather, Strip Tease, Native Tongue, Skin Tight, Double Whammy*, and *Tourist Season*. What you need to know is that he loves the rich and iconoclastic zaniness that is south Florida, has a real fondness for smart hookers with a heart of gold, finds tough-guy baldies especially amusing, and is a bulldoggish environmentalist. In addition to his novels, Hiaasen has also published two collections of his newspaper columns, *Kick Ass* and *Paradise Screwed*, and an eviscerating anti-Disney book called *Team Rodent*. (Caveat emptor: Snakes feature heavily in his books.) Oh, and he goes for one-word titles for his kids' books, largely with heavy environmental messages: *Hoot, Flush, Scat*, and *Chomp*.

Lehane, Dennis. *Live By Night*. New York: William Morrow, 2012. It's not all Tampa, but Lehane's new book is a Prohibition-era crime drama with lots of delicious mobster underbelly, some of it set here (Lehane spends winters in St. Pete's Old Northeast and he's a grad of Eckerd College).

MacDonald, John. *Condominium*. New York: Fawcett, reissue edition, 1985. For most of his life John MacDonald was considered a pulp fiction writer, and prolific, who spent more than half his life in west-central Florida, first in Clearwater, then in Sarasota and Siesta Key. This book still seems fresh, especially in light of recent harrowing hurricane seasons. The setting is Golden Sands, a Sunbelt condo in the path of Hurricane Ella. It's a multi-character disaster book, think *The Towering Inferno*.

Wayne White, Randy. *Gone*. New York: Putnam Adult, 2012. Randy Wayne White was a fishing guide at Tarpon Bay down on Sanibel for 13 years. A prolific mystery novelist, he writes mostly about areas just slightly to the south of Tampa and St. Petersburg, with a new series about Florida fishing guide Hannah Smith, as well as numerous novels featuring super tough-guy Doc Ford solving various mysteries (*Black Widow, Hunter's Moon, The Deadlier Sex, Cuban Death-Lift, The Deep Six, The Heat Islands, The Man Who Invented Florida, Captiva, North of Havana, The Mangrove Coast, Ten Thousand Islands, Shark River, Twelve Mile Limit, Everglades, Tampa Burn*, and *Dead of Night*). In all his books, Florida is one of the main characters, lovingly and lavishly described in all its loony glory. Wayne White is a columnist for *Outside* magazine and *Men's Health* and he's written lots of other books of essays, including *Batfishing in the Rain Forest* and a fish cookbook.

NONFICTION

Klinkenberg, Jeff. *Pilgrim in the Land of Alligators: More Stories about Real Florida*. Gainesville, FL: University Press of Florida, 2011. *Tampa Bay Times* writer Jeff Klinkenberg may have invented the term Real Florida, which means the Old Florida, without Disney, fancy golf courses, or anything glamorous. This book is an assemblage of largely humorous essays he's written for the paper that tell great stories about the people, flora, and fauna in west-central Florida. Klinkenberg wrote two other compelling books of essays entitled *Seasons of Real Florida* and *Dispatches from the Land of Flowers: A Snake Man, a Sad Poet, a Lightning Stalker and Other Stories About Real Florida* (Gainesville, FL: Down Home Press, 2009 and 1996, respectively). He has another out in 2013 called *Alligators in B-Flat*.

Mormino, Gary. *Land of Sunshine, State of Dreams: A Social History of Modern Florida.* Gainesville, FL: University Press of Florida, 2008. A professor emeritus from University of South Florida St. Petersburg, Gary Mormino headed up the Florida Studies program for years. He has a passion for Florida foodways, but in this book explores the explosive growth of the state, from 500,000 inhabitants at the outset of the 20th century to 16 million in 2000. It looks at migration, tourism, the development of the space program and gated communities, and all the other things that have made the fourth-largest state what it is today.

SHELLS

Williams, Winston. *Florida's Fabulous Seashells: And Other Seashore Life.* Tampa: World Publications, 1991. It's light enough to pack in your beach bag, with good color photos and interesting text about marine animals.

Witherington, Blair and Dawn. *Florida's Seashells.* Sarasota, FL: Pineapple Press, 2007. This tome is heftier than *Florida's Fabulous Seashells.*

TRAVEL GUIDES

Murphy, Bill. *Fox-TV's One Tank Trips, Fun Florida Adventures.* St. Petersburg, FL: Seaside Publishing, 2009. An offshoot of a television segment Bill Murphy does, the books showcase Florida-based adventures that are all within a full tank of Tampa. It covers lots of off-the-beaten path attractions, all worthy of your time, from Pioneer Florida Museum in Dade City to the excellent camping at Fort De Soto Park.

WILDLIFE

Adams, Alto. *A Florida Cattle Ranch.* Sarasota, FL: Pineapple Press, 1998. You'll learn about Cracker cows, scrub, and the hardscrabble world of Florida ranching.

Arnov, Boris. *Fish Florida Saltwater: Better than Luck--The Foolproof Guide to Florida Saltwater Fishing.* Houston: Gulf Publishing, 2002. This is a fairly good beginner book: It describes a kind of fish, like amberjack, then tells you how it fights; recommends appropriate tackle, whether you're spinning or plug casting or fly fishing; and discusses technique for live bait or light tackle casting. It also gives catch and size limits and other regulations.

Maehr, David. *Florida's Birds: A Field Guide And Reference.* Sarasota, FL: Pineapple Press, 2005. For birders and rookies alike, birds can be quickly identified in this book via picture (pretty ones with birds grouped by similar species), text, or index. Maps indicate when migratory birds are present or breeding, and where.

Maehr, David. *The Florida Panther: Life and Death of a Vanishing Carnivore.* Washington, DC: Island Press, 1997. The author makes these endangered cougars spring to life in their last frontier in the Big Cypress National Preserve and around the Okaloacoochee Slough.

Simmons, Ernest C. *Birds of Florida's Gulf Coast.* Wilton, NH: Steven M. Lewers + Associates, 2002. This laminated folding guide puts birds into rough groups--wading birds, shore birds, wetland birds, birds of prey, and others.

Sobczak, Charles. *Alligators, Sharks & Panthers: Deadly Encounters with Florida's Top Predator--Man.* Sanibel, FL: Indigo Press, 2006. It chronicles gristly attacks, but with an underlying environmentalist's message about humans mucking about in creatures' natural habitats.

Tekiela, Stan. *Birds of Florida Field Guide.* Cambridge, MN: Adventure Publications, 2005. This is a great small-size book organized by bird color. This makes it easy to narrow things down when you've just spotted a flash of wing color in your binoculars.

Internet Resources

TAMPA

Creative Loafing
http://cltampa.com
The local alternative weekly newspaper has a site that beats the *Tampa Tribune's,* hands down. The writing is provocative and witty, and the paper's arts critics have impeccable taste.

Tampa Bay Convention and Visitors Bureau
www.visittampabay.com
This is a good site for background on the Bay Area as well as travel strategies and accommodations.

ST. PETERSBURG

St. Petersburg/Clearwater Area Convention & Visitors Bureau
www.visitstpeteclearwater.com
Very similar to the Tampa Bay Convention and Visitors Bureau site, this one focuses, not surprisingly, on the beaches. It's easy to book a room from this site, and it features excellent downloadable maps.

Tampa Bay Times
www.tampabay.com
The Gulf Coast's best daily metro paper has an equally superlative website, the place to go if you want to be versed in local politics or find out the day's most exciting events. The paper's movie, book, and pop music reviews are notably good, and a team is working on making the site more usable with the introduction of sortable databases.

GENERAL

Florida Secrets, The Insider's Guide to Unique Destinations
www.floridasecrets.com
The graphics have a cheese factor and it's heavy on the advertising, but the site is a treasure trove of little-known destinations in Florida, divided up on the Gulf Coast by southwest, west-central, eastern, and western Panhandle.

Visit Florida
www.flausa.com
For a good introduction to the Gulf Coast, contact the state's official tourist information organization, Visit Florida (888/735-2872) for a copy of their excellent annual *Visit Florida* guide, the *Florida Events Calendar,* or *Florida Trails.* Online resources include a number of electronic travel guides (for which you can order printed versions if you prefer). Visit Florida also has a 24-hour multilingual tourist assistance hotline at 800/656-8777.

FISHING

Florida Fishing
www.floridafishing.com
It's a clearinghouse of fishing guides, fishing charters, and fishing captains in the state, divided by region. (There's also http://tampabayfish.com, but it doesn't seem to be updated often.)

CAMPING

Florida Association of RV Parks & Campgrounds
www.campflorida.com
It's an easy-to-use comprehensive database of Florida campgrounds, including amenities

information for each site. You can also go on their website and order a print version of the guide. To make reservations at a Florida state campground (or in any state), however, you must utilize www.reserveamerica.com.

PARKS AND FORESTS

Florida State Parks Department
www.floridastateparks.org
Find a park, its affiliated camping and lodging, or get a bead on what events are coming up along the Gulf Coast. The site also has maps and directions to Florida's state parks, and it runs an amateur photo contest of state park photography.

Florida Trail Association
www.floridatrail.org
The Florida Trail Association is a nonprofit that builds, maintains, promotes, and protects hiking trails across the state of Florida, especially the 1,400-mile Florida Trail. From this site you can download all kinds of trail maps and park brochures.

Index

Restaurants Index

Nightlife Index

Shops Index

Hotels Index

www.moon.com

DESTINATIONS | ACTIVITIES | BLOGS | MAPS | BOOKS

MOON.COM is ready to help plan your next trip! Filled with fresh trip ideas and strategies, author interviews, informative travel blogs, a detailed map library, and descriptions of all the Moon guidebooks, Moon.com is all you need to get out and explore the world—or even places in your own backyard. While at Moon.com, sign up for our monthly e-newsletter for updates on new releases, travel tips, and expert advice from our on-the-go Moon authors. As always, when you travel with Moon, expect an experience that is uncommon and truly unique.

MAP SYMBOLS

Expressway	**⟨**	Highlight	✕	Airfield	⚲	Golf Course
Primary Road	○	City/Town	✕	Airport	🅿	Parking Area
Secondary Road	◉	State Capital	▲	Mountain	⬟	Archaeological Site
Unpaved Road	⊛	National Capital	✛	Unique Natural Feature	⛪	Church
Trail	★	Point of Interest			⛽	Gas Station
Ferry	•	Accommodation	⸙	Waterfall		Glacier
Railroad	▼	Restaurant/Bar	▲	Park		Mangrove
Pedestrian Walkway	■	Other Location	⬛	Trailhead		Reef
Stairs	∧	Campground	⛷	Skiing Area		Swamp

CONVERSION TABLES

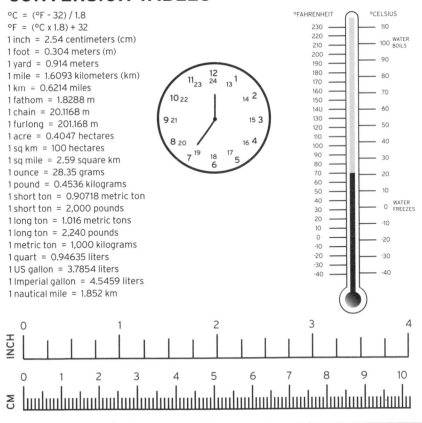

°C = (°F - 32) / 1.8
°F = (°C x 1.8) + 32
1 inch = 2.54 centimeters (cm)
1 foot = 0.304 meters (m)
1 yard = 0.914 meters
1 mile = 1.6093 kilometers (km)
1 km = 0.6214 miles
1 fathom = 1.8288 m
1 chain = 20.1168 m
1 furlong = 201.168 m
1 acre = 0.4047 hectares
1 sq km = 100 hectares
1 sq mile = 2.59 square km
1 ounce = 28.35 grams
1 pound = 0.4536 kilograms
1 short ton = 0.90718 metric ton
1 short ton = 2,000 pounds
1 long ton = 1.016 metric tons
1 long ton = 2,240 pounds
1 metric ton = 1,000 kilograms
1 quart = 0.94635 liters
1 US gallon = 3.7854 liters
1 Imperial gallon = 4.5459 liters
1 nautical mile = 1.852 km

°FAHRENHEIT °CELSIUS

230 — 110
220 —
210 — 100 WATER BOILS
200 —
190 — 90
180 — 80
170 —
160 — 70
150 —
140 — 60
130 —
120 — 50
110 —
100 — 40
90 —
80 — 30
70 —
60 — 20
50 —
40 — 10
30 —
20 — 0 WATER FREEZES
10 —
0 — -10
-10 —
-20 — -20
-30 —
-40 — -30
     — -40

INCH 0 1 2 3 4

CM 0 1 2 3 4 5 6 7 8 9 10

MOON TAMPA & ST. PETERSBURG
Avalon Travel
a member of the Perseus Books Group
1700 Fourth Street
Berkeley, CA 94710, USA
www.moon.com

Editor: Leah Gordon
Series Manager: Erin Raber
Copy Editor: Naomi Adler Dancis
Graphics Coordinator: Kathryn Osgood
Production Coordinator: Domini Dragoone
Cover Designer: Domini Dragoone
Map Editor: Albert Angulo
Cartographers: Heather Sparks, Kaitlin Jaffe, Andy
 Butkovic

ISBN-13: 978-1-61238-524-2
ISSN: 1944-916X

Printing History
1st Edition – 2009
2nd Edition – August 2013
5 4 3 2 1

Text © 2013 by Laura Reiley & Bob Jenkins.
Maps © 2013 by Avalon Travel.
All rights reserved.

AUG 1 5 2013

Front cover photo: Sunshine Skyway Bridge at Tampa
 Bay and St. Petersburg at sunset, © Travel Images/
 UIG, Getty Images
Title page photo: Courtesy of VisitStPeteClearwater.
 com
Front color section: pgs. 2, 3, 23, 25 (right), 26, 27,
 29, 31, and 32 Courtesy of VisitStPeteClearwater.
 com; pg. 22 © Tomasz Zajda/123RF; pg. 24 © Bonnie
 Fink/Dreamstime.com; pg. 25 (left) © 123RF.com;
 pg. 28 Courtesy of visitsarasota.org.

Printed in Canada by Friesens

KEEPING CURRENT

If you have a favorite gem you'd like to see included in the next edition, or see anything
that needs updating, clarification, or correction, please drop us a line. Send your com-
ments via email to feedback@moon.com, or use the address above.